Cybersecurity in Motion

This book advances a central and urgent thesis: in the hyperconnected economy of Logistics 4.0, cybersecurity is no longer a technical safeguard at the periphery of logistics systems but the primary infrastructure of supply chain continuity, economic security, and sustainable development. Digital logistics has evolved into a cyber-physical ecosystem in which data flows, autonomous decisions, and algorithmic coordination shape material reality. In this environment, cyber risk becomes systemic risk, transforming security from an operational concern into a strategic determinant of organisational legitimacy, competitiveness, and resilience. The book reframes cybersecurity as a governance architecture integrating digital infrastructure, risk intelligence, institutional accountability, and technological foresight.

The book offers a synthesis, demonstrating that digitalisation, cybersecurity, and sustainability are mutually reinforcing rather than competing agendas. Without secure digital architectures, transparent ESG reporting, reliable traceability, and accountable automation remain unattainable. Trust is the scarcest resource in digital supply chains, generated through verifiable data, secure infrastructures, and credible governance.

More than a catalogue of tools or regulatory recommendations, the book delivers an integrated analytical architecture for understanding and governing cyber risk in Logistics 4.0 environments. It shows that digital transformation restructures supply chains into cyber-physical systems whose stability, efficiency, and legitimacy depend on the integrity of their digital foundations, and that cybersecurity is a collective supply-chain capability rather than an individual organisational attribute.

The work sets out a governance logic that guides organisations from digitalisation to resilience, treating Information Security Management Systems, standards and security operations frameworks as instruments for stabilising inter-organisational cooperation, maintaining service continuity, and sustaining market legitimacy. It also outlines practitioner and research pathways centred on federated logistics data governance, scenario-based cyber resilience exercises, digital traceability architectures, and integrating cybersecurity metrics into ESG reporting.

Cybersecurity in Motion

Safeguarding the Digital Supply Chain

Justyna Żywiołek, Andrzej Szymonik, and Artur Szymonik

CRC Press
Taylor & Francis Group
Boca Raton London New York

CRC Press is an imprint of the
Taylor & Francis Group, an **informa** business

Designed cover image: Shutterstock ID: 2528234135
First edition published 2027

by CRC Press

2385 NW Executive Center Drive, Suite 320, Boca Raton FL 33431

and by CRC Press

4 Park Square, Milton Park, Abingdon, Oxon, OX14 4RN
CRC Press is an imprint of Taylor & Francis Group, LLC

ISBN: 9781041166702 (hbk)
ISBN: 9781041166719 (pbk)
ISBN: 9781003685784 (ebk)

DOI: 10.1201/9781003685784

Typeset in Caslon
by Deanta Global Publishing Services, Chennai, India

Contents

Preface

In the 21st century, global logistics systems have entered an era of unprecedented digital acceleration. Supply chains that once relied primarily on physical coordination are now governed by data streams, autonomous platforms, algorithmic decision-making, and real-time interoperability. In this hyperconnected environment, cybersecurity emerges not as a technical afterthought but as a structural condition of economic continuity, public trust, and organisational sovereignty. The question is no longer whether digital logistics can be secured—but whether modern economies can function at all without cyber-resilient supply chains. This book, *Cybersecurity in Motion: Safeguarding the Digital Supply Chain*, confronts that challenge at its systemic core.

The chapters in this book present a multidimensional analysis of cybersecurity as the organising principle of digital logistics ecosystems. From architectural vulnerabilities embedded in enterprise resource planning (ERP), warehouse management system (WMS), transportation management system (TMS), and Internet of Things (IoT) platforms, through cascading risks created by third-party integration and human–system interaction, to emerging cryptographic and AI-driven security infrastructures, cybersecurity is treated as a foundational layer of supply chain governance. The book recognises that digital trust has become the scarce resource of global logistics—and that without verifiable data integrity, secure interoperability, and institutionalised cyber governance, neither operational efficiency nor sustainability objectives can be reliably achieved.

The opening chapters establish the technological and organisational foundations of Logistics 4.0, reframing digitalisation as a transformation of logistics ontology rather than a mere upgrade of tools. Cybersecurity is positioned as the design logic of digital architectures, shaping data flows, automation frameworks, and inter-organisational coordination. The discussion then advances into the digital nervous system of modern supply chains, mapping how system interfaces, cloud integration, digital twins, and API ecosystems simultaneously enable real-time logistics intelligence and amplify systemic cyber exposure.

Subsequent chapters investigate the evolving threat landscape in logistics environments, demonstrating how ransomware, social engineering, insider misuse, denial-of-service operations, and supply chain attacks propagate across interconnected ecosystems. These threats are analysed not as isolated IT incidents but as systemic phenomena capable of paralysing entire logistics networks and destabilising markets. The book further explores how Information Security Management Systems and international security governance frameworks function as organisational stabilisers that embed accountability, continuity, and compliance into daily logistics operations.

The later sections focus on emerging cybersecurity technologies and future digital resilience architectures. Cryptography, identity management, blockchain traceability, SIEM and SOC infrastructures, AI-driven threat detection, and post-quantum security are presented as the cognitive and institutional core of cyber-resilient logistics. These technologies are also examined through the lens of sustainability and ESG compliance, redefining secure digital infrastructures as public goods that enable transparent, responsible, and trustworthy global trade.

Across all chapters, the book adopts a pragmatic yet forward-looking stance. It acknowledges the inherent tensions between operational speed and cyber risk, between digital openness and systemic vulnerability, and between global integration and organisational sovereignty. Rather than treating these tensions as irreconcilable, the book offers structured pathways for constructive alignment—grounded in digital architecture design, security governance, and strategic foresight.

Cybersecurity in Motion: Safeguarding the Digital Supply Chain is not merely a technical handbook. It is a strategic framework for an era in which logistics systems have become critical digital infrastructure. Addressed to scholars, practitioners, policymakers, and risk leaders, the book equips its readers with the conceptual clarity and operational instruments necessary to govern cyber risk in motion.

"We cannot solve our problems with the same thinking we used when we created them," Albert Einstein once observed. This book embraces that imperative. It calls for a new paradigm of logistics governance—one in which cybersecurity, sustainability, and digital transformation are no longer treated as competing agendas, but as a single integrated architecture for resilient global commerce.

Justyna Żywiołek
Andrzej Szymonik
Artur Szymonik

About the Authors

Justyna Żywiołek was born on 24 December 1986 in Częstochowa. She completed her master's studies in the field of Metallurgy in 2010. In 2014, she defended her doctoral dissertation with honours in the field of management science, specialising in security science, "The Impact of Information Process Management on the Security of Knowledge Resources in the Enterprise," at the Faculty of Organization and Management of the Lodz University of Technology. Since January 2015, she has been working as an Assistant Professor at the Faculty of Management at the Technical University of Częstochowa. She is a respected researcher in Poland and abroad for her experience in management issues: knowledge and information management and their security. She has published over 160 articles and is the author, co-author, and editor of seven books. She has actively participated in presenting research results at various international conferences. She deals with data protection, is an inspector of personal data protection, and is a leading ISO 27001:2018 auditor. Justyna Żywiołek (PhD Eng.) is a member of ICAA (Intellectual

Capital Association) and EU-OSHA, as well as in organisations operating in Poland promoting information and knowledge security. Guest editor of *Energies MdPI*, *International Journal of Environmental Research* and *Public Health MDPI Journal*, and *Computer Modeling in Engineering and Sciences*. Early Career Editorial Board of *The Journal of Strategic Information Systems* (IFhelp_outline 14.682) and Editorial Advisory Board of the *International Journal of Management and Applied Research* (IF 3.508). Participant in multiple Erasmus+ teacher mobility: Slovenia, Hungary, the Czech Republic, Slovakia, and France.

Andrzej Szymonik is a graduate of the Military Communications Academy (currently known as CSŁiI) in Zegrze and the Military Communications Academy in Sankt Petersburg. In 2001, he defended his doctoral dissertation at the Technical University of Częstochowa. In 2008, the Faculty of Management of the University of Warsaw granted him the degree of Postdoctoral Research Associate (dr hab.) in the field of Management Science. In 2018, he received the title of Professor in the field of Social Sciences at the University of Natural Sciences and Humanities in Siedlce. During 1972–2010, he served in the army and reached the rank of general of the brigade; he was the commander of the Command Support Brigade and the Head of the Science and Military Education Department in the Polish Ministry of National Defence. Currently, he works as an Assistant Professor at the Lodz University of Technology, Faculty of Organization and Management. His achievements include 22 original monographs (details at www.gen-prof.pl), 31 original scientific publications in national and international journals, 85 co-authored scientific publications, and participation in collective studies. He is interested in: security of logistics systems, use of the tools of the fourth industrial revolution in modern logistics, developing models to increase the efficiency and effectiveness of logistics processes in a changing environment and growing customer needs, design for logistics in Industry 4.0, and comprehensive logistics management (Total Logistics Management).

Artur Szymonik was born on 22 May 1985 in Wrocław. He holds a PhD in social sciences in the field of security studies and is currently employed as an Assistant Professor and the Head of the Department of Logistics Systems at the Military University of Land Forces in Wrocław. An officer of the Polish Armed Forces, he also holds master's degrees in law and economics and is a graduate of an Executive Master of Business Administration program. He possesses extensive professional experience in the management of logistics, security, and human resources within both national and international institutional frameworks. He has participated in NATO missions in the Balkans and Afghanistan. He specialises in security studies, public procurement, cybersecurity, and crisis management. As an author of academic publications and a lecturer, he combines his command and managerial experience with research and analytical work, focusing on contemporary challenges in security and logistics.

1

Fundamentals of Cybersecurity in Logistics

1.1 Definitions and Basic Concepts of Cybersecurity in the Context of Logistics

The 21st century in economics is associated with Industry 4.0, which is characterised by the complete integration of information between the physical and digital worlds in the context of manufacturing processes. Industry 4.0 involves advanced digital technologies that influence social, manufacturing, and technological changes. It gives a new face to automation and autonomous processes through the use of intelligent technologies. Industry 4.0 is also another step forward, as the digital revolution encompasses not only product manufacturing methodology, but also Logistics 4.0, which involves the use of new technologies to ensure digital communication and streamline data exchange during processes along the supply chain. At this point, it should be noted that "logistics" in Logistics 4.0 refers to the physical movement and storage of goods and is part of the "supply chain," which also includes processes from the procurement of raw materials from suppliers, through production, to the delivery of the product to the end customer.

Several definitions of Logistics 4.0 can be found in the literature on the subject. Here they are:

- Logistics 4.0 is a logistics system that enables the sustainable fulfilment of individualised customer requirements without increasing costs and supports this development in industry and trade using digital technologies (Helo & Thai, 2024).

DOI: 10.1201/9781003685784-1

- Logistics 4.0 is a concept that emerges in the context of the digital transformation of industry, representing the use of advanced technologies to optimise logistics processes throughout the supply chain. Focusing on efficiency, automation, and integration, this model transforms traditional operations into intelligent, connected, and data-driven systems (Pinherio, 2025).
- Logistics 4.0 is a term referring to modern logistics in the supply chain, including data exchange, digitisation, and cloud computing. Intelligent and digitally connected systems create communication between people, machines, equipment, logistics solutions and products (Gajdzik & Grabowska, 2018).

An analysis of the definitions presented and others leads to the following conclusions:

- Logistics 4.0 concerns information technologies and intelligent resources connected for the purpose of optimising processes in the supply chain and logistics.
- Logistics 4.0 supports the horizontal integration of production systems within Industry 4.0 with suppliers and customers through digital technologies.
- Logistics 4.0 is characterised by digitisation, automation, integration, and flexibility of processes in the supply chain.
- Logistics 4.0 is a continuation of previous logistics systems that were implemented in the three industrial revolutions (Amr et al., 2019).

Logistics 4.0 enables real-time communication, shipment tracking, route optimisation and inventory management through the use of the following technologies.

- IoT in logistics, or the Internet of Things for short, refers to the integration of physical devices within the logistics and transport industry network that communicate with each other and exchange data without human intervention. Essentially, IoT enables devices such as sensors, vehicles, and equipment to connect and synchronise via the Internet, creating a more dynamic, responsive, and integrated logistics environment. All of this is used to analyse traffic conditions in real time and ultimately to increase the efficiency of logistics management within Logistics 4.0 (Chen et al., 2021). IoT technology is transforming the logistics process, advancing various aspects of operations through its innovative applications. Here are some key areas where IoT is having a significant impact (IoT in Logistics, 2025; Rehan, 2025):

- Real-time tracking—IoT enables logistics companies to track shipments and assets in real time, providing up-to-date data on location, temperature, and humidity. This feature streamlines route management, increases delivery accuracy and allows for a more efficient response to potential threats.
- Inventory management—thanks to IoT devices such as RFID tags and sensors, companies can automate inventory tracking and management. This technology ensures accurate inventory levels and notifies of low levels, which translates into effective inventory management.
- Vehicle tracking—IoT solutions enable precise tracking of every vehicle in a logistics company by communicating with logistics managers and providing data on location, speed, and route efficiency.
- Predictive maintenance—by analysing vehicle data, IoT systems can predict when a vehicle will require maintenance before a breakdown occurs, thus minimising downtime.
- Driver behaviour monitoring—IoT devices can monitor driver patterns and behaviour, providing feedback that can lead to safer driving and improved fuel efficiency.

Big data and data analysis have two dimensions. The first refers to the collection of vast amounts of data from, for example, ERP systems, GPS, sensors, and the ability to process data with the following characteristics: speed, variety, and volume. The second involves the ability to draw conclusions from data by applying statistics, mathematics, econometrics, simulation, optimisation or other techniques to help business organisations make better decisions (Wang et al., 2016). Big Data and data analytics are used in logistics in many ways, including route optimisation, last-mile process optimisation, freight tracking, warehouse management, customer service improvement, address verification and standardisation, predictive maintenance, strategic network planning, and operational capacity planning. As technology advances, the role of data analytics in logistics will continue to grow. The integration of artificial intelligence and machine learning with data analytics creates new opportunities for predictive and prescriptive analytics in the supply chain.

Future supply chain management systems will utilise real-time data analysis to enable fully autonomous decision-making, optimising logistics operations and reducing costs. The continuous development of sensors and IoT connectivity will generate even more valuable logistics data for analysis, leading to deeper data-driven insights. Organisations that invest in developing their data analytics capabilities today will be well positioned to lead the logistics industry in the future through innovative supply chain management practices (Lisowski, 2025).

Cloud computing is also referred to as cloud processing or IT cloud. This term refers to computing services offered by external entities, available on demand at any time and regulated according to demand (Rosenberg & Mateos, 2011). Cloud computing is a data processing model based on the use of computing services provided by a service provider in the form of scalable servers, databases, networks with optimal bandwidth and security, software, analytics, etc., via the Internet. Companies offering these services are called cloud providers. The service recipient pays for the use of a specific service, e.g., for the use of IT infrastructure, in accordance with a previously signed agreement, and thus does not incur any investment costs.

Among the areas of application of cloud computing in logistics, the most common are freight transport management, sales and operations planning, customer relationship management, and supply chain, fleet or warehouse resource management.

Cloud computing can be divided according to various criteria.

The first of these is the division of clouds in terms of how they are designed, created, and subsequently managed.

Within these criteria, we distinguish between the following types of cloud (Leończuk, 2012; Malinowska & Rzeczycki, 2016a):

- public cloud, intended for mass users, whose main advantage is universal availability, meaning that anyone with internet access can use it (free email services are a typical example of a public cloud),
- private cloud, i.e., dedicated IT resources or a ready-made solution intended for a single business entity (dedicated resources here refer to the latest IT technologies and highly qualified engineering staff),
- hybrid cloud, combining elements of both models,
- community cloud, in which resources are offered to a group of organisations with common goals and carrying out specific activities (the cloud may be owned by any of the organisations involved, or only one of them, or even an external entity),
- dedicated cloud, in which the service provider allocates a certain part of the cloud to the recipient, who has exclusive access to it,
- virtual private cloud, in which a set of resources is made available on an ad hoc basis for the needs of the service recipient as part of a "public cloud" service, taking into account a specific degree of isolation of these resources.

Another criterion for classifying cloud computing solutions is the issue of access and use of resources and the transfer of responsibility for hardware, licences, and connections to an external provider. Within this framework, we can distinguish the following models (Szymonik, 2018):

- IaaS (Infrastructure as a Service) this type of service involves the provision of dedicated IT infrastructure (physical or virtual) in accordance with the customer's expectations. In this model, the customer receives the hardware platform and the external provider is responsible for its maintenance.
- PaaS (Platform as a Service) is, in a sense, a supplement to the previous model with an application layer (operating system, databases) for which the provider is responsible.
- SaaS (Software as a Service)—the customer receives a service with specific parameters that meets their requirements (in this model, the administration of the infrastructure, operating

system and dedicated applications is the responsibility of the provider; this service shifts responsibility from the consumer to the provider).

The PaaS system in logistics has opened up new opportunities for companies. Businesses can adapt their resources to current needs without having to invest in their own, often costly, IT infrastructure. This solution not only optimises costs but also enables a quick response to market changes. PaaS technology in logistics companies (Słodowska, 2025):

- provides a ready-made IT platform optimised for specific software.
- provides a flexible environment for creating, hosting, and deploying applications, saving the company time and resources.
- manages the execution environment, middleware, operating systems, storage, and network.

The SaaS system combines various technological solutions (ERP, CRM) that enable the integration of all participants in logistics processes. This promotes the creation of long-term and lasting business relationships.

Cloud computing is flexible and scalable, which is why many logistics companies decide to implement it for the following reasons:

- it avoids the costs associated with building IT infrastructure,
- it offers unlimited data storage space,
- it ensures constant access to data,
- it guarantees continuous control over logistics processes in real time,
- it provides a place for efficient communication between all participants in the supply chain,
- allows communication with all business partners within the supply chain and customers within a consistent interface and any device,
- enables cheap and easy data archiving,
- streamlines accounting and reporting processes.

Of course, using external services carries certain risks and inconveniences, which include:

- lack of direct control over the IT system (hardware and software),
- the risk of loss or theft of our information by the cloud service provider,
- disclosure of our company's strategic data (e.g., list of waste markets, list of contractors) to competitors,
- introduction of new solutions that include applications and services that are unnecessary from the user's point of view,
- financial losses resulting from unrealised environmental processes due to unreliable cloud computing services, which may result from intentional or unintentional human actions and unreliable IT equipment,
- price increases for services by the cloud computing owner.

In practice, processes implemented for transport and logistics purposes using cloud computing concern (Grzejszczyk, 2015; Malinowska & Rzeczycki, 2016b; eTower Technologies, 2025):

- monitoring of means of transport and logistics cargo at all stages (traceability),
- inventory management (this allows companies to maintain optimal inventory levels, reduce stock shortages and minimise the risk of excess inventory),
- tracking intermodal transhipments at transhipment points,
- monitoring events in the transport process (damage, incidents, route changes, changes in means of transport),
- supply chain management from raw material procurement to delivery of finished products to customers,
- storage of information about orders, drivers, vehicles, loading, transhipment and unloading locations, trailer equipment,
- infrastructure management (including buildings, equipment, physical security, internal transport, operation, warehouses),
- automatic identification (barcodes, RFID),
- monitoring of risks in transport and logistics.

- Blockchain is a decentralised digital ledger that records transactions across multiple computers. This ensures transparent and secure data management, which is crucial in the logistics industry. This technology (Inbound Logistics, 2025; Chen, 2025):
  - allows products to be tracked throughout the supply chain, from raw materials to shipments around the world, which reduces costs and increases efficiency,
  - increases delivery accuracy,
  - improves supply chain management,
  - provides real-time updates of logistics processes and secure transaction recording,
  - provides all parties involved with access to verified, immutable data, thereby reducing errors and increasing transparency,
  - protects confidential data, reducing the risk of fraud and ensuring transparency and verifiability of all transactions, thereby increasing trust and reliability in the logistics sector,
  - guarantees secure, immutable records in the supply chain,
  - streamlines customs clearance by verifying and sharing data with customs authorities in real time (this reduces delays and ensures faster and more efficient handling of goods).

The blockchain technology market in the transport and logistics industry is estimated to grow by £1.6 billion, reaching a compound annual growth rate (CAGR) of 39.78% between 2022 and 2027. This change highlights the growing importance of blockchain technology in global supply chain management (Inbound Logistics, 2025).

- Augmented Reality (AR) and Virtual Reality (VR)

One of the important components of modern technologies affecting the field of logistics is AR, which allows digital information to be superimposed on the real world, which is extremely useful in the process of order picking and warehouse management. In practice, this technology (Nowak, 2025):

- enables employees wearing smart AR glasses to obtain real-time information about product locations, quantities, and optimal routes, which reduces the time needed to prepare goods for shipment,

- in terms of technical support, assists in diagnosing problems and carrying out repairs by superimposing repair information, diagrams, and operating instructions onto real objects,
- facilitates training—employees using smart AR glasses can learn how to operate new machines, safety procedures and other logistics-related tasks in realistic conditions, which significantly improves the effectiveness of training.

Virtual reality (VR) is an artificial environment generated by computers. This three-dimensional environment allows the user to experience sensory stimuli. The user can interact with the environment in a real or physical way using specialised electronic devices such as goggles, simple head-mounted displays and 3D images. The use of VR in logistics, supply chain management, and freight forwarding has opened up endless possibilities thanks to its diverse applications in various fields of activity (Joshi, 2025). VR drives innovation by providing immersive, interactive experiences that increase operational efficiency, reduce costs and offer advanced training methods. Here are some examples (Printezis, 2025):

- One of the key applications of VR in supply chain management (SCM) is the creation of digital twins, i.e., virtual replicas designed to faithfully reflect a physical object or system. This enables companies to recreate parts of their supply chain in the virtual world, allowing them to test scenarios, model different nodes, modes, flows, and policies, and understand how decisions and disruptions will affect the network's performance. This technology provides comprehensive visibility and traceability, enabling supply chain professionals to identify patterns of highly complex and dynamic behaviour.
- VR allows companies to visualise their designs in a 3D environment, enabling rapid iterations and evaluations. This interactive visualisation enhances the functionality of computer-aided design (CAD) and fosters engagement among engineering staff.
- Virtual reality provides an immersive platform for visualising complex data and processes. This can help supply chain managers better understand and manage their operations.

- VR's audio and video capabilities enable employees to collaborate in a shared virtual environment. This can be particularly beneficial for companies with a global reach.
- Virtual reality (VR) is also changing the way employees are trained. It provides a safe environment where employees can practise and develop their skills without exposing themselves to real-world risks. This realistic and immersive approach accelerates the learning process and improves retention through experiential learning—a hands-on approach to learning that can lead to more efficient work and employee confidence.
- Artificial intelligence (AI) refers to computer systems capable of performing complex tasks that historically were only possible for humans, such as reasoning, decision-making, and problem-solving. Artificial intelligence is (Coursera, 2025; European Parliament, 2025):
  - the theory and development of computer systems capable of performing tasks that historically required human intelligence, such as speech recognition, decision-making, and pattern identification,
  - the ability of a machine to exhibit human-like capabilities such as reasoning, learning, planning, and creativity.

AI is an umbrella term covering a wide range of technologies, including machine learning, deep learning and natural language processing (NLP), which have become an essential part of optimising logistics processes. As practice has shown, AI in logistics can (Messe München, 2025; Murrenhoff et al., 2021):

- recognise various dangerous goods labels,
- distinguish objects without, for example, a serial number or label,
- evaluate data on activity and movements recorded by sensors,
- predict transport arrival times based on data from multiple sources,
- create sales forecasts based on multidimensional data from supply chains and public sources,
- plan breaks for employees using data on machine movement and operation,

- monitor the choice of transport and identify better solutions step by step,
- improve human-machine interaction with trained talking robots,
- personalise recommendations when shopping online, e.g., based on search and purchase history or other online behaviour,
- improve the safety, speed, and efficiency of rail traffic by minimising wheel friction, maximising speed and enabling autonomous driving,
- detect fake news and misinformation by checking social media information, searching for disturbing words and identifying reliable online sources.

Machine learning (ML) is a branch of artificial intelligence dedicated to using data and algorithms to mimic the way humans learn, gradually improving their accuracy. This technology is currently under development, and its application in the logistics sector is becoming increasingly common (i-MAS, 2025; Softweb Solutions, 2025). A practical application of ML is machine vision (MV), which is the practical implementation of machine vision in practice.

MV in logistics is used, among other things (TME, 2025a; Viso.a i, 2025):

- in the picking and sorting of goods to increase order fulfilment speed and optimise space utilisation by monitoring product volume and location in real time,
- in tracking product origin through advanced QR code, RFID, and OCR (optical character recognition) reading, even in low visibility conditions or with damaged labels,
- in scanning shelves, racks, and containers to monitor stock levels in real time,
- to detect misplaced items or incorrect stock levels using 3D imaging and AI-based analytics,
- to automate the inspection process by analysing visual signals such as packaging integrity, label accuracy and product placement,
- to detect microscopic damage to packaging and products.

Automation and robotics are of great importance for the functioning of Logistics 4.0. Their activities are aimed at replacing human labour in specific tasks and sometimes even in entire processes. Automation is closely related to the use of technology and machines to perform tasks that require human intervention. Automation plays a key role in processes such as picking, sorting in postal and courier warehouses, last-mile deliveries, logistics, and e-commerce. Robotisation means nothing more than the use of robots, manipulators, and various types of accompanying devices during the production process. Its aim is to enable the implementation of selected processes without human intervention or with limited intervention. Robotisation combines mechanical, electrical, and software engineering to create robots. These are designed to perform tasks quickly and with high precision, including, for example, enabling fast and accurate selection of products for shipment (Porębski, 2025). Robots have already established a solid foundation in logistics, solving problems such as labour shortages, human error and the need to work 24/7. Not only do they help increase productivity, but they also enable logistics companies to expand their operations and meet high demand. From automated guided vehicles (AGVs) to collaborative robots that move along set routes (AMRs—autonomous mobile robots), the role of robotics in logistics is growing, providing companies with the tools to achieve higher levels of operational efficiency. The growing demand for comprehensive automation in warehouses for operational efficiency in the logistics sector and to alleviate supply chain issues is driving demand for these robots (Jha, 2025).

Autonomous (unmanned) transport is a technology that allows a vehicle to be controlled without the need for human operation. To make this possible, it is necessary to use (Logistyczny.net, 2025): artificial intelligence (AI), machine learning, neural networks, radars, sensors, GPS, and cameras that act as the "eyes" of the control computer.

- artificial intelligence (AI),
- machine learning,
- neural networks,
- radars, sensors, GPS, and cameras that act as the "eyes" of the control computer.

Autonomous transport can take various forms, including (Viva Technology, 2025; Jahani et al., 2025):

- Autonomous vans and lorries—companies such as Tesla, Uber Freight and Aurora are developing autonomous lorries for transporting goods in order to streamline logistics and reduce transport costs.
- Autonomous drones—Aerial deliveries using drones are particularly attractive in areas with difficult terrain or heavy traffic. Although drones are not yet widely used, several companies, including Amazon, are testing drones for fast and light deliveries in suburban and rural areas.
- Last-mile robots—Designed to operate in urban environments, these small, ground-based robots can deliver parcels and food without human assistance. These robots aim to solve the "last-mile problem"—the costly and difficult final stage in the process of delivering a parcel to a customer's door.
- Warehouse robots—these machines move goods around warehouses, streamlining the supply chain. Warehouse robots perform tasks that are often difficult and dangerous for humans, such as organising, retrieving, and transporting large quantities of stock.

Cybersecurity

The tools and technologies presented in Logistics 4.0 are based on digitalisation. The digital technologies used have their advantages, which include: greater efficiency and speed of operation, better control and transparency, cost optimisation, better customer service, data and document security, scalability, and disadvantages such as high implementation costs, complexity and time-consuming implementation, risk of failure and dependence on technology, employee resistance to change, system integration problems, dependence on technology suppliers, and high vulnerability to attacks on IT systems.

In order to protect IT systems, data and digital devices used in logistics and supply chains, we create a set of cybersecurity measures, technologies, and procedures that protect against hacker attacks, viruses, data theft and digital sabotage.

Cybersecurity is not clearly defined. The following terms can be found in the literature on the subject:

- cybersecurity is the resilience of information systems against actions that compromise the confidentiality, integrity, availability, and authenticity of the data processed or related services offered by these systems,
- cybersecurity is the protection of computer systems and networks against cyberattacks—it covers everything from password management to security tools powered by machine learning (cybersecurity enables you to shop, chat, and browse the web without risk) (NordVPN, n.d.),
- cybersecurity is the activity of protecting people, systems, and data from cyberattacks through the use of various technologies, processes, and principles (Jonker et al., n.d.).

An analysis of the definitions presented and others leads to the conclusion that cybersecurity is closely related to the implementation of logistics processes, and moreover (US Bureau of Labour Statistics, 2024):

- it includes protecting information from unauthorised access,
- it protects users (data) from unauthorised access,
- it ensures data availability for authorised users,
- it is closely related to concepts such as:
    - cyberattack—a deliberate action targeting computer systems, networks or electronic devices with the aim of gaining unauthorised access, stealing data or disrupting the normal functioning of IT infrastructure (e.g., paralysing a warehouse system, redirecting transport, stealing data) (Nflo, n.d.a),
    - Vulnerabilities are gaps in IT systems that can be exploited by attackers to gain unauthorised access to data or systems (they pose a serious threat to security as they can be used to carry out various attacks, such as data theft, system takeover or service disruption).—e.g., an unpatched vulnerability in fleet tracking software (Nflo, n.d.c),
    - an IT system threat is a flaw or vulnerability in the physical structure, organisation, procedures, personnel,

management, administration, hardware, or software that can be exploited to cause damage to the IT system or human activity—e.g., hackers, malware, human error (Liderman, 2008, p. 40),
- risk refers to scenarios of events causing losses that occur exclusively in cyberspace, such as phishing, malware, data breaches (Copeland, n.d.),
- data confidentiality means ensuring that data (e.g., about customers, shipments, routes) is only accessible to authorised persons,
- data integrity means guaranteeing that data will not be altered or falsified during processing or transmission,
- availability is ensuring that logistics systems must operate 24/7 and data must be available when needed,
- authorisation is granting appropriate permissions to users (e.g., a driver can only see the route, but not customer data).

Cybersecurity encompasses many issues, which can be summarised in Figure 1.1 (Klimczuk, n.d.; Advisor, n.d.; The Astrology Page, n.d.):

- Standards and structures—the theoretical and practical knowledge required to control the functioning of a given organisation in the context of security. Examples of such documents include:
    - ISO 27001—Information security management system, the main standard for data security, consisting of internal and external audits,
    - ISO 27017—this standard contains guidelines for information security controls applicable to the provision and use of cloud services,
    - ISO 27018—code of practice for personal data protection in cloud computing entities acting as personal data processors,
    - NIS2 (EU)—directive on the security of network and information systems (Resilia, 2025),
    - TPRM—Third Party Risk Management (1ClickVPN, 2025),

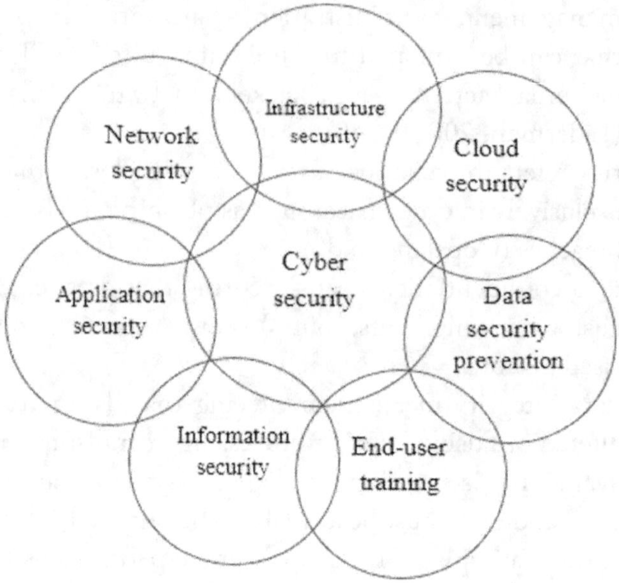

Figure 1.1 Selected areas related to cybersecurity. Source: Based on: Yuchong Li, Qinghui Liu, A comprehensive review study of cyber-attacks and cyber security; Emerging trends and recent developments, ELSEVIER, Energy Reports 7 (2021) 8176–8818, https://doi.org/10.1016/j.egyr.2021.08.126 .

- Technical security—each device must have its own clearly defined physical location, to which access should be restricted to a specific person or group of people.
- IoT security requires the creation of an appropriate system that is resistant to various types of interference. The components of this system include: physical security of devices, appropriate authorisation and identification, security of communication between devices, cloud security, and an integrated IoT security management system.
- Cloud security—a set of procedures, rules, and technologies that protect cloud-based computing environments from cyber threats.
- Application security is the general practice of adding features or functions to software to prevent a variety of threats. These include denial-of-service attacks and other attacks, as well as data breaches or theft.
- Mobile applications are software installed on devices such as phones, smartphones, and tablets, facilitating users' access to

services (e.g., shopping, booking services, banking) or performing tasks that require access to a network or computer.

- Endpoint security is a system that protects devices directly connected to the network from threats. It is a solution that protects not only office devices, but also other devices that are connected via the Internet or other ICT networks (Kubera, 2023).
- Personal data protection—data is vulnerable to leaks as a result of attacks or theft by a company employee or other person, and therefore access to it should be secured. Identity and privileged access management in IT systems is a procedure that prevents unauthorised persons from accessing key resources. It is an essential part of mitigating internal threats, preventing unwanted access to accounts, preventing employees from "borrowing" passwords from colleagues, and identifying individuals hiding behind default or shared accounts.
- Database security encompasses various measures used to protect database management systems from malicious cyberattacks and illegal use. Database security programmes are designed to protect not only the data in the database, but also the data management system itself and any application that accesses it from misuse, damage, and intrusion (Ray, 2023).
- Employee training in cybersecurity covers employee knowledge and awareness of information protection. Knowledge in this area includes basic concepts and principles, legal aspects and practical elements. The topics covered include information technology, the Internet, the methods used by cybercriminals (including elements of psychology, social engineering and manipulation) and ways to protect against cyberattacks.

1.2 Classification of Cyber Threats

In the 21st century, in addition to classic, recurring threats, the supply chain has seen the emergence of threats that disrupt the functioning of IT systems. Bad, distorted or incomplete information can lead to many financial and operational problems, including disruptions in the flow of goods.

The most common threats to IT systems in logistics processes include seven situations:

- cyberattacks on suppliers and partners,
- threats related to hardware and software,
- internal threats,
- data manipulation and information falsification,
- threats related to outsourcing and external suppliers,
- geopolitical and regulatory threats.

The first situation: Cyberattacks on suppliers and partners

In our increasingly digitalised world, logistics is the backbone of global trade, seamlessly connecting manufacturers, suppliers, distributors, and retailers. However, this connectivity comes with a host of cyberattacks targeting the complex network of relationships between links along the supply chain. These attacks can take the form of (Encryption Consulting, 2025; Avetta, 2025):

Malicious software is any programme deliberately created to damage devices, steal data or disrupt their operation. From viruses to ransomware, malicious software exploits vulnerabilities in systems, often spreading silently until it strikes. In 2025, AI-based malware makes detection more difficult, increasing the need for awareness and robust security measures. It can take the form of (Xcitium, 2025): viruses, worms, Trojans, ransomware, spyware, among others.

Attacks on supply chains and partners are largely ransomware (Trend Micro, 2025), which simply target higher levels of the supply chain. The following ransomware threats will directly affect suppliers' vulnerability to attacks:

- the increase in hybrid working and sporting events increases the number of opportunities to hack into often poorly secured networks, endpoints, and users—attackers may change their approach from this point onwards,
- the ongoing convergence of IT/OT (especially in industries with older generation systems) brings with it a number of old firmware vulnerabilities and an increasing number of attacks at the hardware level.

These issues, combined with the rise in sophisticated attacks and the growth of the ransomware economy, create ideal conditions for compromises among both core service providers and supply chain providers.

The number of attacks on organisations originating from external partners and service providers is expected to increase in the coming years as attackers seek weak links in software supply chains, attempting to "attack one to attack all" (Freed, 2025).

The European Union Agency for Cybersecurity (ENISA) has reported that attacks on supply chains are expected to quadruple in 2021, and the risk currently appears to be just as high, if not higher (ENISA, 2021).

- Phishing for login details or sensitive information from employees of companies in the chain—deceptive tricks in which dishonest users impersonate a trusted person to try to obtain data. Fraudsters impersonate credible sources in emails or text messages, attempting to obtain personal information such as passwords or financial details. They often contain links or files that, after a few clicks, can damage your device with malware or redirect you to a fake website pretending to be the real one (NX Lifestyle Logistics, n.d.). In practice, the most common tool is:
  - Phishing—a type of cybercrime that involves obtaining confidential information, such as login details, credit card numbers or personal data, by impersonating trusted individuals or institutions. Attackers use social engineering to manipulate victims and persuade them to disclose sensitive data (Nflo, 2025).
  - Spear phishing—an advanced form of phishing in which attackers target specific individuals or organisations using personalised emails or other forms of communication. Unlike traditional phishing, which is mass-based and impersonal, spear phishing is precisely targeted, which increases its effectiveness (Nflo.pl., 2025).
- Overloading the IT systems of suppliers and partners along the chain means flooding servers with unauthorised traffic, which prevents the planned logistics processes from being carried out. In practice, we most often use the following types of attacks for this purpose (NMFTA, 2025):

  - "denial of service"—consists of overloading the supply chain's resources, preventing it from responding to legitimate service requests,
  - "distributed denial of service"—disrupting the normal traffic of target servers, networks or systems by flooding them with a huge amount of internet traffic (Fortinet, 2025),
  - Both attacks prevent supply chains from functioning properly and can lead to their complete shutdown if they are not quickly identified and stopped.
- Threats related to software supply chain attacks occur when hackers infect legitimate software during its development, update or distribution. Attackers inject their own code into the system or product, which is known as malicious code injection. The software developer may modify the code to perform malicious actions within the application. This enables fraud and information theft or leaves the attacker with a backdoor for remote access to the corporate system. Attacks on software used in the supply chain can occur through (Kalapatapu, 2025; Checkmarx, 2025):
  - breaches of open-source libraries,
  - attacks on development tools and environments, such as code repositories, build servers, and integration services,
  - third-party infiltration,
  - compromising mechanisms used for software updates.

Second scenario: Hardware and software threats.

Hardware-related threats are risks and vulnerabilities that can compromise the integrity, confidentiality, and availability of data, as well as the functionality of computer systems. They include not only risks related to the physical components of systems and devices, but also to software. These threats can take many forms. They include:

Counterfeiting of Components

The complexity of electronic systems, including the integrated circuits used in them, has increased significantly over the last few decades, and they are assembled (manufactured) around the world in order to reduce production costs. Manufacturing involves components such as analogue integrated circuits, microprocessor integrated circuits, memory circuits, programmable logic integrated circuits, and transistors in a global environment.

The international nature of the electronic supply chain also poses challenges, particularly in terms of quality control and transparency of the supply chain involving counterfeit components due to its interconnected nature. As a result, they end up on the market, where the final products manufactured, e.g., laptops and computers, do not guarantee the security of information processed in computer networks. In many cases, the weakness of end devices is exploited by hackers, including along the entire supply chain.

Detecting and avoiding counterfeit components is a difficult challenge, partly because there are so many different types of counterfeits that affect the supply chain. The counterfeiting of integrated circuits (ICs) and semiconductor devices is a serious challenge that threatens the security and reliability of electronic devices, the global economy, intellectual property rights, and the overall sustainability of the electronic supply chain industry. It is extremely important to develop a taxonomy of defects and anomalies found in counterfeit components to enable the detection of these components using a set of testing methods (Guin et al., 2014; Bhure et al., 2024).

Hardware Trojans

Attacks involving the concealment of malicious hardware in integrated circuits have been dubbed "hardware Trojans." They constitute interference with or modification of the original hardware design, which affects the reliability of the electronic system, even in consumer electronics. Hardware Trojans (Secure-IC, 2025a, 2025b):

- are specifically designed to be rarely activated and undetectable by conventional testing practices and verification methodologies,
- are very difficult to locate because they can be placed anywhere in a microprocessor (one may be located in the microprocessor's processor, for example, and another in its power supply),

- consist of a payload (the malicious circuitry) and a trigger (which activates the malicious circuitry).

Attacks on IoT Devices

The Internet of Things (IoT) is a network of devices and software that are connected to each other via the Internet or other communication technologies. In logistics, it enables, among other things, the monitoring of all processes, remote management of individual activities, response to undesirable situations and process optimisation (Dataconsult.pl, 2025). IoT devices are becoming increasingly common in everyday life, making them an attractive target for cybercriminals. The most common threats that IoT device users may face include (Tageldin, 2025; Porady-it.pl, 2025):

- DDoS attacks—distributed denial-of-service attacks can simultaneously attack multiple IoT devices, causing them to crash or become overloaded. Unauthorised individuals can use networks of devices to wreak havoc on computer networks.
- Unauthorised access—weak passwords and a lack of adequate security measures can lead to unauthorised access to devices. Hackers can gain control of devices and use them for their own purposes.
- Malware—IoT devices can be infected with malware that steals personal data or takes control of devices, which in turn can lead to information leaks or data deletion.
- Lack of software updates—many IoT devices do not receive regular updates, making them vulnerable to known security vulnerabilities. Failure to update can lead to hackers exploiting these vulnerabilities.
- Data interception—IoT devices often transmit data through unsecured channels. Interception of this data can lead to privacy violations and theft of sensitive information.

Physical Attacks

A physical attack is any type of action (intentional—human-dependent or accidental) directed and aimed against IT system resources, which include people, computer equipment, network infrastructure or data carriers. These attacks can take various forms, from natural disasters, theft, and vandalism to unauthorised access and manipulation of critical equipment. Physical attacks include (Echelon Protective Services, 2025):

- Theft of equipment, which may include servers, computers, and even external storage devices (e.g., hard drives, USB sticks). Perpetrators may seek to obtain confidential data stored on these devices or disrupt their operation by removing essential equipment.
- Vandalism, in which attackers deliberately damage or destroy hardware components, can lead to data loss, system downtime, and financial consequences for the attacked entity. Such actions may include damage to network cables, destruction of server cooling systems, and damage to USB ports. Vandalism can be a form of sabotage carried out by disgruntled employees.
- Unauthorised access to a secure area poses a potential threat to cybersecurity. Infiltrators can exploit weak entry points or use social engineering tactics to breach physical security measures and gain access to confidential information. In practice, unauthorised access may involve, for example, physically entering a server room or office to tamper with equipment, or connecting unauthorised devices (e.g., hardware keyloggers, malicious USB sticks).
- Electromagnetic interference (EMI)—the use of devices emitting strong electromagnetic fields to damage electronics (TME, 2025b).
- Attacks:
    - environmental—e.g., fires, hurricanes, floods,
    - civilisational (e.g., COVID-19),
    - destructive (e.g., terrorism, crime, sabotage),
    - economic threats, e.g., environmental pollution, faulty structures, construction disasters.

Attacks on firmware and BIOS/UEFI (Krzysztof, 2025):

When thinking about security, most teams focus on application-level vulnerabilities, firewalls, and antivirus tools. However, securing UEFI BIOS firmware is equally important, if not more so. Firmware operates at a fundamental level, below the operating system (OS), which means that traditional security solutions are not always able to detect breaches or malicious activity occurring at this level.

If the firmware is compromised, attackers can:

- gain persistent control over their devices, even after the operating system is reinstalled,
- bypass traditional security measures such as antivirus software,
- disrupt system functions, causing difficult-to-diagnose problems that can cripple devices and networks (Dhillon, 2025).

This is why BIOS and UEFI security must be a priority. Failure to secure these layers can have catastrophic consequences.

Common UEFI attacks currently include (Startup Defense, 2025):

- Rootkits are malicious programmes embedded in the firmware itself, which makes them extremely difficult to detect. Once injected, they can gain complete control over the system and bypass many conventional security measures.
- Exploiting vulnerabilities in UEFI drivers, which help manage various hardware components. If these drivers contain vulnerabilities, attackers can exploit them to inject malicious code into the system.
- Phishing and social engineering tactics—while some attacks on UEFI directly exploit technical vulnerabilities, others take a more human-centric approach. Attackers sometimes combine UEFI with phishing and social engineering tactics to manipulate users and unwittingly facilitate their own attacks.
- Direct attacks with physical access—malicious individuals can change firmware settings or perform malicious installations if they gain physical access to the device. This method is often overlooked, but remains highly effective.

Third scenario: internal threats

Criminals within an organisation can be divided into three general categories (Trevino, 2023):

- Internal employee with malicious intent
  An insider with malicious intent is someone who has access to internal information about the organisation, such as an employee

or contractor, and uses this information to breach confidential data. Their aim is to sabotage the organisation or steal information or money for their own gain. For example, an employee may sell confidential information to a competitor of the organisation for financial gain.

Insiders with malicious intent fall into two subcategories: collaborators and lone wolves. A collaborator is a malicious insider who works with a third party, such as a competitor, to harm the organisation by leaking confidential information or disrupting business operations.

A lone wolf is a malicious insider who acts alone. Lone wolves usually have personal reasons for attacking an organisation, such as dissatisfaction with the company and a desire to disrupt its operations.

- Negligent insider
  A negligent insider is an individual employed by an organisation who does not follow security practices. As a result, they may make a mistake or misjudge a situation, leading to a data breach. For example, they may fall victim to phishing scams and click on a malicious link that compromises the entire organisation's network and systems.

- External employee with internal employee access
  Another common internal threat is an external employee who has gained access to the organisation's systems and data. They are also referred to as moles. To gain access to systems they would not normally have access to, moles impersonate employees or suppliers, making them difficult to detect. Moles are often able to gain access to internal systems by compromising an employee's account or gaining access to the organisation's physical building.

A detailed analysis has shown that the attackers remain the same from year to year. The most harmful of these are (Securivy, 2023):

- privileged users and administrators,
- unaware of the threat, ordinary employees,
- external and temporary employees,
- privileged business users and management.

Internal threats in IT systems can be divided into four groups (Figure 1.2).

Here they are:

1. Data theft, most often involving usernames and passwords. After stealing authentication data, a malicious employee can use it to gain access to the victim's accounts, such as email, bank or work accounts. The insider can then steal confidential information and commit identity theft (Trevino et al., 2023). A similar situation also applies to the theft of company documents, illegal copying of data or the transfer of confidential clauses and agreements to competitors via a computer. These are just some of the practices that are increasingly being carried out by dishonest employees of thousands of national and international companies (Zabezpieczenia.com.pl, n.d.).
2. Abuse of authority involves using privileged access to an account or service in an illegal/inappropriate manner. This type of internal threat is one of the most common. Improper data handling is the second most common type of privilege abuse. It includes careless handling of confidential information—its loss, misplacement, or risky storage. However, unlike illegal abuse of privileges, such incidents are usually unintentional and caused by the unwitting actions of employees.
3. Privilege escalation is a phenomenon whereby an unauthorised user gradually gains broader access to the system—more than the administrator intended. This management error leads to a serious vulnerability in the network's security, exposing it to numerous attacks. An attacker can exploit a vulnerability in the company network to gain access to privileges that allow them to download and install malware, modify the system, and steal important files and sensitive user data. The process usually begins with finding a weak point in the organisation's

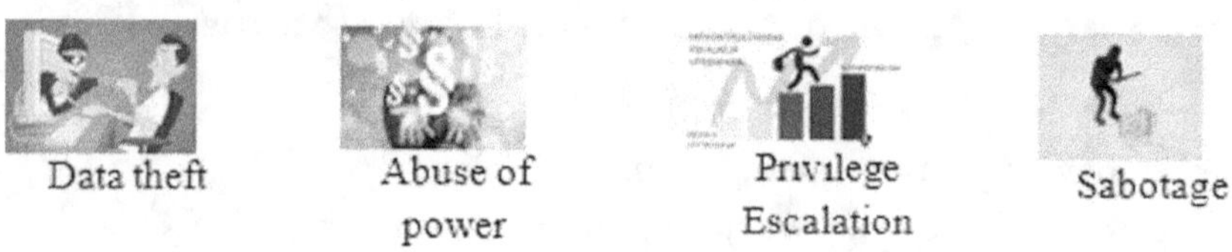

Figure 1.2 Four key types of internal threats. Source: Own work.

infrastructure and then gradually gaining access to higher and higher privileges, known as privilege escalation. This is done without the administrator's knowledge—it is virtually impossible to identify the hacker's actions until the losses and effects of the attack are noticed.

4. Computer sabotage is the deliberate and unlawful causing of serious disruption to the functioning of a system as a result of activities related to computer data, i.e., their entry, transmission, destruction, deletion, damage, alteration or disruption of access to them (Warchoł, 2020). These are actions aimed at disrupting the functioning of a computer system or blocking its operation. It must be directed at computer data or programmes. The methods used by cybercriminals in this area include: computer viruses, worms, logic bombs, denial-of-service attacks (DoS, DDoS), exploiting vulnerabilities in devices, unauthorised alteration of information, unauthorised access to or use of information, data scanning, and exploiting application vulnerabilities (Securivy, n.d.a).

Fourth situation: Data manipulation and falsification of information

Data manipulation attacks occur when an attacker does not obtain data, but makes subtle, discreet modifications in order to achieve some gain or effect. These subtle modifications to data can be just as crippling to an organisation as data breaches (Nettles et al., n.d.). Attacks on data integrity are nothing new, but tactics and targets have changed over time, making such attacks more difficult to detect and even more difficult to stop. The growing amount of digital data being created and applications is contributing to an increasing attack surface. In addition, infrastructures are becoming increasingly cloud-based and software-defined, and greater vulnerabilities in encryption are being identified (Booz Allen Hamilton, n.d.). Manipulation in supply chain IT systems can also affect the flow of goods and information. These activities can lead to wrong decisions, financial losses, disruption of supply flows, and even legal violations.

A similar situation applies to data falsification, where an attacker deliberately alters data, communications or transactions with the intent to mislead, manipulate or disrupt the normal operation of a digital system or network, in business transactions carried out, among others, in the supply chain. This type of attack aims to compromise data integrity, leading to misinformation, unauthorised transactions and breaches of trust in digital environments (ITU Online, n.d.). Data falsification in IT systems in the supply chain is a serious threat that can lead to financial losses, loss of customer trust and even legal liability.

Any manipulation or theft of data can result in:

- overstating or understating inventory levels—e.g., to avoid orders or reduce inventory costs on paper, to mislead suppliers and customers, to force additional orders from trading partners,
- changes to routes in the TMS (Transport Management System)—to delay or extend delivery times, e.g., in the JiT system, to show fuel savings or shorter travel times,
- changes to shipment priorities—to favour certain customers, especially so-called strategic ones,
- termination of contracts, loss of reputation, loss of markets, customers,
- creation of non-existent suppliers or orders—to extort funds or shift responsibility for errors and create confusion in orders,
- falsifying GPS and IoT data from lorries or containers—e.g., concealing unauthorised stops, route changes or theft,
- changing telemetry data in IoT systems to conceal vehicle equipment failure,
- falsifying product quality or compliance certificates (e.g., ISO, CE, HACCP) to place non-compliant goods on the market.

Fifth situation: risks associated with outsourcing and external suppliers

IT outsourcing for logistics companies is a service that involves transferring some or all IT activities to external companies or IT specialists who work as freelancers. This type of solution allows companies to optimise costs and improve efficiency, as they do not have to invest in developing their own IT teams or purchasing equipment or technology. IT outsourcing can include a range of services, such as IT infrastructure management, technical support, data security, software development and cloud services (also known as cloud computing) (Securivy, n.d.b).

According to Eurostat data cited by Operator Chmury Krajowej, over 55.7% of Polish companies used cloud services in 2023, and this number is growing every year (Jadczak, n.d.).

Clouds, obviously, have scalability, but they are also exposed to various threats that can affect the effectiveness, continuity, and efficiency of the supply chain.

The most common cloud security threats include (Euvic, n.d.):

- data breaches, which can result from weak passwords, human error or hacking attempts,
- malware and ransomware attacks that can infect cloud servers and cause serious damage to companies that are links in the supply chain,
- internal attacks in which an employee or contractor intentionally or unintentionally discloses confidential information,
- denial-of-service (DoS) attacks, which can disable cloud services for users,
- loss of control over data and systems as a result of outsourcing data processing to an external company.

Other barriers to the use of the cloud by logistics companies include (Majchrzak, 2019):

- Technical failures. There are concerns about what will happen if the provider is unable to provide services to the company due to a system failure. Supply chain operations are critical to a company's bottom line, and as a result, any delays caused by cloud system malfunctions can have dire consequences.
- Limited customisation options. In most cases, cloud computing offers standardised services that may not suit specific supply chain operations. For example, manufacturing, which consists of unique processes, is difficult to enhance with cloud services. Potential users are concerned that a lack of customisation will lead to negative business consequences.

Sixth situation: Geopolitical and regulatory risks.

In recent years, international supply chains have experienced numerous disruptions that have revealed their vulnerability to a variety of crises, including: the emergence and escalation of tensions between countries, armed conflicts, coups d'état, terrorist attacks, natural disasters, economic crises and pandemics. Such events cause internal problems and disruptions in international relations and pose a threat to global supply chains.

A Reuters Events analysis published at the end of October 2024 identified the eight biggest threats to global supply chains, with geopolitical tensions emerging as the biggest concern (Figure 1.3). In 2024, as many as 33% of logistics and supply chain managers in major global markets, including Europe, North America and the Asia-Pacific region, expressed concerns in this area (Oflakowski, 2025).

The war in Ukraine, growing tensions between the US and China, and the escalation of the conflict in the Middle East are just some of the events illustrating the increase in international tensions. The number of references to geopolitics and political risk in public company documents increased by 600% in the second quarter of 2022 compared to previous years, and remained at an elevated level in 2023. This shows that executives are now paying more attention to the international situation than they did in the past (EY Poland, 2024).

The geopolitical situation also has a huge impact on international transport, and changing alliances, conflicts, and tensions between countries can cause serious disruptions in supply chains. An example is the current trade war between the United States and China, which

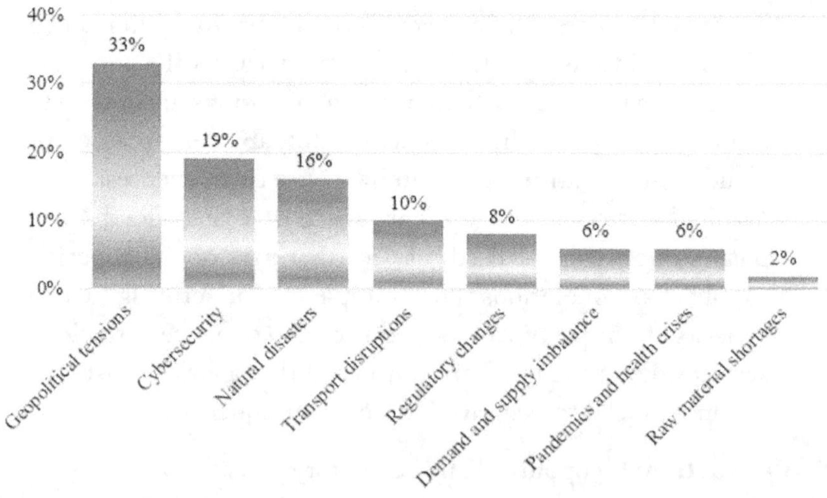

Figure 1.3 The greatest threats to global supply chains. Source: Oflakowski, K. (2025, August 3). *Geopolityka i cyberbezpieczeństwo na szczycie zagrożeń dla TSL*. Logistyka.net.pl. Retrieved 3 August 2025 from https://www.logistyka.net.pl/bank-wiedzy/item/95720-geopolityka-i-cyberbezpieczenstwo-na-szczycie-zagrozen-dla-tsl.

has led to increased transport costs and changes in the flow of goods. In addition, changes in customs policy, such as the introduction of new tariffs or trade barriers, can cause delays in transport processes.

Geopolitical tensions are currently affecting the availability of important transport routes, such as the Strait of Malacca and the Strait of Hormuz, which are crucial for international maritime transport. Blockades, traffic control or regulatory changes often lead to increased transport costs and delivery delays. Carriers and logistics companies must monitor these changes and adapt their transport strategies to the new political realities.

Another example of contemporary geopolitical tensions is drone and missile attacks on Israeli and American ships in the Red Sea and the Gulf of Aden, carried out by Houthi rebels from Yemen, supported by Iran. This has led to the modification of container ship routes transporting goods between Asia and Europe. Ships that would normally sail through the Suez Canal are being redirected to a route around the Cape of Good Hope. By sailing around South Africa, ships take up to 10 days longer, and the impact of the Houthi attacks on maritime transport and supply chains is therefore considered to be greater than that of the coronavirus pandemic. These attacks have so far resulted in the suspension of production at Tesla and Volvo's European plants (Jaworska, n.d.).

Regulatory risks in IT systems used in logistics focus primarily on data protection, cybersecurity, and compliance with evolving standards specific to the industry related to the flow of goods and accompanying information along the supply chain. Failure to comply with these regulations can lead to financial penalties, loss of reputation and even suspension of operations. It should be noted that existing regulations, norms, standards, and legal acts concerning the functioning of logistics (supply chain) are constantly being updated, and new threats are emerging.

1.3 Basic Principles of IT System Protection

IT system protection is a set of applied and implemented measures, mechanisms, tools, and instruments that ensure information security and protect digital data. It should be emphasised that a broader concept than the protection of IT systems is information security, which includes not only actual measures (technical, organisational, and legal), but also policies, philosophies, strategies, general rules, principles, standards, and processes to protect people, systems, and data from cyberattacks.

Effective and rational protection of IT systems is based on several basic rules, which include, among others:

- The Principle of Least Privilege (PoLP), which assumes that each user should only have access to the information and resources necessary to perform their tasks, reduces the risk of data leaks and cyberattacks. Even if a user falls victim to phishing or malware, a potential attacker will not have access to critical data or systems to which the victim did not have access (Siwek, n.d.).
- The CIA triad (Basic Security Model), which contains three basic principles (Geveye, n.d.):
  - confidentiality—this ensures that confidential information remains confidential and is only accessible to authorised persons (in essence, this means that unauthorised persons or systems should not have access to protected data),
  - integrity—focuses on the accuracy and reliability of data (its purpose is to prevent unauthorised changes or modifications to information, ensuring the accuracy and reliability of data),
  - availability—emphasises that information should be accessible and available when needed (this principle ensures that authorised users can use data and resources without hindrance).
- Defence in Depth is a holistic security strategy that involves the use of multiple layers of protection to secure an organisation or individual and their resources. The basic idea behind this concept is simple: if one line of defence is breached, the subsequent layers act as a backup. This approach allows potential threats to be stopped by compensating for possible security gaps. The basic elements of defence in depth include (Rudra, n.d.):
  - physical control,
  - network security control,

  - administrative control,
  - antivirus software,
  - behavioural analysis algorithms (these systems are used to collect and analyse data on user, application, and device behaviour in order to identify suspicious or abnormal behaviour patterns and block them to prevent security breaches).
- Network segmentation—This is an important element of network architecture. It divides a larger network into smaller, isolated segments or subnets. This division helps control traffic flow between different segments and limits the movement of potential cybercriminals within the network. In addition, segmentation improves network performance by reducing congestion and enabling targeted monitoring and troubleshooting within each segment. Its purpose is to improve network security, organisation, and performance. Network segmentation allows users to monitor and manage their networks more easily and effectively. This is essential for businesses that need to protect valuable assets in hybrid and multi-cloud environments, including (Wickramasinghe, n.d.):
  - customer information,
  - financial data,
  - intellectual property.
- Patch Management, Vulnerability Management
  Patch management is a process that an organisation uses to update software, applications, and devices. This process involves searching for, testing, verifying, and applying patches to fix bugs and defects. This helps to eliminate system vulnerabilities, improve system performance, stability, and functionality, and ensure compliance with applicable laws. Timely patch deployment helps protect critical business applications, systems, and other assets from cyber threats such as zero-day attacks, DDoS attacks, SQL injection attacks, and others. This helps minimise system downtime, enabling continuous customer service. To automate this process, you can use patch management software that scans and detects problems and then tests, deploys, and installs patches. The most important

patch management features include (SentinelOne, n.d.; Dissanayake et al., 2022) :

- automatic deployment,
- centralisation,
- prioritisation,
- testing and rollback,
- scheduled and on-demand deployment,
- remote management.

Vulnerability management is a cybersecurity process that helps organisations identify, assess, prioritise, and remove security vulnerabilities across their IT infrastructure. This protects data and systems from cyber threats such as DDoS attacks, phishing, zero-day attacks, etc. It is useful for organisations that operate under strict control, such as healthcare facilities, financial institutions, etc., as well as large enterprises that process large databases. Vulnerability management functions include:

- automatic scanning,
- prioritisation,
- resource detection,
- patching and vulnerability removal,
- compliance reporting.

- The principle of User Awareness refers to the level of knowledge and understanding of information security risks and ways to avoid them by users of IT systems. It includes both knowledge of security rules and procedures and the ability to apply them in practice, which is crucial for the protection of personal data, confidential information and organisational resources. The main goal of awareness is to clearly explain to the user why something is important by providing them with understandable examples to encourage them to change their behaviour and comply with the policy. The goal of awareness is to change behaviour in order to increase the security of the organisation. The key elements of this system include (EITT, n.d.; Ciriello et al., 2024):
    - education—regular training and workshops on threats and best practices in security.

- understanding threats—awareness of potential threats such as phishing, malware, and social engineering attacks.
- application of procedures—the ability to implement security rules in everyday work, such as creating strong passwords and avoiding suspicious links.
- continuous improvement—regularly updating knowledge about new threats and protection technologies.

- Data backup is the process of copying data from an IT system to another location so that it can be recovered if the original data is lost. The purpose of backup is to preserve data in the event of hardware failure, cyberattack, human error, natural disaster or other data loss events. Therefore, backup is an important part of a company's data protection strategy, which usually also includes a business continuity and disaster recovery plan (Moore, n.d.).

  In practice, backup involves following specific rules and strategies. Here they are (Gryczka, n.d.):

1. Cloud storage—this involves storing data on remote servers operated by an external cloud service provider and accessing it from any computer or mobile device with an internet connection.
2. The 3-2-1 backup rule is one of the best rules to follow when planning your backup strategy. This means that you should create three different copies of your data, place them on two different types of storage, and store one copy off-site, i.e., in a different physical location than the others.
3. Hybrid backup solutions are a comprehensive data backup strategy that combines the advantages of on-premises (local) and cloud backup methods.
4. Periodic automatic backups involve regular, scheduled, automatic data backups at specified intervals.
5. Continuous Data Protection (CDP) is an advanced data backup principle that provides real-time or near real-time data protection by continuously recording and backing up data changes as they occur.
6. Backup versioning involves keeping multiple versions of files and data over time.

7. On-site backups, also known as local backups, are a data backup strategy that involves storing copies of data in physical locations at the workplace or on local devices, such as a separate hard drive.
8. Off-site backups involve storing copies of data in a physical location separate from the main data storage site. This strategy provides an additional layer of protection, safeguarding data from on-site failures and threats.
9. A comprehensive backup and recovery plan is essential to mitigate the risks associated with data loss and system failure. Documenting this plan requires a clear plan for regular backups, specifying storage locations, retention policies, and backup methods.

A Business Continuity Plan (BCP) is a comprehensive strategic document that defines procedures and instructions enabling an organisation to continue or quickly resume critical business functions in the event of a major disruption. Unlike traditional contingency plans, a BCP focuses on maintaining the operational continuity of the entire organisation, not just IT systems or individual processes. It covers all critical aspects of the business, from human resources and technical infrastructure to relationships with key suppliers and business partners (Nflo, n.d.b). This plan goes beyond simply responding to incidents, providing a systematic approach to building organisational resilience to a variety of threats and crisis situations, which include (Pohlmann, n.d.):

- a significant cyberattack on your systems (in which a hacker breaks in and shuts down and/or deletes everything),
- a natural disaster (hurricane, flood, fire, snowstorm/ice storm)—damage to your office and/or data centre causing critical infrastructure or services to become unavailable or cease to function,
- failures of systems supporting critical business processes,
- failures of cloud services,
- equipment failures,
- network and Internet disruptions,
- supply chain disruptions, such as supplier failures, transport disruptions and shortages of essential resources.

1.4 The Role of Cybersecurity in the Digital Economy

With the rapid development of the logistics industry, its dependence on advanced IT systems and digital technologies is also growing. Process automation, supply chain management and real-time data analysis are now standard in modern logistics companies. However, increasing digitalisation brings with it cybersecurity risks that are closely linked to market stability, economic confidence, supply continuity and innovation development (Kowalski, n.d.a).

Key areas in which cybersecurity plays a fundamental role in the digital economy and logistics include:

- Data integrity—refers to the accuracy, consistency, and reliability of data. It ensures rational, effective, and informed logistics decision-making, regulatory compliance and risk mitigation throughout the supply chain. Without data integrity, even the most advanced technologies cannot provide accurate information. Data integrity in logistics is characterised by at least five basic principles (Windward AI, n.d.):
  - accuracy—data must accurately reflect actual events in logistics processes (e.g., location of means of transport, weight of cargo, location of goods in a warehouse),
  - consistency—data must remain consistent across all logistics systems, such as procurement, warehouse management, inventory, and transport, even when moving between platforms of different links in the supply chain,
  - completeness—all necessary data should ensure the implementation of logistics processes at different stages in time and space in real time,
  - timeliness—data should be recorded and updated in real time to support effective decision-making, which is key to process optimisation and customer satisfaction,
  - data timeliness—real-time collection, recording, and updating to ensure that information related to logistics processes is accurate, complete, and delivered on time,
  - security—this is not only passwords and antivirus protection, but also a comprehensive set of practices and technologies designed to protect our information from unauthorised access, loss or even theft (Nowicki, n.d.).

Business Continuity is the foundation of success in today's complex, turbulent, and threat-filled business environment. Not only natural disasters and internal failures, but also cyberattacks can disrupt supply chains and halt business operations. At this point, it should be emphasised that all types of downtime can be extremely costly, directly affecting customer satisfaction and company cash flow. One of the key elements of ensuring business continuity is supply chain visibility, which provides real-time insight into inventory levels, shipment status, production schedules and warehouse management. Increased visibility can help create a more responsive and resilient supply chain to better manage the unpredictability inherent in global markets. Key components that enable greater visibility into supply chain operations and are vulnerable to hacker attacks include data integration and (SAP, n.d.; Strawser, n.d.):

- Continuous monitoring—supply chain control involves cloud-connected tools that comprehensively monitor operations. Connecting IoT devices, systems, sensors, suppliers, and partners with centralised logistics process management facilitates active detection of disruptions and response to them.
- Real-time data analytics—implementing advanced data analytics platforms provides logistics companies with an instant view of the entire supply chain network. They receive alerts about delays or potential issues, allowing them to proactively adjust shipping routes and delivery schedules. Real-time visibility allows teams to resolve issues before they escalate into crises.
- Cloud collaboration—the transition to cloud platforms streamlines collaboration by connecting manufacturers, suppliers, distributors, and even customers within a unified system. Real-time sharing of information on inventory levels, delivery schedules, and any unforeseen circumstances makes the supply chain more flexible and resilient to sudden changes.
- Risk management software solutions—implementing advanced software tailored to supply chain risk assessment helps identify gaps in existing networks. This software helps assess supplier stability, the political climate in transit regions,

and even the potential risk of natural disasters. It allows organisations to take preventive measures, such as finding backup suppliers, designating alternative routes, and even implementing redundancy in the system.

- Protection of critical logistics infrastructure, which includes ports, transhipment centres (warehouses), rail and air systems, telecommunications, and ICT networks, has become more complex and multidimensional. Digital monitoring, including advanced camera systems and remote monitoring capabilities, enables real-time surveillance and faster response to incidents, reducing human error and increasing efficiency. However, these advances also require greater expertise in understanding and mitigating digital threats, as digitalisation, while beneficial, brings a number of challenges for critical infrastructure security. The main concern is increased vulnerability to cyber threats such as hacking, phishing, data breaches and ransomware attacks (Smith, n.d.).
- The security of operational technologies (OT—securing systems that control physical industrial processes) and the Internet of Things (IoT—protecting connected devices and their data) is closely linked in logistics to transport (including autonomous vehicles), critical infrastructure, automation, robotisation, manufacturing and processing control systems, energy control, and real-time tracking (Palo Alto Networks, n.d.). The systems presented, which are used in logistics, operate on the basis of data exchange, which is also vulnerable to various types of cyberattacks. The devices used often have weak security and are easy targets for attacks. For example, hacking a temperature sensor can lead to food transport breakdowns, and taking control of an autonomous forklift can lead to physical damage.
- Supply chain security, which is becoming increasingly complex as digitalisation has led to a huge increase in the number of connected devices and suppliers, is important to remember that the supply chain is only as strong as its weakest link, which may be a supplier who has access to company networks or provides them with software solutions or applications. A weakness in a supplier's network or software—or even in an

external supplier's network—can open the door to cybercriminals. This means that a cyber incident can occur a few steps away from a company's main supply chain and still have serious consequences. Cybercriminals often attack smaller, less secure partners (suppliers, subcontractors) to gain access to the systems of a larger logistics company (Bank of America, n.d.).

- Trust in customers and partners is the foundation of any business relationship, including logistics processes throughout the entire supply chain, taking into account both the lower and upper parts. In the digital age of global logistics, where transactions take place instantly and huge amounts of secure data are transmitted through reliable technological systems, transparent operations and compliance with regulatory standards guarantee that companies in the supply chain will deliver on their promises, ensure the quality of their products and services, and respond appropriately to any problems or customer comments (eMudhra, n.d.).
- Every cyberattack, even on the smallest company working with others, can result in financial losses due to downtime, penalties for breaching customer contracts, loss of revenue, compensation payments, or direct costs of restoring systems and data. Business processes based on logistics companies and coordination between different departments are disrupted, delivery schedules are changed, and the exact location of goods becomes unknown. All of this can lead to customer dissatisfaction, loss of trust and a desire to terminate partnerships. This risk of reputational damage is more serious than the financial risk, as trust and partnership are key in business, including logistics. ch partners and investors (AlleM, n.d.).

1.5 Case Study: Analysis of Ransomware Incidents in a Global Company

One of the biggest threats to the logistics sector is ransomware attacks, i.e., malicious software that blocks access to company systems and demands a ransom for restoring access. For logistics companies, such attacks can paralyse operations on a global scale, making it impossible to manage orders, fleets or access to warehouse information, which can lead to serious financial losses (Kowalski, n.d.b). Ransomware attacks have been observed for over 20 years. According to the analysis, their frequency is increasing, as is the size of the ransoms demanded. In 2024, there were 95 active ransomware groups, compared to 68 a year earlier. The record ransom reached USD75 million, and the average demands exceeded USD5.2 million. In 70% of attacks, the victims' data was successfully encrypted. What is particularly important for entrepreneurs is that in 2023, approximately 43% of all cyberattacks targeted SMEs (Kielban & Rachmajda, n.d.). In practice, we encounter many such cases. Three of them are briefly described in Table 1.1 and one detailed case study concerns the transport company KNP Logistics Group.

The incident analysis concerns the British logistics and transport company KNP Logistics Group (KNP for short), which in June 2024 fell victim to the growing ransomware crisis (Breached Company, n.d.). A single hacked employee password gave the Akira ransomware group the keys to destroy what was once one of the largest private logistics companies in the UK. The attack led to the bankruptcy of the Northamptonshire-based company, founded in 1865 (158 years of operation) and which:

- survived world wars, economic crises and countless industry transformations during its century and a half of existence,
- built a reputation as a reliable logistics service provider in the competitive British transport sector, serving customers from various industries, with a large fleet and a significant number of employees.

As a result of a successful hacker attack, which resulted in the loss of 730 jobs, KNP Logistics Group has become an example of how catastrophic basic cybersecurity mistakes can be for a business.

The attack on KNP Logistics Group was carried out by the Akira Ransomware-as-a-Service (RaaS) group, which appeared on the market in March 2023. Since then, the group has become a serious threat, primarily to small and medium-sized enterprises (SMEs), as evidenced by the following figures and actions (R, n.d.):

- revenue—estimated at USD 42 million in the first year of operation,
- number of attacks—over 300 attacks reported in 2024 alone,

Table 1.1 Three Selected Analyses of Ransomware Incidents in International Companies Company

DATE OF THE EVENT	WHO IS AFFECTED?	COUNTRY	CONSEQUENCES
September 2024	Railway infrastructure manager	United Kingdom	Suspension of public Wi-Fi at railway stations A hacker attack linked to an insider at Global Reach, an internet service provider, caused terrorist messages to be displayed on devices connecting to the Wi-Fi network at 19 British railway stations. The incident, identified as cyber vandalism, disrupted public Wi-Fi services managed by Network Rail and operated by Telent. The Wi-Fi service was suspended for several days to allow for an investigation. The attack affected stations in London, Reading, Leeds, and Glasgow Central.
August 2024	The agency overseeing the Port of Seattle and Seattle-Tacoma International Airport	United States	Consequences—disruption to baggage sorting systems, offline display of flight and baggage information, handwritten boarding passes and manual baggage searches. The attack encrypted systems and data, affecting services such as baggage sorting and retrieval, flight and baggage information displays, check-in systems, ticket sales and Wi-Fi. The port refused to pay the ransom and warned of a potential data leak. Some systems, including flight and baggage information displays, were unavailable for about three weeks.
August 2023	Polish State Railways	Poland	Consequences—emergency stoppage of approximately 20 trains. Hackers broke into Polish radio frequencies and caused the emergency stoppage of approximately 20 trains near Szczecin. The saboteurs sent simple “radio-stop” commands to the trains they attacked, triggering the emergency stop function. The attack, which used recordings of the Russian national anthem and a speech by President Putin, disrupted traffic in the north-western part of the country. Connections were restored within a few hours.

Source: Wisdiam. (n.d.). *14 recent cyber attacks on the transport & logistics sector.* Retrieved 2 October 2025 from https://wisdiam.com/publications/recent-cyber-attacks-transport-logistics-sector/.

- targets of attacks—primarily SMEs with fewer than 50 employees (but not exclusively),
- geographical coverage—companies in the UK and the US,
- industry of interest—transport and logistics sector.

Chronology and technical details of the attack on KNP Logistics Group:

The attack on the company (June 2024) began with what cybersecurity experts consider one of the easiest entry points to avoid, namely the interception of authentication data by guessing the password. The Akira ransomware group gained initial access to the KNP network by exploiting an employee's weak password, which was apparently a brute-force attack.

The key attack vectors (methods) used by Akira to gain unauthorised access to the KNP Logistics Group's systems in the analysed case included:

- main entry point—shakedown of employee credentials obtained by guessing the password,
- security vulnerabilities—lack of multi-factor authentication (MFA),
- password weakness—the employee used an easy-to-guess password,
- network access—the attackers were able to move horizontally after gaining access.

Implementation of Akira ransomware in the analysed company

After hacking into the KNP network, the Akira group deployed its signature ransomware, which caused:

- the encryption of critical business data on the company's systems,
- the blocking of internal networks and essential IT infrastructure,
- the deletion of financial data and operating systems,
- the disruption of customer data and service delivery capabilities,
- a ransom demand of approximately £5 million.

Table 1.2 Tactics, Techniques, Procedures, and Consequences of the Attack on KNP

TACTICS, TECHNIQUES, AND PROCEDURES (TTP) CONSEQUENCES	DESCRIPTION OF ACTION/EFFECT
Initial Access	- credential stuffing and brute force attacks on weak passwords, - use of remote access tools and VPN vulnerabilities, - targeted phishing campaigns against specific organisations.
Durability and Lateral Movement	- implementation of backdoors to ensure continuous access, - network reconnaissance and privilege escalation, - exfiltration of confidential data prior to encryption.
Influence and Monetisation (Enforcing Fees, Collecting Ransom)	- double extortion model (encryption + threat of data theft), - targeted ransom demands based on an assessment of the company's revenue, - public leaks to exert additional pressure.
Business Impact Analysis	- operational disruptions: • complete shutdown of IT systems and digital operations, • inability to process customer orders or track shipments, • loss of access to financial documentation and accounting systems, • disruption of the supply chain and logistics coordination; - financial impact: • loss of daily revenue during system downtime, • inability to obtain new, critical funding due to financial data breach, • potential ransom amount (£5 million demand), • administrative and recovery costs; - human cost • 730 jobs lost following the company's bankruptcy, • enormous psychological burden on employees whose passwords were compromised, • loss of institutional knowledge accumulated over 158 years, • disruption to families and employment in the local community.
Management Burden	Company director Paul Abbott revealed the emotional cost of the situation, stating that he did not inform the employee whose password had been compromised and had likely led to the company's downfall, asking, "Would you want to know if it were you?"

Source: Wisdiam. (n.d.). *14 recent cyber attacks on the transport & logistics sector.* Retrieved 2 October 2025 from https://wisdiam.com/publications/recent-cyber-attacks-transport-logistics-sector/.

The attack was particularly devastating because it targeted the company's most important assets—financial systems, customer databases and the operational infrastructure on which the logistics company relied for its day-to-day operations.

The specific tactics, techniques, and procedures, along with the consequences of the malicious attack on KNP, are shown in Table 1.2.

Why data recovery failed:

The data recovery process at KNP failed due to a combination of several key events and factors.

Firstly, the company was already struggling with a difficult market situation, which limited its ability to respond quickly.

Secondly, the scale of the attack was exceptionally serious—cybercriminals paralysed critical financial and operational systems.

Thirdly, the lack of access to backup financing proved to be a problem, as it was impossible to obtain additional funds for reconstruction due to the loss of financial credibility as a result of the attack.

Fourthly, the loss of customer confidence, who, after the data leak, feared for the security of the information entrusted to the bank, ruined any chance of returning to the market.

Bibliography

1ClickVPN. (2025, July 15). *Czym jest zarządzanie ryzykiem stron trzecich (TPRM)?* https://www.1clickvpn.com/pl/blog/what-is-third-party-risk-management-tprm/

Advisor. (n.d.). *Cyberbezpieczeństwo firmy*. Retrieved August 22, 2025, from https://www.advisor.pl/blog/cyberbezpieczenstwo-firmy/

AlleM, N. (n.d.). *Securing the supply chain: Cyber security's importance in logistics*. Retrieved September 29, 2025, from https://www.maersk.com/insights/resilience/2025/04/01/securing-the-supply-chain

Amr, M., Ezzat, M., & Kassem, S. (2019). *Logistics 4.0: Definition and historical background*. ResearchGate. https://www.researchgate.net/profile/Mohammad-Abd-Elkader/publication/336916467_Logistics-40_Definition_and_Historical_Background/links/5dba9cd992851c818019453a/Logistics-40-Definition-and-Historical-Background.pdf

Avetta. (2025, July 19). *Top 5 supply chain cyber risks*. https://www.avetta.com/blog/top-5-supply-chain-cyber-risks

Bank of America. (n.d.). *Meeting the challenges of digital supply chain security*. Retrieved September 28, 2025, from https://business.bofa.com/en-us/content/digital-supply-chain-security.html

Bhure, C., Nicholas, G. S., Ghosh, S., Asadi, N., & Saqib, F. (2024). AutoDetect: Novel autoencoding architecture for counterfeit IC detection. *Journal of Hardware and Systems Security*, *8*, 113–132. https://doi.org/10.1007/s41635-024-00149-3

Booz Allen Hamilton. (n.d.). *Why data manipulation should be your biggest concern*. Retrieved July 30, 2025, from https://www.boozallen.com/c/insight/publication/why-data-manipulation-should-be-your-biggest-concern.html

Breached Company. (n.d.). *The KNP logistics ransomware attack: How one weak password destroyed a 158-year-old company.* Retrieved October 2, 2025, from https://breached.company/the-knp-logistics-ransomware-attack-how-one-weak-password-destroyed-a-158-year-old-company/

Checkmarx. (2025, July 22). *What is a software supply chain security attack?* Retrieved July 22, 2025, from https://checkmarx.com/glossary/what-is-a-software-supply-chain-security-attack/

Chen, M. (2025, August 18). *Blockchain for supply chain: Uses and benefits.* Oracle. https://www-oracle-com.translate.goog/sa/blockchain/what-is-blockchain/blockchain-for-supply-chain/?_x_tr_sl=en&_x_tr_tl=pl&_x_tr_hl=pl&_x_tr_pto=sc

Chen, Y.-T., Sun, E. W., Chang, M.-F., & Lin, Y.-B. (2021). Pragmatic real-time logistics management with traffic IoT infrastructure: Big data predictive analytics of freight travel time for Logistics 4.0. *International Journal of Production Economics, 238*, 108157. https://doi.org/10.1016/j.ijpe.2021.108157

Ciriello, R., Gal, U., Hannon, O., & Thatcher, J. (2024). Responsible social media use: How user characteristics shape the actualisation of ambiguous affordances. *European Journal of Information Systems.* Advance online publication. https://doi.org/10.1080/0960085X.2024.2444249

Copeland, J. (n.d.). *What is technology risk?* SAFE Security. Retrieved August 28, 2025, from https://safe-security.com/resources/blog/what-is-technology-risk-also-known-as-it-risk/

Coursera. (2025, August 21). *What is artificial intelligence? Definition, uses, and types.* https://www.coursera.org/articles/what-is-artificial-intelligence

Dataconsult.pl. (2025, July 28). *Jak IoT wpływa na rozwój logistyki?* Retrieved July 28, 2025, from https://dataconsult.pl/jak-iot-wplywa-na-rozwoj-logistyki/

Dhillon, A. (2025, July 30). *6 unparalleled UEFI BIOS firmware attacks (and their impact).* FirmGuard. https://firmguard.com/the-6-unparalleled-uefi-bios-firmware-attacks-and-their-impact/

Dissanayake, N., Jayatilaka, A., Zahedi, M., & Babar, M. A. (2022). Software security patch management - A systematic literature review of challenges, approaches, tools and practices. *Information and Software Technology, 144*, 106771. https://doi.org/10.1016/j.infsof.2021.106771

Echelon Protective Services. (2025, July 29). *What is a physical attack in cyber security?* Retrieved July 29, 2025, from https://echelonprotectiveservices.com/what-is-a-physical-attack-in-cyber-security/

EITT. (n.d.). *Co to jest user security awareness?* Retrieved August 31, 2025, from https://eitt.pl/slownik/user-security-awareness/

eMudhra. (n.d.). *Digital trust in logistics: Streamlining operations securely.* Retrieved September 29, 2025, from https://www.emudhra.com/en/blog/digital-trust-in-logistics-streamlining-operations-securely

Encryption Consulting. (2025, July 19). *Top 10 supply chain attacks that shook the world.* https://www.encryptionconsulting.com/top-10-supply-chain-attacks-that-shook-the-world/

eTower Technologies. (2025, August 18). Cloud computing revolutionizing the logistics industry. https://www-etowertech-com.translate.goog/industry-news/cloud-computing-revolutionizing-the-logistics-industry.html?_x_tr_sl=en&_x_tr_tl=pl&_x_tr_hl=pl&_x_tr_pto=sc

European Parliament. (2025, August 21). *Sztuczna inteligencja: co to jest i jakie ma zastosowania?*. https://www.europarl.europa.eu/topics/pl/article/20200827STO85804/sztuczna-inteligencja-co-to-jest-i-jakie-ma-zastosowania

European Union Agency for Cybersecurity (ENISA). (2021). *ENISA threat landscape for supply chain attacks*. Publications Office of the European Union. https://doi.org/10.2824/168593

Euvic. (n.d.). *Bezpieczeństwo chmury obliczeniowej Jak chronić dane w dobie cyfrowej transformacji?* Retrieved August 2, 2025, from https://www.euvic.com/pl/post/bezpieczenstwo-chmury-obliczeniowej-jak-chronic-dane-w-dobie-cyfrowej-transformacji/

EY Poland. (2024, February). *Odporność łańcuchów dostaw, napięcia polityczne i wymogi ESG. Geopolityczne ryzyka w 2024 r.* EY Poland Newsroom. Retrieved August 3, 2025, from https://www.ey.com/pl_pl/newsroom/2024/02/eyparthenon-geopolityka-2024

Fortinet, Inc. (2025, July 19). *DDoS attack meaning*. Retrieved July 19, 2025, from https://www.fortinet.com/uk/resources/cyberglossary/ddos-attack

Freed, M. (2025, July 19). *Defending against supply chain and ransomware attacks*. Cybereason. https://www.cybereason.com/blog/defending-against-supply-chain-and-ransomware-attacks

Gajdzik, B., & Grabowska, S. (2018). Leksykon pojęć stosowanych w Przemyśle 4.0. *Zeszyty Naukowe Politechniki Śląskiej, seria: Organizacja i Zarządzanie*, *132*, 231.

Geveye, M. O. (n.d.). *Understanding the core principles of information security*. Retrieved August 31, 2025, from https://www.centraleyes.com/core-principles-of-information-security/

Grupa Transportowa. (n.d.). *Wpływ sytuacji geopolityczno-ekonomicznej na sprawność transportu i łańcuch dostaw*. Grupa Transportowa Aktualności. Retrieved August 11, 2025, from https://www.grupatransportowa.pl/aktualnosci/wplyw-geopolityki-na-transport-i-lancuch-dostaw

Gryczka, A. (n.d.). *9 data backup strategies and techniques*. Retrieved September 1, 2025, from https://www.future-processing.com/blog/9-data-backup-strategies-and-techniques/

Grzejszczyk, E. (2015). Modelowanie procesów logistycznych ITS w chmurze obliczeniowej na przykładzie firmy spedycyjnej. In *Prace naukowe Politechniki Warszawskiej* (No. 106, p. 24).

Guin, U., DiMase, D., & Tehranipoor, M. (2014). Counterfeit integrated circuits: Detection, avoidance, and the challenges ahead. *Journal of Electronic Testing*, *30*, 9–23.

Helo, P., & Thai, V. V. (2024). Logistics 4.0—digital transformation with smart connected tracking and tracing devices. *International Journal of Production Economics*, *275*, 109336. https://doi.org/10.1016/j.ijpe.2024.109336

IoT in logistics: What it is, applications, and benefits. (2025, August 15). Inbound Logistics. Retrieved August 15, 2025, from https://www.inboundlogistics.com/articles/iot-in-logistics/

i-MAS. (2025, August 22). *The role of machine vision in logistics and supply chain improvement.* https://i-mas.com/en/the-role-of-machine-vision-in-logistics-and-supply-chain-improvement/

Inbound Logistics. (2025, August 18). *Blockchain in logistics: Definition, role in logistics, and benefits.* https://www-inboundlogistics-com.translate.goog/articles/blockchain-in-logistics/?_x_tr_sl=en&_x_tr_tl=pl&_x_tr_hl=pl&_x_tr_pto=sc

Inbound Logistics. (2025, August 18). *Blockchain in logistics: Definition, role in logistics, and benefits.* https://www-inboundlogistics-com.translate.goog/articles/blockchain-in-logistics/?_x_tr_sl=en&_x_tr_tl=pl&_x_tr_hl=pl&_x_tr_pto=sc

ITU Online. (n.d.). *What Is a falsification attack?* Retrieved July 30, 2025, from https://www.ituonline.com/tech-definitions/what-is-a-falsification-attack/

Jadczak, A. (n.d.). *Aż 55,7% polskich przedsiębiorstw korzysta już z usług cloud computing.* ITwiz. Retrieved August 2, 2025, from https://itwiz.pl/az-557-polskich-przedsiebiorstw-korzysta-z-uslug-cloud-computing/

Jahani, J., Khosravi, Y., Kargar, B., Ong, K. L., & Arisian, S. (2025). Exploring the role of drones and UAVs in logistics and supply chain management: A novel text-based literature review. *International Journal of Production Research*, *63*(5), 1873–1897. https://doi.org/10.1080/00207543.2024.2373425

Jaworska, M. (n.d.). *Łańcuchy dostaw w obliczu napięć geopolitycznych.* ElektronikaB2B. Retrieved August 4, 2025, from https://elektronikab2b.pl/biznes/57088-lancuchy-dostaw-w-obliczu-napiec-geopolitycznych

Jha, M. (2025, August 21). *5 key trends in logistics automation and autonomous robots.* RTInsights. https://www.rtinsights.com/5-key-trends-in-logistics-automation-and-autonomous-robots/

Jonker, A., Lindemulder, G., & Kosinski, M. (n.d.). *What is cybersecurity?* IBM. Retrieved July 11, 2025, from https://www.ibm.com/think/topics/cybersecurity

Joshi, N. (2025, August 20). *Optimize your logistics and supply chain operations with VR.* Allerin. https://www.allerin.com/blog/optimize-your-logistics-and-supply-chain-operations-with-vr

Kalapatapu, P. (2025, July 20). *Top 15 software supply chain attacks: Case studies.* Cisco Blog. Retrieved July 20, 2025, from https://outshift.cisco.com/blog/top-10-supply-chain-attacks

Kielban, Ł., & Rachmajda, D. (n.d.). *Cyberatak na wynajem: dlaczego MŚP są dziś łatwym celem.* Retrieved October 1, 2025, from https://www.poradnikbiznesu.info/cyberbezpieczenstwo/cyberatak-na-wynajem-dlaczego-msp-sa-dzis-latwym-celem/

Klimczuk, O. (n.d.). *Co się składa na cybersecurity?* Security Bez Tabu. Retrieved August 11, 2025, from https://securitybeztabu.pl/co-sie-sklada-na-cybersecurity/

Kowalski, A. (n.d.a). *Cyberbezpieczeństwo w sektorze logistycznym—jak chronić dane i operacje*. Retrieved September 11, 2025, from https://logistica.pl/cyberbezpieczenstwo-w-sektorze-logistycznym-jak-chronic-dane-i-operacje/

Kowalski, A. (n.d.b). *Cyberbezpieczeństwo w sektorze logistycznym—jak chronić dane i operacje*. Retrieved October 2, 2025, from https://logistica.pl/cyberbezpieczenstwo-w-sektorze-logistycznym-jak-chronic-dane-i-operacje/

Krzysztof, B. (2025, July 29). *Różnice pomiędzy BIOS, a UEFI*. Bitdefender. https://bitdefender.pl/roznice-pomiedzy-bios-a-uefi/

Kubera, G. (2023, August 13). *Ochrona punktów końcowych - co trzeba o niej wiedzieć*. Computerworld. https://www.computerworld.pl/news/Ochrona-punktow-koncowych-co-trzeba-o-niej-wiedziec,411609.html

Leończuk, D. (2012). Możliwości zastosowania technologii cloud computing w logistyce. *Logistyka*, *5*, 627.

Liderman, K. (2008). *Analiza ryzyka i ochrona informacji w systemach komputerowych*. Wydawnictwo Naukowe PWN.

Lisowski, E. (2025, August 17). *Analityka Big Data w logistyce: 10 przypadków użycia*. Addepto. Retrieved August 17, 2025, from https://addepto.com/blog/10-use-cases-of-big-data-in-logistics/

Logistyczny.net. (2025, August 24). *Autonomiczny transport drogowy i jego wpływ na logistykę* [*Autonomous road transport and its impact on logistics*]. https://www.logistyczny.net/logistyka/autonomiczny-transport-drogowy-i-jego-wplyw-na-logistyke

Majchrzak, T. (2019). Cloud computing w zarządzaniu łańcuchem dostaw. *Logistyka*, *3*, 16.

Malinowska, M., & Rzeczycki, A. (2016a). Rozwiązania cloud computing w logistyce—stan obecny i tendencje rozwojowe. *Przegląd Techniczny i Logistyczny*, *4*, 167.

Malinowska, M., & Rzeczycki, A. (2016b). Rozwiązania cloud computing w logistyce—stan obecny i tendencje rozwojowe. *Przegląd Techniczny i Logistyczny*, *4*, 169.

Messe München. (2025, August 22). *Artificial intelligence AI in logistics: potentials & application examples*. transportlogistic. https://www.transportlogistic.de/en/industry-insights/detail/artificial-intelligence-revolutionizes-logistics.html

Moore, J. (n.d.). *Data backup explained: A comprehensive enterprise guide*. Retrieved September 1, 2025, from https://www.techtarget.com/searchdatabackup/definition/backup

Murrenhoff, A., Friedrich, M., & Witthaut, M. (2021). *Future challenges in logistics and supply chain management: Künstliche Intelligenz in der Logistik* (Whitepaper). Institut für angewandte Logistik (IML), Fraunhofer. https://doi.org/10.24406/IML-N-462112

National Motor Freight Traffic Association (NMFTA). (2025, July 19). *Supply chain cybersecurity: A comprehensive guide*. Retrieved July 19, 2025, from https://www.nmfta.org/supply-chain-cybersecurity-a-guide/

Nettles, R. A., Merulla, C., & Warzala, S. (n.d.). *Data manipulation: Attacks and mitigation*. CSIAC. Retrieved July 30, 2025, from https://csiac.dtic.mil/articles/data-manipulation-attacks-and-mitigation/

Nflo. (2025, July 19). *Co to jest phishing i jak się przed nim ochronić?—Działanie, rozpoznanie, dobre praktyki i co robić po ataku*. https://nflo.pl/baza-wiedzy/co-to-jest-phishing-i-jak-sie-przed-nim-ochronic-dzialanie-rozpoznanie-dobre-praktyki-i-co-robic-po-ataku/

Nflo. (n.d.a). *Ataki cybernetyczne—wszystko co musisz wiedzieć. Praktyczny przewodnik po atakach hakerskich*. Retrieved August 28, 2025, from https://nflo.pl/baza-wiedzy/atak-cybernetyczny-kompendium/

Nflo. (n.d.b). *Co to jest i jak działa BCP (Business Continuity Plan)? Kluczowe elementy*. Retrieved September 2, 2025, from https://nflo.pl/baza-wiedzy/czym-jest-bcp-dzialanie/

Nflo. (n.d.c). *Czym jest zarządzanie podatnościami IT (Vulnerability Management) i dlaczego jest kluczowe dla cyberbezpieczeństwa?* Retrieved August 27, 2025, from https://nflo.pl/baza-wiedzy/czym-jest-zarzadzanie-podatnosciami-it-vulnerability-management-i-dlaczego-jest-kluczowe-dla-cyberbezpieczenstwa/

Nflo.pl. (2025, July 22). *Co to jest spear phishing?* Retrieved July 22, 2025, from https://nflo.pl/slownik/spear-phishing/

NordVPN. (n.d.). *Co to jest cyberbezpieczeństwo?* Retrieved July 27, 2025, from https://nordvpn.com/pl/cybersecurity/

Nowak, J. (2025, August 20). *AR and VR technologies in logistics: Discover the wide range of applications*. Logiscom. https://logiscom.pl/logistyka/technologie-ar-i-vr-w-logistyce-poznaj-szerokie-zastosowanie/

Nowicki, T. (n.d.). *Bezpieczeństwo danych w logistyce. Jak chronić informacje klientów i dane operacyjne?* Retrieved September 14, 2025, from https://logistyka24.com.pl/bezpieczenstwo-danych-w-logistyce-jak-chronic-informacje-klientow-i-dane-operacyjne/

NX Lifestyle Logistics. (n.d.). *Unmasking phishing attacks*. Retrieved September 19, 2025, from https://nxlifestylelogistics.ch/cybersecurity/unmasking-phishing-attacks/

Oflakowski, K. (2025, August 3). *Geopolityka i cyberbezpieczeństwo na szczycie zagrożeń dla TSL*. Logistyka.net.pl. Retrieved August 3, 2025, from https://www.logistyka.net.pl/bank-wiedzy/item/95720-geopolityka-i-cyberbezpieczenstwo-na-szczycie-zagrozen-dla-tsl

Palo Alto Networks. (n.d.). *What is the difference between IoT and OT security?* Retrieved September 27, 2025, from https://www.paloaltonetworks.com/cyberpedia/iot-security-vs-ot-security

Pinherio, D. (2025, August 29). *Logistics 4.0: What it is, how it works and what impacts it will have on the future of the logistics chain*. CargoSapiens. Retrieved August 29, 2025, from https://cargosapiens-com.translate.goog/en/blog/logistica-4-0/?_x_tr_sl=en&_x_tr_tl=pl&_x_tr_hl=pl&_x_tr_pto=sc

Pohlmann, J. (n.d.). *Business continuity planning: Why it's essential for sustainable success*. Retrieved September 2, 2025, from https://linfordco.com/blog/business-continuity-plan-bcp-importance-soc-2/

Porady-it.pl. (2025, July 29). *Fakty i Mity o bezpieczeństwie urządzeń IoT.* Retrieved July 29, 2025, from https://porady-it.pl/fakty-i-mity/fakty-i-mity-o-bezpieczenstwie-urzadzen-iot/

Porębski, K. (2025, August 22). *Automatyzacja i robotyzacja procesów magazynowych.* https://webmakers.expert/blog/automatyzacja-i-robotyzacja-procesow-magazynowych

Printezis, A. (2025, August 21). *The impact of virtual reality on supply chain management.* SupplyChainBrain. https://www.supplychainbrain.com/blogs/1-think-tank/post/40101-the-impact-of-virtual-reality-on-supply-chain-management

R, P. (n.d.). *Akira Ransomware: Zmieniająca się siła w domenie RaaS.* Retrieved September 30, 2025, from https://bitdefender.pl/akira-ransomware-zmieniajaca-sie-sila-w-domenie-raas/

Ray, T. (2023, August 14). *Database security.* Imperva. https://www.imperva.com/learn/data-security/database-security/

Rehan, S. (2025, August 17). *Sensors and Internet of Things (IoT) in logistics.* AZoSensors. Retrieved August 17, 2025, from https://www.azosensors.com/article.aspx?ArticleID=2825

Resilia. (2025, July 19). *Unijne wytyczne dla bezpieczeństwa cyfrowego. Co musisz wiedzieć o dyrektywnie NIS2?* https://resilia.pl/blog/dyrektywa-nis2-informacje-co-trzeba-wiedziec/

Rosenberg, J., & Mateos, A. (2011). *Chmura obliczeniowa: Rozwiązania dla biznesu* (p. 26). Helion.

Rudra, A. (n.d.). *What is defense in depth security?* Retrieved August 31, 2025, from https://powerdmarc.com/what-is-defense-in-depth-security/

SAP. (n.d.). *Co to jest widoczność w łańcuchu dostaw i dlaczego jest ważna?* Retrieved September 14, 2025, from https://www.sap.com/poland/resources/supply-chain-visibility

Secure-IC. (2025a, July 27). *Hardware Trojans or the threat of malicious circuits.* Secure-IC Blog. Retrieved July 27, 2025, from https://www.secure-ic.com/blog/hardware-trojans/hardware-trojans

Secure-IC. (2025b, July 27). *Hardware Trojans.* Secure-IC Applications. Retrieved July 27, 2025, from https://www.secure-ic.com/applications/challenges/hardware-trojans/

Securivy. (2023, November 28). *Zagrożenia wewnętrzne—statystyki i przewidywania—AKTUALIZACJA.* Securivy Blog. Retrieved July 30, 2025, from https://securivy.com/blog/zagrozenia-wewnetrzne-statystyki-i-przewidywania-aktualizacja/

Securivy. (n.d.a). *Na czym polega usługa outsourcingu informatycznego?* Securivy Blog. Retrieved August 2, 2025, from https://securivy.com/blog/outsourcing-it-na-czym-polega/

Securivy. (n.d.b). *Zagrożenia związane z niekontrolowaną eskalacją uprawnień.* Securivy Blog. Retrieved July 30, 2025, from https://securivy.com/blog/zagrozenia-zwiazane-z-niekontrolowana-eskalacja-uprawnien/

SentinelOne. (n.d.). *Patch management vs vulnerability management: 19 differences.* Retrieved August 31, 2025, from https://www.sentinelone.com/cybersecurity-101/patch-management-vs-vulnerability-management/

Siwek, Ł. (n.d.). *Zasada minimalnego dostępu i uprawnień*. Vida. Retrieved August 31, 2025, from https://www.vida.pl/zasada-minimalnego-dostepu-i-uprawnien/

Słodowska, J. (2025, 15 kwietnia). *Chmura obliczeniowa w logistyce i transporcie*. Polcom. https://polcom.com.pl/cloud-computing/chmura-obliczeniowa-w-logistyce-i-transporcie-co-warto-wiedziec/

Smith, J. (n.d.). *The impact of digitalization on critical infrastructure security*. Retrieved September 27, 2025, from https://www.mirrorreview.com/impact-of-digitalization/

SoftWeb Solutions. (2025, August 22). *Machine vision in logistics: What is machine vision, components, benefits, and applications*. https://www.softwebsolutions.com/resources/machine-vision-in-logistics.html

Startup Defense. (2025, July 29). *UEFI attack anatomy: Comprehensive security guide*. https://www.startupdefense.io/cyberattacks/uefi-attack

Strawser, B. (n.d.). *Ensuring business continuity for logistics: Key strategies*. Retrieved September 14, 2025, from https://bryghtpath.com/business-continuity-for-logistics/

Szymonik, A. (2018). Wybrane najnowsze rozwiązania wykorzystywane w logistyce. *Gospodarka Materiałowa i Logistyka*, *11*, 540–551.

Tageldin, L. (2025). Internet of things security: Threats, recent trends, and mitigation approaches. *Advances in Internet of Things*, *15*, 1. https://doi.org/10.4236/ait.2025.151001

The Astrology Page. (n.d.). *Co to jest bezpieczeństwo aplikacji? - definicja z techopedia*. Retrieved August 12, 2025, from https://pl.theastrologypage.com/application-security

TME. (2025a, 20 września). *Zaawansowane systemy wizyjne w logistyce* [*Advanced vision systems in logistics*]. https://www.tme.eu/pl/news/library-articles/page/69972/zaawansowane-systemy-wizyjne-w-logistyce/

TME. (2025b, July 29). *Zakłócenia elektromagnetyczne (EMI): identyfikacja i metody zapobiegania w elektronice*. https://www.tme.eu/pl/news/library-articles/page/68660/zaklocenia-elektromagnetyczne-emi-identyfikacja-i-metody-zapobiegania-w-elektronice/

Trend Micro. (2025, July 19). *Czym jest ransomware?* https://www.trendmicro.com/pl_pl/what-is/ransomware.html

Trevino, A. (2023, July 17). *Niezbędne informacje o zagrożeniach wewnętrznych*. Keeper Security Blog. Retrieved July 30, 2025, from https://www.keepersecurity.com/blog/pl/2023/07/17/everything-you-need-to-know-about-insider-threats/

Trevino, A., Cutler, A., & Guccione, D. (2023, July 14). *How does indentity theft happen online*. Keeper Security Blog. Retrieved July 30, 2025, from https://www.keepersecurity.com/blog/2023/07/14/how-does-identity-theft-happen-online/

U.S. Bureau of Labor Statistics. (2024, September). *Information security analysts*. Occupational Outlook Handbook. Retrieved March 9, 2025, from https://www.bls.gov/ooh/computer-and-information-technology/information-security-analysts.htm

Ustawa z dnia 5 lipca 2018 r. o krajowym systemie cyberbezpieczeństwa, Dz.U. 2018 poz. 1560.

Viso.ai. (2025, September 21). *Popular applications of computer vision in Logistics*. Retrieved September 21, 2025, from https://viso.ai/applications/computer-vision-in-logistics/

Viva Technology. (2025, August 25). *Autonomous delivery: Robots delivering the future of logistics*. https://vivatechnology.com/news/autonomous-delivery-robots-delivering-the-future-of-logistics

Wang, G., Gunasekaran, A., Ngai, E. W. T., & Papadopoulos, T. (2016). Big data analytics in logistics and supply chain management: Certain investigations for research and applications. *International Journal of Production Economics*, *176*, 98–110. https://doi.org/10.1016/j.ijpe.2016.03.014

Warchoł, A. (2020, March 12). *Vademecum Bezpieczeństwa Informacyjnego*. Uniwersytet Komisji Edukacji Narodowej w Krakowie. Retrieved July 30, 2025, from https://vademecumbezpieczenstwainformacyjnego.uken.krakow.pl/2020/03/12/sabotaz-komputerowy/

Wickramasinghe, S. (n.d.). *What is network segmentation? A complete guide*. Retrieved August 31, 2025, from https://www.splunk.com/en_us/blog/learn/network-segmentation.html

Windward AI. (n.d.). *Data integrity, what is data integrity?* Retrieved September 12, 2025, from https://windward.ai/glossary/what-is-data-integrity/

Wydajna chmura obliczeniowa w logistyce i transporcie—co warto wiedzieć? (2025, sierpnia 17). Beyond.pl. https://www.beyond.pl/baza-wiedzy/poradniki/wydajna-chmura-obliczeniowa-w-logistyce-i-transporcie-co-warto-wiedziec/

Xcitium. (2025, July 19). *What is malicious software? Your 2025 guide to understanding malware*. https://www.xcitium.com/blog/pc-security/what-is-malicious-software/

Zabezpieczenia.com.pl. (n.d.). *Informatyka śledcza, czyli jak ochronić firmę przed nieuczciwymi pracownikami*. Retrieved July 30, 2025, from https://www.zabezpieczenia.com.pl/ochrona-informacji/informatyka-%C5%9Bledcza-czyli-jak-ochroni%C4%87-firm%C4%99-przed-nieuczciwymi-pracownikami

Źródło: Li, Y., & Liu, Q. (2021). A comprehensive review study of cyber-attacks and cyber security: Emerging trends and recent developments. *Energy Reports*, *7*, 8176–8188. https://doi.org/10.1016/j.egyr.2021.08.126 -rys.1.1

2

The Digital Architecture of Modern Supply Chains

This chapter explores the structural and technological foundations of today's digital supply chains. It begins by describing the architecture of logistics systems, detailing how interconnected components—such as transport management systems (TMS), warehouse management systems (WMS), enterprise resource planning (ERP), RFID, and IoT devices—work together to enable real-time operations. The integration of these technologies is positioned as both a performance driver and a potential security risk, given the expanding digital attack surface. The chapter discusses the importance of secure IT system integration, focusing on data flow management, system interoperability, and access control. It also addresses the risks introduced by digitalisation, including system misconfigurations, weak authentication mechanisms, and supplier vulnerabilities. To ground these concepts, the chapter presents a case study of a 3PL operator that implemented an ERP system to enhance service delivery but faced unexpected cybersecurity challenges. The example demonstrates how operational improvements can expose new security gaps if cybersecurity is not considered at every stage of digital transformation. This chapter ultimately prepares readers to recognise the dual role of digital architecture as both an enabler of efficiency and a source of risk in supply chain management.

In the era of global digital transformation, supply chains are no longer a series of isolated functions but have evolved into highly integrated, data-driven ecosystems. Logistics, as one of the central components of these supply chains, plays a strategic role in ensuring speed, flexibility, and responsiveness to market demands. However, with the growing reliance on digital tools and interconnected platforms, logistics systems have become increasingly vulnerable to cyber threats. This chapter aims to explore the architecture of modern logistics systems,

DOI: 10.1201/9781003685784-2

the technologies that enable them, and the cybersecurity implications arising from their integration and digitalisation.

The logistics sector has undergone a fundamental transformation in recent years. Traditional, paper-based and manually operated logistics processes have given way to automated, real-time systems capable of processing vast amounts of data across global networks. Technologies such as Warehouse Management Systems (WMS), Transport Management Systems (TMS), Enterprise Resource Planning (ERP), Internet of Things (IoT), and Radio Frequency Identification (RFID) have become indispensable components of modern logistics infrastructure. These technologies not only enhance operational efficiency but also enable predictive analytics, dynamic routing, inventory optimisation, and end-to-end visibility.

However, the increasing complexity of these systems and their interdependence with external platforms (such as e-commerce portals, supplier systems, and customer interfaces) introduces significant challenges. The integration of multiple IT systems—often developed by different vendors, operating on different standards, and maintained by separate teams—creates an extended attack surface that is difficult to monitor and secure. As logistics organisations adopt cloud-based platforms and open APIs for greater interoperability, they must also navigate a growing set of cybersecurity risks, including unauthorised access, data leaks, ransomware, and supply chain attacks.

Understanding the structure and components of logistics systems is critical for identifying vulnerabilities and designing secure architectures. Modern logistics networks are composed of several interrelated subsystems, each performing a distinct function but dependent on shared data and real-time coordination. Warehousing, transportation, inventory management, order fulfilment, and customer service are all managed through digital platforms that must operate seamlessly. Any disruption in one node—whether from system failure or cyber incident—can propagate rapidly across the entire network, causing delays, financial loss, and reputational damage.

Furthermore, the reliance on third-party logistics (3PL) providers, outsourcing of IT functions, and use of cloud services complicate the security landscape. In many cases, logistics companies entrust sensitive operational data to external partners, making it essential to ensure robust access controls, encryption protocols, and incident response strategies. Cybersecurity is no longer just an IT function; it is a core component of risk management and operational continuity in logistics.

This chapter is structured to provide a comprehensive overview of the digital architecture that underpins modern supply chains. It begins by describing the structural design and key components of logistics systems, followed by an in-depth look at enabling technologies such as WMS, TMS, ERP, RFID, and IoT. The next section explores the integration of these systems and its impact on security, highlighting the challenges associated with multi-system environments. The fourth section addresses the broader challenges and risks that arise from the digitalisation of logistics, including those related to regulatory compliance, legacy infrastructure, and organisational culture. Finally, the chapter concludes with a real-world case study of a 3PL operator that implemented an ERP system, shedding light on both the benefits and cybersecurity pitfalls of digital transformation.

By the end of this chapter, readers will have a clear understanding of how digital architecture shapes the functioning of supply chains, the role of specific technologies in enabling logistics operations, and the critical importance of integrating cybersecurity considerations into the design, implementation, and management of these systems. In a world where disruptions can originate from malicious cyber actors just as easily as from physical events, securing the digital backbone of logistics is essential not only for individual organisations but for the stability and resilience of entire supply chains.

2.1 Structure and Components of Logistics Systems

In the digital economy, logistics systems have become the operational core of global supply chains. A logistics system can be defined as a coordinated set of resources, technologies, and processes that manage the flow of goods, services, and information from point of origin to point of consumption. Unlike traditional logistics, which relied heavily on manual coordination and paper-based transactions, modern logistics systems are digitally enabled, highly automated, and increasingly intelligent. They enable not only the efficient movement of products but also real-time decision-making, predictive planning, and visibility across the entire supply network.

Modern logistics systems comprise multiple interdependent subsystems that work together to support end-to-end supply chain functionality. The key subsystems include:

- **Warehousing**: Facilities and systems responsible for the receipt, storage, picking, and dispatch of goods. Advanced warehouses operate with automated picking systems, robotics, and real-time inventory tracking.
- **Transportation**: Involves the planning, execution, and monitoring of goods movement across various modes (road, rail, sea, air). Digital transportation management systems (TMS) optimise routing, reduce costs, and enhance delivery performance.
- **Inventory Management**: Ensures optimal stock levels are maintained to meet demand without overstocking. Systems use predictive analytics and AI to balance supply and demand efficiently.
- **Order Management**: Coordinates customer orders from placement to fulfilment. It integrates with e-commerce platforms, inventory systems, and customer service tools.
- **Procurement and Supplier Management**: Digital platforms manage purchasing, supplier evaluation, and collaboration across global sourcing networks.

These components are supported by both physical infrastructure (warehouses, transport fleets, logistics hubs) and digital infrastructure (software platforms, sensors, data analytics, communication systems). The integration of physical and digital elements allows logistics to function as a dynamic, data-driven system.

The transformation from traditional logistics to Logistics 4.0 marks a shift toward full digital integration, real-time data exchange, and intelligent automation. Logistics 4.0, often seen as part of the broader Industry 4.0 movement, introduces technologies like cyber-physical systems, machine learning, digital twins, and autonomous logistics assets. These advancements enable predictive maintenance, self-optimising networks, and enhanced visibility into logistics operations.

Traditional logistics was characterised by segmented operations, limited real-time insight, and siloed data. Logistics 4.0, by contrast, is marked by its ability to sense and respond dynamically across the

Table 2.1 Core Components of a Modern Logistics System

SUBSYSTEM	KEY FUNCTIONS	ENABLING TECHNOLOGIES
Warehousing	Storage, picking, dispatch	WMS, RFID, Robotics, IoT
Transportation	Routing, shipment tracking, fleet operations	TMS, GPS, Fleet Management Systems
Inventory Management	Stock control, demand forecasting	ERP, AI, Predictive Analytics
Order Management	Order processing, customer communication	CRM, E-commerce Integrations
Procurement	Supplier selection, purchasing coordination	SRM, E-Sourcing Platforms

value chain. This capability is made possible by the seamless integration of smart devices, cloud computing, and interoperable systems.

Modern logistics systems operate across multiple layers, each with specific responsibilities and digital dependencies:

- **Operational Layer**: Focuses on day-to-day activities within logistics facilities (e.g., warehouse operations, vehicle loading, dispatch). Technologies like barcode scanners, warehouse robots, and IoT devices are key enablers.
- **Tactical Layer**: Handles planning activities such as regional routing, inventory positioning, and service level management. Digital twins, transport planning tools, and inventory optimisation software operate here.
- **Strategic Layer**: Involves long-term decisions like facility location, outsourcing strategy, infrastructure investments, and risk mitigation planning. Business intelligence platforms, simulation tools, and advanced analytics support this layer.

Table 2.2 Evolution from Traditional Logistics to Logistics 4.0

ASPECT	TRADITIONAL LOGISTICS	LOGISTICS 4.0
Coordination	Manual, fragmented	Integrated, real-time
Data Access	Paper-based, delayed	Cloud-based, instant
Decision-Making	Reactive	Predictive, AI-assisted
Asset Utilisation	Static	Dynamic, optimised via IoT
Customer Experience	Basic shipment tracking	Real-time updates, self-service platforms

The interaction between logistics functions and IT systems is not merely supportive—it is fundamental. Logistics operations today are impossible to manage without robust IT infrastructure. Enterprise systems (such as ERP and SCM software), connected sensors, AI-powered analytics, and mobile apps collectively form the digital nervous system of logistics. These technologies allow for real-time coordination between supply chain partners, seamless data sharing, and rapid adaptation to disruptions.

In summary, understanding the structure and components of logistics systems is essential for grasping where vulnerabilities may lie and how to reinforce them with cybersecurity measures. As the next sections will show, the more digital and integrated the system becomes, the greater the need for a resilient and secure digital foundation.

Modern logistics systems operate as complex cyber-physical environments, where each compodigitally orchestrated ecosystem reacts to real-time information from both internal and external sources.

Interdependencies between subsystems are not only functional but also temporal and technological. For example, a Warehouse Management System (WMS) must be synchronised with the Tra so that picking and packing align with scheduled pickups and delivery slots. At the same time, the Order Management System (OMS) must integrate with the ERP platform to ensure consistency in financial transactions, product availability, and service level commitments.

This interconnectivity implies massive volumes of data being exchanged and the need for consistency, integrity, and resilience. Therefore, logistics system architecture must support high-frequency data synchronisation, prevent data duplication or inconsistency, and remain robust against both technical and cybersecurity disruptions.

It is also essential to recognise that logistics system architecture is not one-size-fits-all—it varies by industry, company size, and digital maturity. E-commerce companies often employ highly integrated and automated platforms compared to traditional B2B logistics providers who may still rely on hybrid or legacy systems. This creates divergent needs in terms of integration complexity, scalability, and security readiness.

2.1.1 System Interfaces and Data Flows

One of the critical elements in logistics system architecture is the design and security of system interfaces (APIs). These determine how effectively and securely different components exchange information. For instance, the interface between WMS and ERP must allow seamless two-way data exchange related to stock levels, batch numbers, and order statuses—with zero latency and no data loss.

Mismanagement of such interfaces can create a domino effect—for example, if WMS sends incorrect data to TMS, it can generate flawed shipping documentation, delay deliveries, and negatively impact the customer experience. Therefore, governance of data flow and interface monitoring becomes a cornerstone of digital logistics operations.

2.1.2 Digital Twins in Logistics

An increasingly important innovation in logistics architecture is the deployment of digital twins—virtual representations of physical logistics operations. Digital twins allow for real-time monitoring, simulation of future scenarios, and optimisation of ongoing processes.

For example, a logistics centre may use a digital twin to simulate operations during a high-demand period such as Black Friday. This model can identify bottlenecks, assess resource allocation, and provide recommendations for layout adjustments or shift planning. When combined with AI algorithms, the digital twin becomes a predictive and autonomous management tool.

Digital twins also contribute to risk reduction. By simulating cyberattack scenarios or system outages, logistics operators can proactively design resilience strategies and reduce response time in crisis situations.

2.1.3 Multi-Source Data Integration

Another vital aspect of system architecture is the ability to integrate diverse data sources, both internal (ERP, CRM, MES) and external (weather data, courier tracking systems, or 3PL partners). This enables the development of predictive logistics models that go beyond historical performance and provide real-time, data-informed decision-making.

For instance, if a weather alert indicates a severe storm in a delivery region, the logistics system can proactively reroute shipments or adjust delivery windows. Similarly, integrating supplier systems with ERP allows for automated replenishment and reduced stockouts.

However, these benefits come with cybersecurity trade-offs. The more systems are exposed to external data, the more vulnerable they become. Hence, architectural design must include built-in safeguards, such as encrypted data channels, multi-factor authentication, and role-based access controls to protect critical flows from compromise.

2.1.4 Use Cases—Architecture in Practice

To further understand the complexity and variability of logistics architecture, it is useful to examine several real-world scenarios:

- **E-commerce Distribution Center**: Operates through a tightly integrated environment combining WMS, TMS, and OMS. Every customer order triggers an automatic sequence of operations—item picking, packaging, labelling, and carrier assignment. Real-time data flow between systems ensures high throughput and customer satisfaction.
- **Third-Party Logistics (3PL) Provider**: Must support *multi-client operations* through a flexible, scalable architecture. Separate WMS instances may be deployed for each client, with centralised dashboards for performance monitoring, billing, and service-level reporting.
- **Automotive Parts Manufacturer**: Integrates ERP and MES systems with downstream logistics partners to enable *just-in-time delivery.* Real-time stock visibility allows customers to plan production schedules while ensuring minimal inventory costs.

Each of these cases demonstrates not only the operational dependency on digital infrastructure but also the need for tailored architectural strategies that align with security, scalability, and business goals.

As logistics architecture becomes increasingly layered and modular, it is useful to distinguish between its three core operational levels:

strategic, tactical, and operational. Each layer interacts with others and depends on digital systems to coordinate actions, plan resources, and manage risks in a synchronised way.

2.1.4.1 Strategic Layer

The strategic layer involves long-term decisions that define the overall structure and capabilities of the supply chain. These include:

- The selection of warehouse and distribution centre locations
- Outsourcing strategies (e.g., whether to rely on 3PLs or operate in-house logistics)
- Network design and transport mode optimisation
- Investments in infrastructure and IT platforms

Sustainability planning, carbon footprint management, and ESG-related logistics innovation.

This layer is supported by business intelligence systems, advanced analytics, scenario modelling tools, and digital dashboards. Strategic logistics planning must incorporate risk analysis, including geopolitical risks, cybersecurity exposure, and supply chain dependency vulnerabilities.

2.1.4.2 Tactical Layer

The tactical layer translates strategic plans into actionable workflows and resource allocation. It includes:

- Regional inventory distribution and replenishment planning
- Transportation route optimisation and carrier selection
- Demand forecasting and capacity management
- Service-level agreement (SLA) monitoring with suppliers and partners

At this level, digital systems such as transport management systems (TMS), advanced planning systems (APS), and vendor collaboration portals are essential. Data from IoT sensors, GPS trackers, and AI forecasting engines are aggregated to support responsive logistics decisions.

Tactical activities benefit heavily from predictive analytics, especially in industries with high variability in customer demand or seasonal fluctuations. Companies with robust tactical logistics platforms can often absorb disruptions more easily and react faster to external shocks, such as port congestion, fuel shortages, or cyberattacks on partner networks.

2.1.4.3 Operational Layer

The operational layer is the foundation of logistics execution. It encompasses:

- Day-to-day warehouse operations (inbound, storage, outbound)
- Vehicle dispatch and route tracking
- Order fulfilment, packaging, and returns management
- Real-time incident response (e.g., damage reports, delays, system failures)

This layer is powered by WMS, barcode scanning systems, RFID, warehouse robotics, mobile apps, and human-machine interfaces. Any disruption at this level—whether due to a technical fault or cyber incident—can cascade upwards, affecting both tactical execution and strategic outcomes.

2.1.5 Real-Time Responsiveness as a Competitive Advantage

One of the most valuable outcomes of a well-architected logistics system is real-time responsiveness. This capability allows organisations to react dynamically to internal anomalies or external changes—such as shifts in demand, delays, security alerts, or environmental factors.

For instance, a retailer using an integrated WMS–TMS system can detect a picking error in the warehouse and reroute a replacement item via express courier, avoiding a missed delivery. A manufacturer might use digital twins and MES (Manufacturing Execution Systems) to halt or divert production when sensors detect abnormal inventory movement in the supply chain.

The architecture that supports real-time logistics must be designed with latency minimisation, data prioritisation, and resilience in mind. Systems must prioritise critical information flows—such as stockout alerts, delivery confirmations, or cybersecurity incident flags—over less time-sensitive data.

Table 2.3 Key Capabilities Enabled by Real-Time Logistics Architecture

CAPABILITY	EXAMPLE APPLICATIONS	ENABLING TOOLS
Dynamic Routing	Avoiding traffic, weather, or depot congestion	TMS, GPS, AI-based route planners
Inventory Visibility	Adjusting stock across locations in real time	WMS, RFID, ERP
Customer Communication	Providing live delivery tracking and ETA updates	CRM systems, mobile apps
Incident Response	Reacting to cyber breaches or physical delays	SIEM, SOC, alert systems
Predictive Maintenance	Detecting and replacing failing assets early	IoT sensors, analytics platforms

The integration of these tools into a cohesive architecture is not trivial. It requires strong governance frameworks, agile IT development teams, and a cybersecurity strategy that adapts alongside technical innovation.

2.1.6 The Security Lens: Why Architecture Shapes Cyber Resilience

Digital architecture in logistics is not only about efficiency and speed—it is increasingly about defensive capability. Every subsystem added to the logistics chain—whether a scanner, drone, or cloud database—introduces a new potential entry point for cyber threats (Table 2.4).

Poorly designed architecture may lack segmentation, allowing lateral movement across systems if a breach occurs. Without role-based

Table 2.4 Security Principles in Logistics System Architecture

SECURITY PRINCIPLE	IMPLEMENTATION EXAMPLE	KEY BENEFIT
Zero Trust Architecture	Access control based on user identity and device context	Reduces internal and external threats
Network Segmentation	Isolated networks for warehouse, office, and cloud environments	Prevents lateral movement in attacks
Least Privilege Access	Grant access strictly as needed by role	Minimises potential misuse of credentials
Encryption in Transit	TLS/SSL protection of API and system communication	Secures data against interception
Continuous Monitoring	Integration with SIEM and threat intelligence feeds	Enables early detection and response

access controls, end-to-end encryption, and continuous monitoring, even the most advanced logistics platform can become a liability.

Architecture must support:

- *Zero Trust principles* (never trust, always verify)
- *Data segregation* between customers, vendors, and internal users
- *Authentication layers* suited to different device types (e.g., mobile, desktop, IoT)
- *Audit logs* and *forensics readiness* for compliance and incident response

Without embedding these principles into logistics architecture from the ground up, the operational benefits of digital transformation can be quickly negated by cyber disruptions, data breaches, or compliance failures.

2.1.7 Architectural Agility and Scalability

Finally, a future-ready logistics system must be scalable and modular. As business models shift—e.g., from B2B to omnichannel retail—logistics systems must adapt without requiring complete rebuilds.

Modular architecture allows the organisation to:

Add or remove functions (e.g., last-mile drone delivery, cold chain sensors)
Switch technology vendors with minimal disruption
Support acquisitions or international expansion
Comply with changing regulations (e.g., GDPR, NIS2, CTPAT)

The move toward microservices architecture, API-first platforms, and edge computing supports this agility. Logistics organisations that embrace these architectural principles will be better positioned to innovate while maintaining security and compliance.

2.2 Key Technologies Supporting Logistics (WMS, TMS, ERP, RFID, IoT)

The digital transformation of the logistics sector is not a future trend—it is a current and pressing necessity. As global supply chains grow more complex, fragmented, and vulnerable to both physical and digital disruptions, the need for robust, integrated technological systems becomes paramount. The transition from traditional logistics to Logistics 4.0 has shifted the paradigm from linear, reactive operations to dynamic, data-driven ecosystems. In this environment, technology is no longer a supporting tool but the structural foundation upon which logistics performance, competitiveness, and security are built.

This chapter explores the fundamental technologies that underpin modern logistics architecture and ensure seamless, resilient, and intelligent supply chain operations. These include Warehouse Management Systems (WMS), Transport Management Systems (TMS), Enterprise Resource Planning (ERP), Radio Frequency Identification (RFID), and the Internet of Things (IoT). Each of these technologies addresses specific logistics functions—such as inventory management, shipment coordination, or data consolidation—but their true power emerges through integration. When deployed synergistically, these systems transform disconnected processes into a unified logistics intelligence framework.

The rapid pace of digitalisation has pushed logistics beyond mechanisation and automation. Technologies now enable real-time visibility, predictive analytics, remote asset control, and autonomous decision-making. For instance, RFID-enabled pallets can provide exact item locations at any time; IoT sensors can detect temperature deviations in cold chain logistics; and ERP-TMS integrations can instantly reroute shipments to avoid geopolitical disruptions or cyber risks.

However, the widespread adoption of these technologies also introduces new layers of complexity—particularly in the context of cybersecurity, interoperability, and governance. Each new integration point creates a potential vulnerability. Systems that were once isolated are now connected to global networks, partner APIs, and mobile platforms—exposing them to threats such as ransomware, data theft, and system sabotage.

Therefore, understanding logistics technologies is not solely a matter of operational excellence—it is a strategic imperative. Logistics professionals, supply chain managers, and technology architects must have a clear, structured view of how these systems function individually, how they interact, and how they can be secured against misuse or attack.

This section begins by defining the core functions of each major technology and identifying the role it plays within the wider logistics system. It proceeds to examine the operational, tactical, and strategic benefits of these systems, supported by real-world applications and use cases. We also discuss the technological dependencies that exist between systems—such as WMS-ERP synchronisation—and how these relationships shape workflow automation, data accuracy, and decision support.

Furthermore, the section emphasises the need for interoperability and scalability. Logistics systems must not only function within a single warehouse or regional network but must be able to scale across multiple geographies, languages, compliance frameworks, and partner platforms. This requires adherence to industry standards, such as GS1 for RFID, as well as secure, API-first architectures that allow modular expansion without compromising integrity.

In addition, this chapter addresses the role of these technologies in resilience planning. In a world increasingly shaped by disruption—pandemics, cyberattacks, political instability, climate events—logistics organisations must leverage technology to monitor risk, simulate alternative scenarios, and maintain operational continuity. Technologies such as AI-powered TMS or sensor-integrated WMS can dramatically reduce the impact of external shocks by enabling proactive responses rather than delayed reactions.

Finally, it is important to note that technology adoption is not uniform across industries or regions. While some logistics providers and manufacturers operate fully digitised, cloud-native platforms, others are in transitional phases—facing challenges related to legacy systems, skills gaps, and capital investment. Therefore, the technologies presented here are not only described in terms of their capabilities but also contextualised with regard to implementation barriers, maturity stages, and risk profiles.

In summary, the technologies outlined in this section represent the building blocks of the modern digital supply chain. They are essential not only for improving logistics efficiency and transparency but also for ensuring the agility, resilience, and security of global operations. By mastering these technologies and understanding their interdependencies, supply chain professionals will be equipped to design and manage logistics systems that meet the demands of tomorrow's digital economy.

The transformation of logistics into a data-driven, intelligent, and highly responsive sector is grounded in the integration of advanced digital systems. Technologies such as Warehouse Management Systems (WMS), Transport Management Systems (TMS), and Enterprise Resource Planning (ERP) solutions play a foundational role in ensuring both operational efficiency and strategic agility. Their significance lies not only in automating routine tasks but in enabling real-time visibility, predictive analytics, and seamless collaboration across supply chain actors.

Warehouse Management Systems have become the nerve centre of intralogistics. They orchestrate the full cycle of warehouse activities, from goods receipt to dispatch, managing stock locations, replenishment, order picking, and returns. A modern WMS is far more than a database—it is a dynamic control tower capable of interacting with sensors, conveyors, and autonomous mobile robots. Cloud-based deployments offer scalability and accessibility, particularly important for logistics providers operating across multiple warehouse sites. Crucially, WMS platforms improve order accuracy, optimise storage space, and allow for responsive inventory allocation based on live data.

In environments where speed and accuracy are paramount—such as e-commerce, pharmaceuticals, and fast-moving consumer goods—a well-integrated WMS can become a competitive differentiator. However, as WMS systems interface with third-party APIs, mobile devices, and IoT infrastructure, they must be carefully protected from unauthorised access or system compromise. A manipulated WMS could not only distort inventory data but misroute entire shipments or halt automated fulfilment.

Transport Management Systems complement WMS platforms by overseeing the outbound flow of goods. A TMS allows logistics managers to plan and optimise routes, select carriers, consolidate shipments, and monitor freight in transit. It connects upstream with ERP systems and downstream with GPS tracking devices, offering real-time insight into fleet location, estimated arrival times, and delivery performance. In global supply chains, TMS also handles multimodal transport coordination, customs documentation, and compliance with regional regulations.

Modern TMS platforms increasingly incorporate artificial intelligence to predict disruptions, suggest alternative routes, and minimise transportation costs while maintaining service levels. For instance, when a traffic incident is detected along a planned route, the system can recommend a detour and notify both the carrier and recipient automatically. These capabilities significantly enhance delivery reliability and customer satisfaction.

Yet, like WMS, the connectivity that makes TMS powerful also introduces cyber risks. If API channels to carriers are not secured, or if driver applications are compromised, attackers could intercept shipment data, manipulate delivery routes, or even stage fraudulent pickups. Ensuring the integrity of these systems demands robust identity management, encrypted communication protocols, and anomaly detection mechanisms.

Enterprise Resource Planning systems serve as the overarching integrator, harmonising data across logistics, finance, procurement, and production functions. In the logistics context, ERP ensures that stock levels are synchronised between warehouses, orders are processed with real-time inventory validation, and procurement is aligned with actual demand. ERP systems generate unified reports that allow supply chain leaders to evaluate cost structures, supplier performance, and logistics KPIs with a holistic view.

When integrated properly, ERP becomes the backbone of digital supply chain management. It enables automated responses to supply and demand fluctuations, coordinates replenishment cycles, and supports forecasting models. For example, a drop in safety stock detected in the WMS can trigger a replenishment request in the ERP system, which in turn initiates an order to a preferred supplier and books the inbound transport—all within the same digital ecosystem.

However, because ERP systems manage such sensitive and wide-reaching data, they are highly attractive to cybercriminals. A compromised ERP may expose not only logistics operations but also financial accounts, HR records, and strategic business information. Securing ERP platforms involves layered access control, continuous monitoring, and advanced threat detection technologies, especially when these systems are exposed to cloud environments or mobile interfaces.

The integration of WMS, TMS, and ERP technologies enables logistics organisations to shift from isolated, reactive operations to intelligent, end-to-end supply chain orchestration. Yet this transformation requires careful architectural planning. Each system must be interoperable, secure, and aligned with the organisation's logistics strategy. The next section will further develop this foundation by examining the role of tracking and sensor-based technologies—specifically RFID and IoT—and how their deployment adds new layers of real-time awareness and control to logistics infrastructure.

Among the most transformative technologies in the logistics sector are those that bridge the physical and digital realms through real-time identification, tracking, and data collection. Two such innovations—Radio Frequency Identification (RFID) and the Internet of Things (IoT)—have redefined visibility, control, and responsiveness in logistics operations. They enable logistics systems to move beyond static databases and rely instead on dynamically captured data from physical objects, vehicles, or infrastructure.

RFID technology enables the non-contact identification of items using electromagnetic fields. Unlike traditional barcodes, RFID tags do not require line-of-sight scanning and can be read simultaneously in batches, dramatically increasing the speed and accuracy of warehouse or in-transit processes. An RFID system typically consists of three components: tags (attached to goods or containers), readers (placed at control points or gates), and software integrated with logistics platforms such as WMS or ERP. When a pallet passes through a loading dock equipped with RFID sensors, the system can automatically log its movement, update the inventory, and trigger the next logistical step—all without manual intervention.

The use of RFID has become especially prominent in high-volume, high-velocity supply chains where time efficiency and data reliability are paramount. Industries such as retail, automotive, and pharmaceuticals have adopted RFID to gain visibility into inventory levels, improve shrinkage control, and enable traceability from origin to point of sale. In cold chain logistics, RFID sensors equipped with temperature monitoring allow real-time alerts if thermal thresholds are exceeded, thus protecting product quality and compliance with safety standards.

However, the benefits of RFID are closely linked to its integration into the broader logistics ecosystem. Without proper synchronisation with the WMS or ERP system, RFID data may be underutilised or even introduce inconsistencies. Moreover, security concerns arise from the wireless nature of RFID communication. Unprotected RFID channels could be exploited to intercept or clone tag information, leading to data leaks or inventory manipulation. As a result, RFID implementation must include encryption of data exchange, secure middleware platforms, and physical protection of strategic readers.

While RFID focuses on identification, the Internet of Things expands the logistics infrastructure with a wide network of interconnected sensors, devices, and control systems that continuously generate and transmit data. IoT in logistics encompasses everything from vehicle telematics and warehouse environmental monitoring to smart containers and predictive maintenance systems. These interconnected objects allow logistics operations to shift from reactive to proactive modes, where conditions are anticipated and managed in real time.

IoT applications are particularly powerful in fleet management. Embedded sensors in trucks can transmit data about speed, location, fuel consumption, and engine condition. This information, processed through a TMS or dedicated fleet platform, enables route optimisation, driver behaviour analysis, and maintenance scheduling. In warehousing, IoT devices monitor temperature, humidity, and lighting to optimise storage conditions and energy use, contributing to both efficiency and sustainability.

The integration of IoT into logistics architecture transforms the traditional logistics centre into a cyber-physical system—a smart warehouse capable of autonomous adjustment based on sensor input. For example, a warehouse might detect that a section is overstocked, automatically suggest inventory reallocation, and initiate internal movements using automated guided vehicles. When connected to AI modules, the system may also predict future demand peaks and adjust space planning or labour allocation accordingly.

Nevertheless, IoT-based logistics infrastructure introduces significant cybersecurity challenges. Each sensor or device becomes a potential entry point for malicious actors. Without standardised protocols, outdated firmware, or unsecured network connections, the IoT layer can become the weakest link in the digital chain. Attackers may exploit vulnerable devices to infiltrate core logistics systems or cause operational disruption. Therefore, secure IoT deployment requires a layered defence strategy: segmenting networks, implementing device-level authentication, and continuously monitoring data flows for anomalies.

A critical aspect of successful logistics digitalisation lies in the seamless integration of these technologies. WMS, TMS, ERP, RFID, and IoT systems must not operate in isolation but as part of a unified, interoperable platform. Integration ensures that data captured in one part of the supply chain is immediately usable in another, enabling synchronised decision-making. For instance, a temperature alert from an IoT sensor in a refrigerated truck should instantly update the shipment status in the TMS, notify the recipient through the CRM, and trigger a compliance report in the ERP system.

Achieving such integration is technically and organisationally complex. Different systems may be built on incompatible architectures, use diverse data formats, or be operated by separate vendors. Bridging these gaps requires the use of middleware, standard communication protocols such as REST APIs or EDI, and enterprise service buses (ESBs). It also demands cross-departmental collaboration, clear data governance policies, and a unified cybersecurity framework that spans the entire system landscape.

The benefits of well-executed integration are substantial. It enables end-to-end visibility across the supply chain, reduces latency in information flow, and improves the quality of analytics. With integrated systems, organisations can automate complex workflows, minimise manual intervention, and create digital twins that simulate logistics operations in real time. Moreover, integrated architectures facilitate business continuity planning, as disruption in one area can be rapidly addressed by rerouting resources or rebalancing capacity elsewhere.

At the same time, integration multiplies risk exposure. The more systems are connected, the broader the attack surface. If one component—such as an unsecured RFID reader or an IoT gateway—is compromised, the breach can propagate across the entire logistics network. This makes architectural planning not only a question of efficiency but one of security resilience. Cybersecurity-by-design becomes an imperative rather than an afterthought.

In summary, the deployment of RFID and IoT technologies, combined with the integration of core logistics systems, creates an environment of operational intelligence and flexibility. These technologies empower logistics organisations to achieve higher service levels, reduce costs, and respond dynamically to market demands. However, their adoption must be accompanied by a clear understanding of system dependencies, security vulnerabilities, and organisational readiness. In the following sections, we will explore how these technologies are embedded into logistics strategies and how they support broader goals such as sustainability, customer-centricity, and risk mitigation.

The integration of advanced logistics technologies offers transformative potential, but the path to successful implementation is far from straightforward. Many organisations struggle to move beyond fragmented digital solutions toward a truly connected and intelligent logistics ecosystem. Despite growing investment in WMS, TMS, ERP, RFID, and IoT technologies, achieving full interoperability remains a complex endeavour, shaped by organisational culture, legacy systems, infrastructure constraints, and varying levels of digital maturity.

One of the most significant challenges in technology integration is the coexistence of old and new systems. Many companies operate legacy ERP or warehouse platforms that are not designed to interact with modern cloud-based applications or mobile devices. Retrofitting these systems to support APIs, real-time data synchronisation, or advanced analytics often requires costly customisation and exposes the organisation to increased vulnerability if integration is done hastily or without proper security planning.

Additionally, the diversity of stakeholders within a supply chain—including third-party logistics providers, subcontractors, suppliers, and customers—complicates integration. Each participant may use different software, standards, and communication protocols. Creating a shared information environment where these disparate systems can securely exchange data calls for standardised formats such as EDI or XML, and governance models that define data ownership, access rights, and compliance responsibilities.

From an organisational perspective, successful digital integration is not solely a technical project—it requires a transformation in decision-making, roles, and workflows. Employees must be trained not only to use new tools but to trust automated insights and adapt to data-driven operations. Resistance to change, siloed departments, and lack of top-down leadership support are often more decisive barriers than technical complexity alone.

Cybersecurity considerations further complicate integration. As systems become interconnected, a vulnerability in one platform may cascade across the entire digital supply chain. For example, a compromised handheld scanner with access to the WMS could become a gateway to the ERP, exposing financial or customer data. To mitigate these risks, organisations must adopt zero-trust architectures, monitor integration points in real time, and ensure that each data flow—especially those crossing organisational boundaries—is encrypted and auditable.

To support implementation and risk management, various maturity models have been developed to assess an organisation's readiness for digital integration. One such model evaluates logistics technology deployment across five levels: fragmented, reactive, standardised, integrated, and intelligent. In the fragmented stage, systems operate independently, often with manual processes bridging them. At the reactive stage, basic interfaces exist, but data exchange is irregular or delayed. Standardised systems use common formats and protocols but lack centralised coordination. Integrated systems share real-time data and workflows across platforms, while intelligent systems add layers of artificial intelligence, predictive analytics, and autonomous decision-making.

Many organisations in emerging economies remain at the reactive or standardised levels, often due to budget constraints, infrastructural gaps, or limited access to high-quality technical talent. However, leading global firms are moving toward intelligent logistics ecosystems, where AI engines interpret sensor data, optimise network flows, and identify emerging risks without human intervention. These firms treat data not as a by-product of logistics operations, but as a strategic asset.

A comparative look at implementation practices across regions reveals marked differences. In Germany, for instance, logistics firms benefit from state-supported initiatives such as "Industrie 4.0" and maintain high levels of technology adoption, particularly in manufacturing-linked logistics. Japanese companies emphasise precision and integration with lean production systems, while the US market is characterised by aggressive investment in AI-driven platforms and last-mile optimisation. In contrast, small-to-medium enterprises (SMEs) in Central and Eastern Europe often lack access to capital and skilled integrators, making them reliant on modular SaaS solutions with limited customisation options.

Table 2.5 summarises typical integration challenges and strategic responses across different organisational maturity levels:

Another important implementation consideration is scalability. A logistics platform designed for regional operations may fail when extended globally due to language, compliance, or infrastructure gaps. Therefore, integration projects must adopt a modular and service-oriented architecture that allows new components, users, or markets to be added without rebuilding the system from scratch. Microservices, cloud computing, and edge processing all play critical roles in supporting scalable logistics systems.

In conclusion, while the deployment of individual logistics technologies such as WMS, TMS, RFID, and IoT provides localised benefits, it is their seamless integration that delivers strategic advantage. However, this integration is not automatic—it requires careful planning, strong leadership, robust cybersecurity, and a long-term commitment to digital transformation. Organisations that succeed in building connected, intelligent logistics environments will gain superior control over their supply chains, enhanced resilience against disruption, and improved service performance in an increasingly volatile global market.

The next chapter will explore how the very technologies and interconnections that support efficiency and visibility in logistics can also become sources of vulnerability. We will examine the nature of cyber threats in logistics systems, the types of attacks most commonly faced, and real-world incidents that illustrate the potential consequences of failing to protect the digital supply chain.

Table 2.5 Digital Maturity Stages and Their Organizational Implications

MATURITY LEVEL	COMMON CHALLENGES	STRATEGIC FOCUS
Fragmented	Siloed data, manual processes	Identify digital priorities, centralise data
Reactive	Delayed visibility, ad hoc connections	Implement basic APIs, train staff
Standardised	Inconsistent workflows, multiple platforms	Align systems with shared protocols
Integrated	Complex architecture, security vulnerabilities	Strengthen governance, adopt monitoring tools
Intelligent	High complexity, AI bias or error propagation	Ensure explainability, build digital culture

2.3 IT System Integration and Its Impact on Security

The digital transformation of supply chains relies not merely on the adoption of advanced technologies but on their successful integration into a cohesive and interoperable ecosystem. While logistics organisations increasingly deploy systems such as WMS, TMS, ERP, and IoT platforms, the real value lies in connecting these components to enable seamless data exchange, synchronised operations, and end-to-end visibility. However, as integration intensifies, so too does the complexity of managing information flows and ensuring their security. In today's logistics environments, where digital systems operate across organisational boundaries and national jurisdictions, IT integration becomes both a driver of efficiency and a potential vector of vulnerability.

This chapter explores the dual nature of IT system integration within logistics. On the one hand, integration enables enhanced agility, automation, and real-time responsiveness, allowing companies to react swiftly to disruptions, optimise resources, and deliver superior customer service. On the other hand, interconnected systems inherently expand the attack surface, expose new entry points for cyber threats, and create interdependencies that can lead to cascading failures.

Many logistics enterprises underestimate the security implications of linking internal and external platforms. For example, a poorly secured API connection between a company's ERP system and a third-party transport provider's platform can serve as a backdoor for unauthorised access, leading to data breaches or even operational sabotage. Similarly, IoT-enabled logistics assets, if not properly segmented and monitored, can be exploited to inject malicious code into enterprise systems.

Therefore, understanding the *security implications of system integration* is no longer optional—it is essential. This chapter investigates the architecture of integrated logistics IT environments, identifies common integration patterns and their associated risks, and outlines strategies for mitigating security threats without compromising performance or scalability. By examining real-world cases of cyber incidents linked to integration failures, we will illustrate how weak system architecture can undermine not just data confidentiality and integrity, but also the continuity of physical logistics operations.

As organisations strive to build more intelligent, data-driven logistics networks, the need to design integration architectures that are secure-by-design becomes paramount. This chapter will provide a conceptual and practical foundation for evaluating integration decisions not only in terms of technological functionality, but also through the lens of cyber risk, resilience, and regulatory compliance.

As logistics systems grow increasingly interconnected, the boundaries between different digital platforms, applications, and service providers become increasingly blurred. In modern supply chains, data flows no longer remain confined within organisational silos; instead, they are continuously exchanged among multiple systems, departments, and external partners. While this digital integration enhances visibility, responsiveness, and decision-making accuracy, it also significantly elevates the complexity of managing cybersecurity.

System integration in logistics often involves the orchestration of various specialised platforms: Warehouse Management Systems (WMS) must communicate with Transport Management Systems (TMS), which in turn link to Enterprise Resource Planning (ERP) solutions, customer relationship platforms (CRM), and, increasingly, external systems owned by third-party logistics (3PL) providers, suppliers, and even customers. These interactions occur via APIs, middleware, file transfers, IoT protocols, and cloud service connections—each of which introduces potential vulnerabilities.

One of the most critical aspects of system integration is ensuring *data integrity and trust across platforms.* In many cases, supply chain disruptions do not result from system failures per se, but from data mismatches or corrupted transactions due to insecure or incompatible integration logic. For example, if an unauthorised modification occurs during the handoff of shipment data between a TMS and ERP system—whether due to malicious interference or software error—the result can be the misrouting of goods, delays, or erroneous billing. When such failures occur in real time and across global operations, the consequences quickly escalate.

Another common integration scenario is the use of *shared cloud platforms* or *multi-tenant environments* where logistics organisations access applications hosted by third-party providers. While these models reduce costs and increase scalability, they also concentrate risk. A vulnerability in the cloud provider's infrastructure can affect multiple clients simultaneously, and data leakage between tenants can occur if isolation mechanisms are flawed.

The problem is further compounded when logistics systems are connected via *legacy interfaces*, often lacking proper encryption, authentication, or monitoring. Older protocols such as FTP or SOAP may still be used for exchanging critical shipment data or financial documentation. In such cases, attackers may intercept or manipulate data transmissions without being detected—especially if no end-to-end visibility is maintained across systems.

To clarify how various types of integration introduce specific security risks, Table 2.6 summarises common integration patterns and their associated vulnerabilities:

As Table 2.6 illustrates, the very mechanisms that allow systems to communicate effectively can become entry points for cyber threats if not properly secured. In particular, application programming interfaces (APIs), now ubiquitous in logistics integration, have emerged as a major attack vector. Poorly designed or insufficiently monitored APIs can be exploited through techniques such as broken authentication, parameter tampering, or excessive data exposure. In one documented case, an attacker exploited a misconfigured API in a major freight management system to gain unauthorised access to shipment records across multiple accounts.

IoT integration presents another layer of complexity. The continuous flow of sensor data from RFID systems, GPS trackers, temperature

Table 2.6 Integration Types, Use Cases, and Associated Security Risks

INTEGRATION TYPE	TYPICAL USE CASE	POTENTIAL SECURITY RISK
API-Based integration	Real-time data exchange between ERP and TMS	API abuse, injection attacks, weak access control
File-Based Batch Transfer (FTP/SFTP)	Scheduled data sync (e.g., order batches)	Data interception, file tampering, spoofing
Cloud-to-Cloud Saas Connection	Linking WMS to cloud-based analytics or CRM	Insecure tokens, lack of tenant isolation
IoT System Bridging	Sensor data flow from warehouse to central WMS	Device hijacking, network injection, lack of segmentation
Third-Party Portal Access	3PL or carrier access to client ERP	Credential theft, excessive permissions, session hijack
Legacy System Bridges	Custom adapters for older platforms	Hardcoded credentials, no encryption, protocol spoofing

loggers, and mobile devices often bypasses traditional firewalls and antivirus filters. If these data streams are not authenticated, encrypted, or validated, they can serve as channels for injecting false information or launching denial-of-service attacks. For example, maliciously spoofed temperature data in a pharmaceutical cold chain could result in unnecessary product destruction or regulatory violations.

Integration also affects the ability of organisations to monitor security incidents holistically. In fragmented systems, each platform may have its own logs, threat detection tools, and user access policies, making it difficult to correlate events or detect coordinated attacks. If a breach occurs within one system and propagates to another—say, from a compromised CRM portal to an ERP environment—response efforts may be delayed due to lack of centralised visibility.

To address these challenges, security must be embedded directly into the design and operation of integration architectures. This principle, often referred to as "security by design," implies that every integration point—whether an API, message queue, or file drop folder—should be treated as a critical asset requiring authentication, encryption, auditing, and anomaly detection. Moreover, the use of integration gateways, secure service buses, and data loss prevention (DLP) tools can help enforce consistent policies across systems.

An essential component of secure integration is identity and access management (IAM). Organisations must ensure that only authorised systems and users can access specific datasets or functions, and that privileges are assigned based on strict need-to-know principles. For instance, a third-party transport provider granted API access to shipment schedules should not be able to view customer billing records or HR data stored within the same ERP platform.

Finally, effective integration requires collaboration between cybersecurity teams and logistics process owners. Too often, integration projects are driven solely by IT or vendor teams, with insufficient understanding of operational dependencies or threat models. Cybersecurity teams must be involved from the initial architecture planning phase, participating in threat modelling, interface testing, and contingency planning.

The abstract nature of integration-related threats often obscures their real-world consequences—until a breach occurs and cascades across interdependent systems. The logistics sector has seen a growing number of cyber incidents that originated not from a direct assault on core infrastructure but from vulnerabilities in the interfaces linking disparate systems. These events reveal how seemingly routine integrations, if poorly secured, can be leveraged to compromise entire operations.

One illustrative example is the 2017 cyberattack on a global shipping and logistics company that resulted in severe operational disruption across ports, warehouses, and customer service systems. Although initially attributed to the spread of the NotPetya malware, post-incident forensic analysis revealed that one of the key entry points was an insecure integration bridge between the company's internal ERP system and a third-party customs clearance application used in Eastern Europe. The attackers exploited this trust channel—based on outdated authentication and unencrypted file transfers—to introduce malware into the corporate network. Within hours, it propagated through WMS and TMS platforms, halting cargo movement and affecting thousands of clients worldwide.

This case underscores a critical insight: the weakest component in an integrated logistics architecture can compromise the entire system, especially when trust assumptions are not rigorously validated. It also highlights the need for system designers to treat every integration—regardless of vendor reputation or business necessity—as a potential attack vector.

To mitigate these risks, logistics organisations must adopt a set of secure integration architecture principles. First among them is the use of segmentation: systems should be divided into trust zones, and data flows across these zones should be explicitly controlled, logged, and monitored. For instance, an API connection between a TMS and an external carrier portal should pass through an API gateway that performs rate limiting, schema validation, token verification, and anomaly detection.

Second, integration design must support resilience and failover. Redundant paths, timeouts, and rollback mechanisms should be in place so that a disruption in one component does not bring the entire logistics operation to a halt. For example, if real-time inventory updates from a regional warehouse fail to reach the ERP system due to an integration fault, the system should fall back on cached data and trigger alerts for manual intervention rather than processing orders blindly.

Third, data validation and sanitisation are essential. All inputs received from external systems—be it XML, JSON, or file-based—must be rigorously checked to prevent injection attacks, malformed records, or protocol spoofing. Even trusted partners may inadvertently introduce corrupted or malicious data due to software bugs or misconfigurations.

An increasingly important tool in managing integration-related security is the Security Information and Event Management (SIEM) platform. SIEM solutions collect, aggregate, and correlate logs from multiple systems—including WMS, TMS, ERP, API gateways, and IoT platforms—to detect anomalies that might indicate a breach. For instance, if an API call is observed from an unusual IP address, outside standard business hours, requesting excessive records from the WMS, the SIEM can generate an alert and forward it to the Security Operations Center (SOC) for investigation.

Modern SIEM systems leverage machine learning to identify suspicious patterns across large datasets. In logistics, they might detect signs of API scraping, unauthorised access attempts to IoT devices, or unusual sequences of file transfers between integration points. The key advantage of SIEM in the integration context is its ability to bridge the gap between systems that would otherwise operate in monitoring silos.

Complementing SIEM, the Security Operations Center (SOC) plays a central role in incident response. A SOC team monitors dashboards, investigates alerts, and coordinates containment and remediation efforts. For logistics organisations with global operations, a SOC must be capable of tracking integration events across multiple time zones, languages, and regulatory environments. Integration-related incidents may not present as overt system failures but as subtle inconsistencies in data flows, requiring highly skilled analysts to interpret.

To support SOC operations, integration logs and metadata must be retained, normalised, and contextualised. This means including not just raw request data, but also attributes such as originating user identity, authentication method, system role, data classification level, and business impact scores. In a forensic scenario, such metadata is invaluable for reconstructing the timeline and scope of an attack.

An emerging best practice is the use of "integration twins"—digital replicas of data flows and system interactions used to simulate integration behaviour under different threat conditions. These twins can help test resilience, validate failover logic, and expose latent vulnerabilities before deployment. While still a developing field, digital twins for integration are especially promising in high-stakes logistics environments such as pharmaceuticals, defence, and perishable goods.

Finally, integration security cannot be an afterthought—it must be governed as part of the broader risk management framework. This includes periodic risk assessments, vendor audits, penetration testing of integration points, and continuous training for both IT and operations personnel. Cyber risks should be included in Service Level Agreements (SLAs) with integration partners, and compliance with standards such as ISO/IEC 27001, NIST SP 800-53, or TISAX must be verifiable across the digital supply chain.

The complexity and scope of system integration in modern logistics require a structured approach to designing, maintaining, and evaluating digital security across all connection points. Integration is no longer a one-time technical project but a continuous, evolving process that demands vigilance and strategic foresight. The final component of a secure integration strategy lies in implementing robust governance structures, conducting regular security audits, and embedding cyber resilience principles into architectural decisions.

One of the first and most critical recommendations is to adopt secure integration lifecycle management. This means that every stage of the integration process—from initial planning to decommissioning—should include dedicated security checkpoints. During the planning phase, organisations must identify all data flows, define trust boundaries, and assign data sensitivity levels. In the implementation phase, each interface should undergo code review, authentication testing, and simulation under attack scenarios. Once deployed, integration points should be continuously monitored, logged, and patched.

To operationalise this approach, logistics organisations are increasingly implementing Security-by-Design Frameworks tailored to integration projects. These frameworks enforce a minimum baseline of protection, such as mutual TLS (Transport Layer Security), API key rotation, multi-factor authentication for partner access, and audit trails for each external interaction. When working with third-party vendors or logistics service providers, integration checklists become contractual requirements to ensure that external systems uphold the same level of cybersecurity as internal ones.

A key organisational measure is to formalise cross-functional governance teams, bringing together logistics operations, IT integration architects, cybersecurity officers, and compliance personnel. These teams are tasked with overseeing integration risk assessments, change approvals, and post-incident reviews. Their role is particularly important in environments involving multiple integration partners, where assumptions about shared responsibility can lead to gaps and confusion during a cyber event.

To evaluate the health and risk posture of integrated systems, periodic integration security audits must be conducted. Such audits include the review of:

- Interface authentication and encryption mechanisms
- Change management logs across systems
- API gateway configurations and rate limits
- Cross-system access controls and privilege escalation risks
- End-to-end traceability of data movement between platforms
- Vulnerability scans of legacy connectors and middleware
- Penetration testing of external-facing portals or service endpoints

Audits must also address regulatory alignment, particularly in sectors where logistics intersects with sensitive data (e.g., pharmaceuticals, defence, finance). Compliance with data protection regulations such as GDPR, HIPAA, or customs-related security mandates like AEO (Authorised Economic Operator) should be built into integration design, not retrofitted afterwards.

In addition to audits, organisations should simulate cyber incidents involving integration points to test response readiness. For example, if an API credential is compromised, can the security team detect and revoke it in time? If an IoT sensor is hijacked and begins sending invalid shipment data, does the WMS flag the inconsistency before customer delivery? Such scenarios expose not only technical but also procedural weaknesses that can be improved through tabletop exercises and red teaming.

The culmination of these measures is the creation of resilient integration environments, capable of adapting to changes, detecting anomalies, and withstanding attacks without systemic failure. Table

2.7 outlines best practices for building and maintaining secure integrated logistics systems.

To conclude, integration has become a defining characteristic of the digital supply chain, and with it, a defining risk factor. A logistics network can only be as secure as its weakest integration point. As attackers increasingly exploit the complexity and opacity of inter-system communication, defenders must respond with clarity, structure, and resilience.

System integration must evolve from an enabler of efficiency to a cornerstone of cybersecurity architecture. Organisations that build their logistics strategies with this mindset will not only protect their operations from disruption, but also earn the trust of partners, regulators, and customers in an era where digital confidence is paramount.

2.4 Challenges and Risks of Logistics Digitalisation

The digital transformation of logistics represents one of the most profound structural shifts in the history of supply chain management. Technologies such as cloud-based platforms, autonomous vehicles, smart sensors, and AI-driven optimisation engines have redefined how goods are sourced, stored, tracked, and delivered. At the same

Table 2.7 Best Practices for Securing Integrated Logistics Environments

AREA	BEST PRACTICE
Architecture Design	Apply zero-trust principles, segregate systems by trust levels, use secure APIs
Authentication & Access	Implement multi-factor authentication, use role-based access control (RBAC)
Data Security	Encrypt all data in transit and at rest, validate inputs, sanitise data formats
Monitoring & Response	Deploy SIEM systems, set up integration-specific alerts, ensure SOC coverage
Vendor Management	Audit partner systems, define integration SLAs with security clauses
Lifecycle Management	Apply version control for APIs, monitor deprecations, manage key rotation
Compliance	Align with ISO 27001, NIST, GDPR, AEO, or sector-specific regulations
Business Continuity	Test failover paths, use integration twins for simulation, document recovery flows

time, this transformation introduces a new layer of complexity and risk, creating both unprecedented opportunities and significant vulnerabilities.

While digitalisation enables real-time visibility, operational efficiency, and enhanced responsiveness, it also expands the attack surface, increases interdependencies, and introduces systemic fragility into global logistics networks. The convergence of operational technology (OT) and information technology (IT), the rise of edge computing, and the outsourcing of critical functions to third-party digital platforms all contribute to a volatile risk environment. A single point of failure—whether a software misconfiguration, a cyberattack, or a failed integration—can propagate quickly, causing cascading disruptions across interconnected systems.

Moreover, logistics digitalisation is not a one-size-fits-all journey. Organisations differ in their digital maturity, strategic objectives, and regulatory constraints. Small and medium-sized enterprises may struggle with the cost and complexity of advanced platforms, while large multinationals face governance challenges in standardising cybersecurity policies across geographically dispersed units and external partners.

This chapter explores the multifaceted risks associated with logistics digitalisation—from cybersecurity threats and data breaches to technological obsolescence, vendor lock-in, and skill gaps within the workforce. It examines how these risks manifest at different levels of the supply chain, and how organisations can develop holistic strategies to anticipate, manage, and mitigate them. Special attention is given to the human factor, organisational culture, and regulatory pressure as invisible yet critical determinants of risk exposure.

In the context of increasingly automated and data-driven logistics, the ability to recognise and respond to digital threats is no longer an IT concern alone—it is a core element of supply chain resilience, business continuity, and strategic competitiveness. Understanding the risk landscape is the first step toward building secure, sustainable, and future-ready logistics systems.

The increasing reliance on digital technologies in logistics brings a fundamental shift in how supply chains are designed, executed, and managed. While digitalisation unlocks immense potential in terms of automation, visibility, and customer responsiveness, it also introduces a variety of new risk dimensions that must be carefully understood and managed. These challenges are not purely technical—they span organisational, operational, regulatory, and strategic domains. This section examines the core categories of risk associated with logistics digitalisation and explores how they impact supply chain performance and resilience.

One of the most immediate challenges is the expansion of the digital attack surface. As logistics systems become more interconnected—linking internal WMS, TMS, and ERP systems with external carriers, platforms, and sensors—the number of potential entry points for cyberattacks increases exponentially. A single compromised API or IoT device can serve as a backdoor into critical logistics infrastructure. In many cases, logistics firms underestimate how easily a vulnerability in one node can propagate through an entire digital supply network.

Compounding this risk is the fragmentation of security governance. With many logistics organisations relying on third-party logistics providers (3PLs), software vendors, and cloud service platforms, the responsibility for securing data and systems becomes distributed—and often ambiguous. Without centralised oversight and consistent security standards across the network, gaps in protection inevitably emerge. This fragmentation also complicates incident response, as visibility is limited, and accountability may be unclear in the event of a breach.

Another critical area of concern is data integrity and reliability. As logistics firms collect and process vast volumes of data in real time—from shipment statuses to predictive maintenance indicators—the value of this data grows, but so does its fragility. Errors in data transmission, deliberate tampering, or mismatched formats between integrated systems can lead to misrouted shipments, stock imbalances, or operational delays. These types of disruptions, while less visible than cyberattacks, can cause significant reputational and financial damage.

Digitalisation also brings the threat of technological obsolescence and vendor lock-in. As supply chains become dependent on proprietary platforms or SaaS solutions, they risk losing operational flexibility. For example, a logistics firm that builds its processes entirely around a single WMS vendor may find it difficult to switch providers or integrate with newer systems down the line. This lock-in can be exploited commercially or become a security risk if the vendor fails to keep the software up to date.

A less discussed but equally important challenge is the skills gap in the logistics workforce. The shift toward digital tools requires new competencies in data analytics, cybersecurity, system integration, and automated decision-making. Many logistics professionals—especially in mid-size or traditional firms—lack the training to effectively manage digital systems or recognise digital threats. The result is a growing reliance on IT departments or external consultants, which may slow decision-making or introduce operational blind spots.

Moreover, the pace of digital innovation often outstrips regulatory adaptation. While certain industries (such as pharmaceuticals or defence logistics) are subject to strict compliance regimes, others operate in jurisdictions with weak or fragmented cybersecurity laws. This inconsistency creates compliance risks, particularly when logistics data crosses international borders. Firms may inadvertently violate privacy laws (e.g., GDPR) or fail to meet sector-specific cybersecurity requirements, resulting in fines or legal disputes.

To illustrate how these risks interact in real-world environments, consider the following classification, which groups the challenges of logistics digitalisation into five primary categories (Table 2.8):

What makes these challenges particularly difficult to manage is their interdependence. A security failure may be caused not only by a missing firewall but by a lack of employee awareness. A regulatory breach may result not from a failure to follow the law but from an inability to monitor data flows across complex international logistics networks. Digitalisation, therefore, demands not only better technologies but also systemic thinking.

One of the emerging responses to these risks is the development of enterprise-wide digital risk management frameworks. These frameworks integrate risk identification, assessment, mitigation, and monitoring into all layers of logistics planning and execution. Key features often include risk mapping, scenario analysis, and real-time dashboards for threat intelligence and incident reporting.

Still, many organisations fall short in implementing such frameworks due to siloed operations. IT departments may develop technical controls, while logistics managers focus on operational KPIs—often with limited overlap. Bridging this gap requires not just tools but also

Table 2.8 Categories of Risk in Logistics Digitalisation

RISK CATEGORY	DESCRIPTION	POTENTIAL IMPACT
Cybersecurity Risks	Threats from hackers, malware, phishing, and insider attacks targeting digital systems	Data loss, operational disruption, reputational damage
Data Quality and Integrity	Errors, inconsistencies, or tampering in real-time logistics data	Misdirected shipments, stockouts, poor decision-making
Technological Dependence	Reliance on specific platforms or vendors with limited flexibility	Obsolescence, vendor lock-in, integration difficulties
Workforce & Skills Gaps	Lack of qualified personnel to manage, secure, or optimise digital logistics systems	Process inefficiencies, increased human error, compliance risk
Regulatory & Legal Risks	Exposure to differing national standards or evolving cybersecurity/data protection regulations	Fines, litigation, loss of market access

a cultural shift that places cybersecurity and digital resilience at the core of supply chain strategy.

In the next section, we will examine each of the five risk categories in more detail, providing examples of how they manifest in logistics operations and offering practical mitigation approaches used by industry leaders.

The increasing complexity of digital logistics ecosystems requires organisations to move beyond traditional operational risk thinking. In a world of interconnected platforms, cloud-based processes, and algorithm-driven decisions, the risks are neither static nor isolated. They are dynamic, often latent, and tightly interwoven with everyday business activity. This necessitates a paradigm shift in how logistics leaders conceptualise, detect, and manage digital risk.

One of the key challenges is the invisibility of certain threat vectors. Unlike physical theft or mechanical breakdowns, digital disruptions often lack immediate, tangible symptoms. A misconfigured API may not result in system failure but could silently leak sensitive shipment data for weeks. An unauthorised script running in a partner's TMS may slightly alter temperature tracking reports without triggering obvious alarms. These subtle yet impactful vulnerabilities highlight the need for sophisticated detection systems and a deep cultural awareness of digital hygiene across all levels of the logistics organisation.

The interdependence of digital logistics components further amplifies systemic vulnerability. Modern supply chains rely on seamless data exchange across transport systems, warehouse sensors, inventory dashboards, and external customs portals. This mesh of platforms, often built and maintained by different vendors and stakeholders, lacks uniform security standards. The risk does not lie solely in individual components, but in the interfaces between them—where responsibility is unclear, visibility is limited, and assumptions about trust prevail.

The human element adds yet another layer of complexity. Operators, drivers, warehouse managers, and even third-party contractors often have varying levels of digital literacy. Without adequate training, even the most secure infrastructure can be compromised by social engineering, credential sharing, or negligent behaviour. Furthermore, in logistics environments where time pressure is constant and efficiency is king, security protocols are sometimes bypassed in the name of operational urgency. This tension between speed and safety must be addressed structurally, through system design and management policy, rather than individual enforcement.

An increasingly common risk vector comes from the proliferation of embedded systems and edge devices such as RFID readers, autonomous forklifts, and smart pallets. These tools often operate on proprietary protocols, run outdated firmware, and remain invisible to central IT monitoring. A compromised RFID reader may serve as an unnoticed gateway into the broader network. Furthermore, their sheer volume makes centralised patching and auditing practically difficult, if not impossible. Securing this new digital terrain requires device discovery tools, segmentation strategies, and partnerships with vendors who understand security as part of product design—not a feature to be added later.

To understand the interplay between these dimensions of risk and different logistical domains, Table 2.9 offers a matrix view of how specific functions in the logistics value chain are exposed to different categories of digital risk.

This view reveals that every function in a modern supply chain is simultaneously a potential target, conduit, and amplifier of digital risk. No node is isolated. This interconnected vulnerability is particularly acute in global logistics operations where data must flow not only within the firm but also across partners, authorities, and digital platforms—many of which operate under different cybersecurity cultures, standards, and resource levels.

It is worth noting that not all risks carry the same probability or impact. Cyberattacks are statistically less frequent than data inconsistencies, but their impact is often catastrophic. On the other hand, vendor lock-in and workforce skill gaps are chronic rather than acute—they accumulate over time, quietly eroding flexibility, security, and responsiveness. Therefore, organisations must calibrate their risk mitigation strategies not only according to likelihood but also to the potential disruption amplitude and long-term strategic consequences.

Effective mitigation demands an architectural mindset. Logistics digitalisation must not be implemented as isolated tools or siloed systems, but as interconnected ecosystems with shared control principles. In practical terms, this means the establishment of shared data schemas, standard authentication mechanisms, encrypted interfaces, and cross-domain monitoring. The governance of these environments cannot be assigned solely to IT or cybersecurity teams; it must be elevated to strategic oversight, including risk officers, compliance specialists, and logistics executives who understand both the physical and digital layers of supply chain functionality.

Another key consideration is the pace of innovation. Many logistics firms face a situation in which digital change is being driven by competition or customer expectation, rather than by internal readiness. The deployment of AI-based forecasting, for instance, may outpace the team's ability to validate the data quality it depends on. Similarly, the integration of autonomous vehicles may proceed without clear security policies for firmware updates, remote overrides, or sensor spoofing. In such environments, innovation itself becomes a source of risk.

The final section of this chapter will present a set of forward-looking recommendations on how to systematically manage digital risks in logistics. These recommendations will be supported by examples from industry leaders, lessons learned from documented incidents, and a discussion of the strategic importance of embedding security into the DNA of supply chain digitalisation.

The mitigation of digital risks in logistics cannot rely on piecemeal interventions or reactive protocols. Instead, it must be guided by a holistic, anticipatory strategy that is aligned with the pace of

Table 2.9 Digital Risk Exposure across Key Logistics Functions

LOGISTICS FUNCTION	CYBERSECURITY RISK	DATA INTEGRITY RISK	VENDOR LOCK-IN RISK	SKILLS GAP RISK
Warehouse Operations	IoT device hijacking, ransomware	RFID data drift, system syncing errors	WMS feature dependency	Low familiarity with digital dashboards
Transportation Management	GPS spoofing, API breach	Real-time route data corruption	TMS vendor transition complexity	Poor interpretation of alerts
Inventory Control	Credential leakage to internal users	Mismatch in stock records across platforms	SaaS limitations in multi-warehouse support	Limited audit trail awareness
Order Processing	Phishing attacks on customer portals	Order misrouting due to duplicated data	CRM module dependency	Lack of knowledge in ERP workflows
Cross-border Clearance	Malware from unsecured customs integration	Loss of regulatory documents	Dependency on legacy EDI systems	Weak knowledge of compliance software

technological evolution and grounded in the realities of global supply chain operations. This requires not only technical adaptation but a redefinition of organisational culture, decision-making processes, and performance indicators that include digital resilience as a core value.

One of the most effective strategic frameworks that has emerged is the integration of digital risk governance within broader enterprise risk management (ERM). Rather than treating cybersecurity, data quality, vendor risk, and skill development as independent categories, leading logistics firms embed them into an interconnected risk register with clear ownership, impact assessments, and response plans. This allows for proactive scenario modelling, prioritisation of critical vulnerabilities, and alignment between operational functions and digital oversight.

Moreover, there is a growing recognition that digital risk must be addressed at both the strategic and operational layers of the logistics enterprise. Strategically, executive leadership must be involved in defining digital transformation roadmaps that balance innovation with control. Operationally, frontline staff must be equipped with the tools, training, and support systems necessary to detect and respond to digital anomalies as part of their daily routines.

Several logistics organisations have adopted the concept of a Digital Control Tower—not only for real-time visibility but also for integrated risk monitoring. These control towers aggregate operational data, cybersecurity telemetry, supplier feeds, and regulatory alerts into a unified platform. By doing so, they enable predictive analytics that not only optimise logistics flows but also anticipate disruptions. For example, if a cybersecurity tool detects increased traffic to a WMS port combined with delayed warehouse scans, the system may flag a potential breach or system malfunction before service-level agreements are compromised.

The value of such predictive capabilities is amplified when paired with cross-functional incident response protocols. A logistics firm may designate specific response teams not only for cybersecurity incidents but also for data quality failures, partner system outages, and regulatory non-compliance. These teams operate on pre-established playbooks, reducing confusion during crises and accelerating resolution times.

To support these structures, the development of digital twin environments has gained traction. By creating virtual models of supply chain processes—including their digital dependencies—firms can test the impact of different threat scenarios without risking real-world operations (Table 2.10). This approach is particularly useful in identifying failure points in integrations, evaluating the propagation of delays or attacks, and improving response coordination between IT and logistics departments.

One powerful illustration of these principles in practice is the case of a global 3PL provider that underwent a complete digital transformation of its cross-dock operations. As part of the project, it replaced legacy WMS and tracking systems with AI-enhanced platforms, integrated third-party customs software via secured APIs, and trained its operational managers in basic cybersecurity awareness. However, during a routine audit six months later, it discovered that one of its subcontracted carriers had maintained direct database access without proper encryption. The oversight did not result in a breach, but the potential severity prompted a redesign of all partner access protocols, implementation of token-based authentication, and the introduction of real-time access logging. The lesson: risk often emerges not from the planned architecture, but from the exceptions and assumptions made during rapid deployment.

Table 2.10 Strategic Recommendations for Managing Digital Risks in Logistics

STRATEGIC AREA	RECOMMENDATION
Governance	Integrate digital risk into enterprise-wide risk management systems with executive ownership
Monitoring	Deploy digital control towers with integrated cybersecurity and operational anomaly detection
Training	Develop logistics-specific cybersecurity education for staff at all levels
Technology Architecture	Design modular systems with secure APIs, open standards, and failover capabilities
Vendor Management	Establish vendor evaluation frameworks including security posture, data handling, and lifecycle policies
Innovation Management	Synchronise digital adoption plans with readiness assessments and phased implementation models
Simulation & Testing	Use digital twins and red team exercises to test cyber resilience and recovery protocols
Cultural Change	Promote a mindset where every employee is a digital risk manager

Another example comes from a last-mile delivery startup that suffered a data loss incident when a cloud provider decommissioned a storage region without notice. The firm had failed to implement redundancy across zones, assuming that their SLA guaranteed availability. Following the incident, the company adopted a multicloud strategy with automated replication and diversified vendors based on regional legal constraints. This shift not only reduced operational risk but also improved performance and customer experience in key markets.

The convergence of such experiences points to a clear conclusion: digital risk is no longer optional, and neither is its management. Logistics organisations that fail to anticipate and adapt to the digital threat landscape risk systemic disruption, regulatory sanctions, reputational damage, and competitive disadvantage. In contrast, those that embed security, adaptability, and digital literacy into their strategic DNA stand to lead in a market that increasingly values trust, transparency, and technological maturity.

In closing, logistics digitalisation represents both a frontier of opportunity and a battlefield of risk. By investing in strategic foresight, architectural discipline, and cultural change, logistics leaders can transform this duality into a foundation for long-term resilience and innovation. The future of logistics will not belong to the fastest or the cheapest—but to those who can move fast securely, scale wisely, and respond intelligently to digital disruption.

2.5 Case Study: ERP Implementation in a 3PL Operator and Its Impact on Data Security

The growing complexity of supply chain operations, intensified by globalised trade and real-time customer expectations, has led third-party logistics (3PL) providers to invest heavily in enterprise resource planning (ERP) systems. These platforms offer the promise of end-to-end integration, process automation, and enhanced decision-making based on accurate, centralised data. However, the implementation of ERP systems in 3PL environments is far from a purely operational undertaking—it is also a major transformation in how data is generated, accessed, and secured.

Unlike manufacturers or retailers, 3PL operators function within highly dynamic and externally dependent ecosystems. They must manage not only their own processes, but also those of their clients, subcontractors, customs agents, carriers, and technology partners. ERP implementation in such an environment poses unique challenges, particularly related to data governance, multi-party access, and cybersecurity compliance. Any misconfiguration, oversight, or unmitigated vulnerability in this context can quickly escalate into cross-client breaches, service failures, and regulatory exposure.

This chapter presents a comprehensive case study of an ERP system deployment in a mid-sized European 3PL firm operating across multiple warehouses and transport hubs. The study explores the project's strategic drivers, system architecture, integration process, and most importantly, the impact on data security during and after implementation. Drawing on interviews with project stakeholders, internal documentation, and incident logs, the case identifies key vulnerabilities encountered throughout the rollout—ranging from insecure legacy system integration to overly permissive user roles.

The analysis also highlights successful mitigation strategies, such as phased migration, role-based access control (RBAC), and continuous auditing mechanisms. It reveals how the ERP system became both a risk surface and a tool for managing risk—illustrating the dual role of digital systems in contemporary logistics. By examining this real-world scenario, the chapter provides valuable insights into how 3PLs can navigate the digital transition securely, and how ERP systems, when deployed thoughtfully, can become pillars of both operational efficiency and cyber resilience.

In 2019, a mid-sized European third-party logistics (3PL) operator specialising in e-commerce and industrial sectors launched a full-scale ERP (Enterprise Resource Planning) implementation initiative. The primary goal was to consolidate dispersed warehouse, transport, and financial operations into a unified platform that would enable real-time, 24/7 access to operational data and increase transparency across services provided to B2B clients. Prior to this, the company relied on various decentralised systems: separate WMS (Warehouse Management Systems) for each distribution centre, a standalone TMS (Transport Management System) for fleet coordination, and a range of spreadsheets and custom databases for finance, HR, and planning.

Although the main motivation for change was operational integration and improved customer service quality, the organisation recognised early the potential risks of migrating all business-critical data into a single, centralised environment. In particular, concerns were raised regarding new threat vectors, increased points of integration with external systems, and a lack of clarity over user data access rights.

The project began with a comprehensive pre-implementation assessment, mapping core operational processes to be migrated and classifying the types of data to be managed in the new system. Special attention was paid to sensitive datasets such as client contracts, personal data of drivers and warehouse workers, transport history logs, customs documentation, and internal cost structures. The audit also revealed several vulnerabilities in the existing IT infrastructure, including the absence of centralised access control, duplicated user credentials across multiple systems, and insufficient network segmentation between branches.

The company selected a globally recognised ERP provider offering logistics-focused modules for warehousing, transportation, and contract management. A SaaS (Software-as-a-Service) model hosted in a GDPR-compliant European cloud region was chosen to ensure scalability and elasticity. However, this transition required a rethinking of the company's approach to data control, which had previously been localised on physical servers at each site.

In the first implementation phase, the focus was placed on warehouse operations, encompassing receiving, storage, picking, packing, and outbound shipping. Data migration was based on manual mapping and validation between legacy WMS and the central ERP system. This phase exposed a significant security gap: the lack of a standardised access permission structure. In local systems, user rights were often assigned ad hoc, without clear alignment to official job roles. As a result, seasonal workers and shift supervisors had access to full order histories and financial records—clearly unacceptable under the new system.

The implementation team, in cooperation with the information security department, began developing a Role-Based Access Control (RBAC) structure. Operational roles were clearly defined, matched to permission sets, and users were systematically assigned to roles using the principle of least privilege (PoLP). Although this principle was initially met with resistance by team leaders who valued operational flexibility, it became a crucial safeguard against unauthorised access to customer data.

Parallel to the internal role standardisation, the integration of the ERP with client-side systems—such as EDI, APIs, and B2B portals—proved to be a security-critical element. Previously, most external data transfers were conducted over VPN connections or through static file exchanges via SFTP or email. The ERP migration required a shift to REST API-based integration secured through tokens, certificates, and IP whitelisting. Penetration testing by an external auditor revealed that one client-side integration allowed visibility into another client's contract data due to a misconfigured API endpoint. This issue was immediately remediated, leading to a new policy for reviewing all partner-facing interfaces and tightening API access controls.

Table 2.11 summarises the main data security risks identified during the ERP implementation project and the mitigation actions taken.

Thanks to early identification of gaps and the adoption of best practices, the ERP implementation did not result in any serious data breaches. However, the experience confirmed that ERP deployments in logistics must treat information security not as a parallel track, but as an integral component embedded from the initial planning phase through post-deployment operations.

Following the go-live phase of the ERP system, the 3PL operator entered a critical period of system stabilisation and user adaptation. During this time, both internal operations and client-facing processes underwent significant shifts. While many initial efficiencies became quickly evident—such as faster invoice processing, real-time inventory visibility, and automated shipping label generation—the ERP deployment also revealed several post-implementation challenges, particularly in the domain of data security and access governance.

One of the most pressing issues emerged when internal audits detected anomalies in access logs. Several employees from regional warehouses had accessed contract data unrelated to their assigned accounts. While no malicious activity was found, the incident highlighted a misalignment between role configurations and organisational policy. In response, the company deployed an advanced identity governance system integrated with the ERP platform. This system enabled time-limited access tokens, automated de-provisioning of

Table 2.11 Key Data Security Risks Identified during ERP Implementation

PROJECT PHASE	SECURITY RISK	POTENTIAL IMPACT	MITIGATION ACTIONS
Data Migration	Excessive user permissions	Breach of customer confidentiality	Implementation of RBAC and PoLP
EDI/API Integration	Inadequate API access controls	Cross-client data exposure	Tokenised authentication and IP whitelisting
Cloud Hosting	Lack of internal network segmentation	Increased lateral movement in case of breach	Deployment of virtual security zones
File Transfer	Unencrypted data in transit	Potential document interception	Introduction of TLS, SFTP, and secure VPN usage
Identity Management	Manual user account administration	Human error and unauthorised access	Centralised Identity and Access Management (IAM) system

accounts upon job role change, and quarterly certification campaigns to ensure role-to-user consistency.

A more serious event occurred when a phishing campaign targeted email accounts associated with the ERP's client notification module. An attacker successfully spoofed the domain used for sending shipment confirmations and lured a client into clicking a malicious link. Although no ERP data was compromised directly, the reputational damage triggered an immediate review of communication workflows. The company introduced SPF, DKIM, and DMARC records for email authentication, implemented two-factor authentication (2FA) across all user accounts, and launched mandatory phishing awareness training for all administrative and customer-facing staff.

From a systems monitoring perspective, the organisation realised that its traditional Security Information and Event Management (SIEM) tool was not fully optimised for cloud-based ERP platforms. Alerts related to suspicious behaviour—such as repeated login attempts from unexpected geographies or abnormal data exports—were not reaching the security team in real time. In collaboration with the ERP vendor and a third-party MSSP (Managed Security Service Provider), the company deployed a cloud-native SIEM solution specifically tailored for SaaS environments. This transition resulted in faster detection times and improved incident triaging, especially during non-business hours.

A continuous improvement loop was established, combining monthly incident reviews with quarterly penetration testing. Each test iteration helped to refine access control policies, validate encryption configurations, and assess the resilience of API endpoints. Over time, this practice evolved into a formalised ERP Security Maturity Model, guiding the organisation through successive phases of risk mitigation, audit readiness, and regulatory compliance (e.g., ISO/IEC 27001, GDPR).

To better understand the long-term security posture of the organisation post-ERP implementation, Table 2.12 summarises the major categories of incidents encountered, their frequency, severity, and organisational impact.

As these events demonstrate, the post-deployment phase is not merely about system operation—it is where resilience is tested and where vulnerabilities not visible during the implementation phase often emerge. The company's ability to respond effectively hinged on two strategic elements: its investment in adaptive governance tools and its shift toward a culture of shared responsibility for digital risk.

This case study also underscores an often-overlooked truth in ERP deployments: the system itself is not inherently secure or insecure; it is the surrounding ecosystem—comprising people, policies, and integrations—that determines the actual level of protection. In the 3PL's case, success was ultimately driven by leadership commitment to transparency, cross-departmental cooperation, and continuous risk-based adaptation.

Based on this experience, the company articulated a set of guiding principles for future digital system implementations:

Security must be embedded from day zero: Waiting until system go-live to address security introduces unmanageable retrofitting costs and unnecessary risk.

Operational ownership of cybersecurity is critical: IT and security teams must collaborate with logistics managers to translate abstract risks into operational safeguards.

Automation reduces human error: Wherever possible, account provisioning, data encryption, and incident detection must be automated to avoid policy drift.

Security is not a one-time configuration: With evolving threats and changing business needs, system security must be continuously evaluated, tested, and improved.

Table 2.12 Post-Implementation Incident Overview and Lessons Learned

INCIDENT TYPE	FREQUENCY (12 MONTHS)	SEVERITY	ROOT CAUSE	CORRECTIVE MEASURES IMPLEMENTED
Unauthorised Data Access	3	Medium	Role misconfiguration in RBAC	Identity governance automation, role audits
Phishing-Based Spoofing	1	High	Lack of email authentication protocols	SPF, DKIM, DMARC, 2FA, staff training
API Misuse Attempt	2	Medium	Inadequate rate limiting and input validation	Revised API gateway rules, token rotation policies
Credential Sharing (Internal)	4	Low	Informal practices among shift workers	User behaviour monitoring, policy enforcement
Forgotten Access Removal	2	Medium	Manual deactivation failures post-departure	Lifecycle automation, HR-IT system synchronisation

External partners require internal standards: No integration—whether with a client, vendor, or customs system—should bypass enterprise-wide security baselines.

The strategic outcome of this project was more than just a successful ERP implementation. It resulted in a more security-conscious organisation, one that viewed technology not only as a driver of efficiency but as a vector of responsibility. The ERP system became a central nervous system for operations—but its ability to function securely and ethically depended entirely on the quality of its governance and the vigilance of its users.

As digital transformation continues to accelerate across the logistics sector, this case illustrates how 3PL operators can navigate complexity without sacrificing control. When ERP systems are designed and operated through the lens of cybersecurity, they become enablers of trust, scalability, and long-term resilience—not liabilities.

Bibliography

Abeyratne, S. A., & Monfared, R. P. (2016). Blockchain ready manufacturing supply chain using distributed ledger. *International Journal of Research in Engineering and Technology*, *5*(9), 1–10.

Aceto, G., Persico, V., & Pescapé, A. (2018). The role of information and communication technologies in healthcare: Taxonomies, perspectives, and challenges. *Journal of Network and Computer Applications*, *107*, 125–154.

Alam, M., Ahmed, Z., Shah, S., Patel, A., & Khoso, I. (2021). Cybersecurity challenges in smart logistics. *Computers & Industrial Engineering*, *158*, 107408.

Alicke, K., Barriball, E., & Trautwein, V. (2020). How COVID-19 is reshaping supply chains. *McKinsey Quarterly*, *3*, 1–11.

Bag, S., Pretorius, J., Gupta, S., & Dwivedi, Y. K. (2021). Role of institutional pressures and digital technologies in sustainable supply chain management. *International Journal of Production Economics*, *231*, 107830.

Ben-Daya, M., Hassini, E., & Bahroun, Z. (2019). Internet of things and supply chain management: A literature review. *International Journal of Production Research*, *57*(15–16), 4719–4742.

Boddy, J., & Boddy, C. (2020). Ransomware and the logistics sector. *Computers & Security*, *95*, 101857.

Büyüközkan, G., & Göçer, F. (2018). Digital supply chain: Literature review and a proposed framework. *Computers in Industry*, *97*, 157–177.

Choi, T. M., Wallace, S. W., & Wang, Y. (2018). Big data analytics in operations management. *Production and Operations Management*, *27*(10), 1868–1883.

Christopher, M. (2016). *Logistics and supply chain management* (5th ed.). Pearson.

CISA. (2023). *Cross-sector cybersecurity performance goals*. U.S. Department of Homeland Security.

Dalenogare, L. S., Benitez, G. B., Ayala, N. F., & Frank, A. G. (2018). The expected contribution of Industry 4.0 technologies. *International Journal of Production Economics*, *204*, 383–394.

Dubey, R., Gunasekaran, A., Childe, S. J. (2019). Big data analytics capability in supply chain agility. *Journal of Business Research*, *98*, 311–320.

ENISA. (2023). *Threat landscape for supply chain attacks*. ENISA.

Fosso Wamba, S., & Queiroz, M. (2020). Blockchain in operations and supply chain management. *International Journal of Production Research*, *58*(7), 1–18.

Ghadge, A., Kara, M., Moradlou, H., & Goswami, M. (2020). Cyber risk management in supply chains. *Production Planning & Control*, *31*(2–3), 207–220.

Ghobakhloo, M. (2020). Industry 4.0, digitization, and opportunities. *Journal of Manufacturing Technology Management*, *31*(1), 1–24.

Gunasekaran, A., Subramanian, N., & Ngai, E. (2019). Quality management in the digital supply chain. *International Journal of Production Economics*, *207*, 1–11.

Hofmann, E., & Rüsch, M. (2017). Industry 4.0 and logistics. *Computers in Industry*, *89*, 23–34.

ISO/IEC. (2022). *ISO/IEC 27001:2022 Information security management systems*. ISO/IEC.

Ivanov, D. (2020). Predicting the impacts of epidemic outbreaks on supply chains. *Transportation Research Part E*, *136*, 101922.

Kache, F., & Seuring, S. (2017). Challenges and opportunities of digital information. *International Journal of Operations & Production Management*, *37*(1), 10–36.

Khan, S., & Haleem, A. (2021). Digital twin for supply chain resilience. *International Journal of Logistics Management*, *32*(2), 575–601.

Kshetri, N. (2018). Blockchain's roles in strengthening cybersecurity. *International Journal of Information Management*, *43*, 243–256.

Lee, H. L., & Whang, S. (2000). Information sharing in a supply chain. *Management Science*, *46*(5), 626–643.

Lu, Y. (2017). Industry 4.0: A survey. *Journal of Industrial Information Integration*, *6*, 1–10.

Manavalan, E., & Jayakrishna, K. (2019). Internet of Things embedded sustainable supply chain. *Computers & Industrial Engineering*, *127*, 925–953.

Marcucci, E., Le Pira, M., & Gatta, V. (2017). Smart urban freight planning. *Transportation Research Procedia*, *25*, 3433–3448.

Marr, B. (2016). *Big data in practice*. Wiley.

Min, H. (2015). *The essentials of supply chain management*. Pearson.

NIST. (2023). *SP 800-53 Rev. 5: Security and privacy controls*. NIST.

OECD. (2023). *Digital security risk management*. OECD.

Queiroz, M., Telles, R., & Bonilla, S. (2019). Blockchain in supply chain management. *International Journal of Production Economics, 207*, 170–184.

Radanliev, P., De Roure, D., Nurse, J., & Burnap, P. (2020). Supply chain cyber risk. *Technological Forecasting and Social Change, 154*, 119968.

Saberi, S., Kouhizadeh, M., Sarkis, J., & Shen, L. (2019). Blockchain technology and sustainable supply chains. *International Journal of Production Research, 57*(7), 2117–2135.

Sheffi, Y. (2015). *The power of resilience*. MIT Press.

Son, B., Choi, H., & Kim, S. (2021). Digital twin-based logistics systems. *IEEE Access, 9*, 12033–12045.

Tang, C. (2006). Perspectives in supply chain risk management. *International Journal of Production Economics, 103*(2), 451–488.

World Economic Forum. (2023). *Global cybersecurity outlook*. World Economic Forum.

Zhong, R. Y., Xu, X., Klotz, E., & Newman, S. T. (2017). Intelligent manufacturing in the context of Industry 4.0. *Engineering, 3*(5), 616–630.

Zsidisin, G. A., & Ritchie, B. (2009). *Supply chain risk management*. Springer.

Żywiołek, J., & Schiavone, F. (2019). Knowledge management and information security in smart organizations. *Management & Marketing: Challenges for the Knowledge Society, 14*(3), 362–376.

3

Threats and Incidents in the Logistics Environment

3.1 Common Types of Attacks and Vulnerabilities in the Sector

The logistics industry, operating within a vast and interconnected digital supply chain, is vulnerable to a range of cybersecurity threats that can have far-reaching consequences (Okoli et al., 2024). A cybersecurity threat refers to any possible malicious attack aimed at unlawfully accessing data, disrupting digital operations, or damaging information. Cyber threats can originate from a variety of actors, including corporate spies, hacktivists, terrorist groups, hostile nation-states, criminal organisations, lone hackers, and disgruntled employees. Threats can:

- be accidental or intentional;
- come from outside the system or from inside it (Ghelani, 2022);
- arise as a result of the user's unawareness or naivety (Jeske & van Schaik, 2017);
- be driven by the desire for profit, applause or revenge.

Threat awareness is crucial to planning effective protection strategies. Cyberattacks on supply chains exploit existing system vulnerabilities, aiming to compromise the security and reliability of products or services. Logistics companies are a crucial link in this process, making them an attractive target for criminals seeking to exploit vulnerabilities in transportation, warehousing, and distribution. Such attacks can result in the introduction of compromised goods into circulation, disruptions in delivery, and a loss of trust in logistics companies (Okoye et al., 2024). Supply chain connections amplify the impact of such attacks.

DOI: 10.1201/9781003685784-3

The vast majority of actions aimed at the security of computer systems are considered criminal offences by law. Examples of illegal behaviour include:

- hacking into a computer system;
- unauthorised acquisition of information;
- destruction of data and programmes;
- sabotage (paralysis of operation) of the system;
- software piracy, software theft;
- computer fraud and computer forgery;
- computer espionage.

The 21st century has seen the emergence of numerous threats to IT systems. This is (and continues to be) driven by the development of new communication techniques and technologies, including mobile devices, the Internet of Things, cloud computing, and big data. In practice, we encounter an increasingly wide range of cybersecurity threats. Here are some common threats logistics companies face:

1. Social engineering attacks involve manipulating and misleading victims to gain confidential information or access to their devices (Wang et al., 2021). These are carried out by, among other things, persuading users to open infected links or by deceiving them into accessing the computer directly. The most commonly used social engineering methods include:
   - Phishing attacks—involve the use of fraudulent emails, messages, or websites to trick individuals into disclosing confidential information, such as login credentials or financial data. Considering the diversity of stakeholders involved in logistics, including employees, suppliers, and partners, phishing attacks pose a significant risk. Successful phishing attacks can lead to unauthorised access to critical systems, breaches of confidential information, and potential disruptions in the supply chain (Okoye et al., 2024).
   - Spear phishing—is a specific type of phishing targeted at a particular individual or group. The attacker uses information about the victim to make their message appear credible (Eftimie et al., 2022). For example, a logistics

department employee may receive an email that looks like a reminder about an unpaid invoice from an actual business partner of the company.
- Smishing—is a type of phishing carried out through SMS messages. Attackers exploit the characteristics of mobile devices, including the common use of shortened links (e.g., bit.ly), to persuade users to click and disclose sensitive data (Rahman et al., 2023).
- Vishing—a term derived from the combination of the words *voice* and *phishing*. It is a form of telephone fraud aimed at extracting confidential information. The perpetrator typically impersonates an employee of a public or financial institution and, under the pretext of a supposed verification process, asks the victim to provide or confirm information that is actually used to take over their account or perform unauthorised transactions (Ashfaq et al., 2024).

2. Malware is a specially designed tool intended to cause harm to the user (Alenezi et al., 2020). It can be used to steal data, break system security mechanisms, or monitor the activity of the person using the computer. The most common types include:
   - Ransomware is a type of malicious software that encrypts files or entire systems and demands a ransom for the decryption key. The critical nature of logistics operations makes ransomware a serious threat, as an attack can disrupt the flow of goods, compromise tracking systems, and halt essential services. Ransomware attacks can result in downtime, financial losses, reputational damage, and the potential leakage of confidential data, affecting both internal operations and relationships with customers and partners (Odimarha et al., 2024); Ransomware-as-a-Service (RaaS) is a cybercriminal business model that enables individuals with little to no technical knowledge to carry out attacks. All that is required is registration on an RaaS platform and payment—usually a percentage of the ransom obtained. Modern ransomware campaigns are becoming increasingly sophisticated and precisely

targeted. They often use methods similar to spear phishing, involving the distribution of specially crafted emails designed to entice the victim into clicking a malicious link or opening an infected attachment. This is how ransomware infiltrates the victim's system. Every organisation, regardless of size, should be aware of this threat and implement protective measures—including developing an effective backup strategy and data recovery procedures in the event of an incident.

- A Trojan horse is a type of malicious software that disguises itself as a legitimate file or application in order to gain access to the victim's system (Nelson et al., 2023). Once executed, it can be used to steal personal data, install additional malicious programmes, or take control of the user's computer.
- Spyware is software installed on a computer without the user's consent or knowledge. Its primary purpose is to monitor the victim's activity, such as visited websites, and transmit the collected data to the programme's creator (Naser et al., 2023). It is most commonly used to obtain passwords, financial information, and other confidential data that can be sold or used in subsequent attacks.

3. Internal threats (Falkevych & Lisnyak, 2023) refer to situations in which an organisation's employees—either knowingly or accidentally—compromise the security of systems and data. These threats may stem from the actions of individuals with malicious intent or from unintentional mistakes. Employees with access to confidential logistics information may contribute to data leaks, unauthorised access, or disruptions in the functioning of logistics processes. In the first case, the threat results from deliberate violations of security rules; in the second, from carelessness or a lack of awareness.
4. Web application exploits are one of the most frequently used attack vectors by cybercriminals (Priyanka & Smruthi, 2020). They provide access to valuable data and are often relatively easy to exploit. A successful attack can result in serious consequences—from financial losses, through a weakened company

reputation, to a loss of customer trust. The most significant and common vulnerabilities in web applications include:

- SQL Injection (Priyanka & Smruthi, 2020)—is an attack technique targeting web applications by exploiting flaws in the handling of database queries. The hacker inputs crafted data that alters the way the SQL query operates. As a result, they can gain unauthorised access to information and then read, modify, delete it, and in some cases even execute their own code within the database. This type of attack can cause serious and lasting damage.
- Remote Code Execution—is a type of vulnerability that allows an attacker to execute their own code on the system where the vulnerable application is running. These vulnerabilities pose a serious threat to AI (Artificial Intelligence) and ML (Machine Learning) systems, especially in GPU-accelerated environments, where the computational power of GPUs can be exploited for malicious purposes (Szabo & Hadad nextsecai, 2025).
- Cross-Site Scripting (XSS) (Priyanka & Smruthi, 2020)—is a type of attack on web applications that targets the website's users. A cybercriminal injects a malicious script into an apparently safe site, making every visitor a potential victim. Defending against XSS can be challenging because the malicious code affects the visited pages rather than the user's device directly. As with other threats, awareness, and proper knowledge play a key role in protection.

5. Supply Chain Attacks (also referred to as third-party attacks, value chain attacks, or "backdoor" attacks) occur when a cybercriminal gains access to the logistical processes carried out between a supplier and a recipient by taking control of an intermediary company (Arulkumar S et al., 2024). Hackers infiltrate one link in the chain and then use this position to further penetrate and interact with other connected entities. In practice, such attacks may include:
   - Third-Party Access—organisations often grant their partners, suppliers, or subcontractors access to their own IT systems. If a hacker takes control of a trusted partner's

network, they can exploit its legitimate permissions to infiltrate the company's infrastructure.

- Trust in Third-Party Software—almost every company relies on solutions developed by external entities. Injecting malicious code into a programme or its update enables the installation of a harmful component which, as part of trusted software, can provide access to the company's confidential data.
- Hardware Attacks—these target physical devices, such as keyloggers (Singh et al., 2021), which capture data entered by the user. Compromising such a device gives cybercriminals the ability to use it as a gateway into the entire supply chain, increasing the scale and impact of the attack.

6. Denial of Service (DoS) Attacks—these involve disrupting the operation of computer systems or network services by consuming all available resources (Salim et al., 2020). As a result, users lose access to the service, and its functionality on the Internet becomes paralysed. Such attacks typically lead to network bandwidth overload and the exhaustion of computer resources such as CPU and RAM. The most common DoS threats include:
   - Distributed Denial of Service (DDoS)—these attacks leverage the simultaneous activity of multiple computers (usually infected devices or cloud resources) to generate massive requests directed at a chosen service. Since both the application and the system it runs on, as well as the network infrastructure, have limited bandwidth, the influx of such a large number of requests leads to overload and prevents legitimate users from accessing the service.
   - Ransom Denial of Service (RDoS)—these attacks involve demanding a ransom in exchange for stopping or not initiating a DoS/DDoS attack against an organisation. They can occur independently or in combination with ransomware, increasing pressure on the victim and forcing them to pay.
7. Man-in-the-Middle (MitM) Attacks—these involve secretly intercepting communication between two parties so that neither realises someone is interfering with the data exchange

(Muzammil et al., 2024). This allows a cybercriminal to eavesdrop on conversations, steal confidential information, and even impersonate one of the participants. This technique can be used in various ways to take control of devices or obtain valuable data, which is why several types of MitM attacks are distinguished:

- IP Spoofing—every device connected to the Internet has a unique IP address. A cybercriminal can impersonate such an address to mislead systems or users and thereby gain access to confidential information (Fonseca et al., 2021).
- Domain Name System (DNS) Cache Poisoning—this technique involves redirecting a user to a fake website instead of the one they intended to visit (Alharbi et al., 2022). The victim believes they are using a secure and trusted site, while in reality, they are landing on a page controlled by a cybercriminal. The most common goal of such an attack is to capture login credentials or divert traffic from a legitimate site to a fraudulent one.
- HTTPS Spoofing—when browsing the Internet, for example during online shopping, the "HTTPS" indicator in a website's address suggests that the connection is encrypted and theoretically secure ("S" stands for Secure). However, in a Man-in-the-Middle attack, a cybercriminal can trick the browser into displaying a fake security confirmation. As a result, the user ends up on an unsecured site, giving the attacker the ability to monitor communication and intercept transmitted data (Zhang et al., 2020).
- Email Interception—cybercriminals can break into email accounts of financial institutions or other organisations to monitor correspondence and transactions with clients. They often also spoof bank email addresses, sending forged messages from them. As a result, unsuspecting clients may hand over their authentication data or funds directly to fraudsters.
- Wi-Fi Eavesdropping—a hacker can create a fake network with a name similar to a public one (e.g., "Hotel," "Station") and intercept users' logins, passwords, or

payment card details. Another method is exploiting vulnerabilities in a legitimate router's security, which enables monitoring of network traffic and can lead to severe data leaks (Hu et al., 2023).

- Browser Cookie Theft—cookies store important information related to website usage. They may contain login details, addresses, or saved products in an online shopping cart, making repeat purchases easier. If a hacker gains access to these cookies, they can retrieve this data and potentially impersonate the user.

The rise of digitalisation has contributed to increasingly frequent, costly, and dangerous cyber incidents, including those related to ensuring supply continuity within logistics chains. Protecting data privacy, availability, and integrity has become a key priority for both institutions (including the military) and individuals. An effectively developed security strategy not only prevents data loss, theft, or corruption, but also mitigates the impact of potential security breaches or crisis situations.

It should be emphasised that one of the most effective tools for protecting our devices, data, and privacy remains common sense. Only when combined with appropriate techniques and tools does it provide real protection against various types of cyberattacks.

3.2 Security Gaps at the Interface between Supply Chain Partners

Modern organisations increasingly view the quality of relationships with business partners as a key factor determining their competitiveness and ability to adapt in a dynamic and unpredictable environment. The functioning and development of enterprises largely depend on interactions with other economic entities. For this reason, relationships within the supply chain should be treated as a fundamental element of supply chain management in every organisation. Strong business-to-business (B2B) relationships represent an effective business strategy, playing a significant role in the internationalisation processes of enterprises and constituting a primary area of interest for contemporary corporate marketing (Jamaluddin & Saibani, 2021).

From a relational perspective, effective collaboration among supply chain partners facilitates access to complementary resources, enhances organisational capabilities, and ultimately drives improvements in productivity, competitiveness, and profitability (Acquah, 2023). Consequently, efficient management of exchanges within the supply chain—encompassing both risk-sharing and information flow—constitutes a critical prerequisite for achieving competitive advantage and is fundamentally conditioned by the quality of relationships among network participants.

In modern supply chains, resource sharing constitutes an integral component of cooperative relationships (Wu et al., 2014). This sharing encompasses both tangible elements—such as warehouse space, technical equipment, and logistics services—and intangible components, including information exchange and financial flows. Resource Dependence Theory highlights the reliance of supply chain participants on data regarding demand and inventory levels provided by retailers operating at the downstream end of the supply stream (Celtekligil, 2020). Furthermore, aggregated information obtained from all partners within the supply chain is utilised in planning, production, and inventory replenishment processes (Töyli et al., 2013). Partners who derive benefits from collaboration tend to engage in long-term cooperation, fostering greater synergistic effects and enhancing the overall efficiency of the system.

It is worth emphasising that the advancement of information technologies, particularly the emergence of the Internet, has enabled supply chain participants to utilise new, previously inaccessible channels of communication and information exchange. This development has significantly enhanced the potential for collaboration and increased the level of integration within supply networks.

In the context of supply chains, an interface refers to the mechanisms and structures that facilitate the exchange of information, services, and physical goods between independent economic entities (Stefansson & Russell, 2008). Modern supply chains are characterised by a high degree of complexity and integration, making the interface a critical area from both operational and security perspectives.

In business practice, the exchange of information and services between partners is carried out using various technological solutions:

- Application Programming Interface (API)—enables direct communication between partners' IT systems, ensuring the automation of processes such as orders or stock updates (Nawaz et al., 2023).
- Electronic Data Interchange (EDI)—standards for electronic exchange of documents (e.g., invoices, bills of lading), allowing for cost reduction and shortening the transaction processing time (Newman & Bruce, 2015).
- ERP/CRM systems—integrate the company's internal processes (ERP–resource planning, CRM–customer relationship management) and enable their connection with partner systems (Myataza et al., 2024).
- Cloud solutions—cloud platforms are currently one of the main environments for exchanging data and services, offering scalability and ease of access, while generating new challenges in terms of security and data control (Ugbebor, 2024).

Each of the mentioned solutions not only improves the efficiency of cooperation, but also increases the scope of potential threats related to unauthorised access, data manipulation or interruption in the availability of services (Table 3.1).

The inter-organisational interface, representing the point of contact between systems, processes, and organisational structures of different entities within the supply chain, is particularly vulnerable to security gaps. These vulnerabilities stem from the heterogeneity of technological environments, differences in security management policies, and the complexity of processes coordinating collaboration. From a logistical and organisational perspective, five principal categories of inter-organisational interfaces can be distinguished (Stefansson & Russell 2008; Mentzer et al., 2001):

1. Technical Interfaces—these encompass IT infrastructure, software, and tools that enable the integration of partner systems. They include network connections, communication protocols, APIs, and data exchange systems. The quality and security of these interfaces are critical for ensuring business process continuity.
2. Institutional Interfaces—these refer to procedures, policies, and formal arrangements governing collaboration (e.g., SLA

Table 3.1 Supply Chain Interface Categories

INTERFACE CATEGORY	CHARACTERISTIC	EXAMPLES
Technical	Based on tools and systems that support data exchange and process standardisation, they enable the integration of partner technologies.	ERP systems, EDI, SCM platforms, blockchain, shared databases.
Institutional	A formal framework regulating cooperation between entities, defining roles, responsibilities, and rules of operation.	Contracts, SLAs, quality procedures, industry standards, legal regulations.
Logistics	Touchpoints related to the flow of material goods and services along the supply chain.	Warehouses, distribution centres, transshipment points, transport systems.
Procedural	Mechanisms for coordinating operational and planning activities, integrating partner processes.	Production planning, VMI (Vendor Managed Inventory), CPFR (Collaborative Planning, Forecasting, and Replenishment), delivery scheduling.
Human	Based on interpersonal interactions, building trust, communication, and organisational culture.	Project meetings, inter-company teams, informal networks, manager-manager relationships.

Source: Own elaboration based on Stefansson and Russell (2008) and Mentzer et al. (2001).

agreements, security standards, and joint risk control mechanisms). They play a key role in maintaining consistency of actions among entities with varying levels of organisational maturity.

3. Logistical Interfaces (Material/Physical)—these are associated with the flow of physical goods at points of contact such as warehouses, distribution centres, or transport terminals. The efficiency of these interfaces determines delivery timeliness and the overall fluidity of the supply chain.
4. Process (Operational) Interfaces—these include mechanisms for coordinating operational activities such as production planning, delivery scheduling, inventory management, and demand forecasting. Practical examples include VMI (Vendor Managed Inventory) and CPFR (Collaborative Planning, Forecasting, and Replenishment), which aim to eliminate barriers to inter-firm collaboration.

5. Human Interfaces—these concern direct interactions between employees of different organisations, including knowledge exchange, decision-making, and coordination of activities. Although often underestimated, they significantly influence efficiency and trust levels in partner relationships.

The literature on the subject identifies five basic categories of security vulnerabilities, which correspond to the previously mentioned interface categories.

Technical vulnerabilities in supply chain security management encompass both deficiencies in IT infrastructure and irregularities in the implementation of integration solutions between organisational systems. One of the most frequently identified issues involves insufficient protection of system interfaces, including APIs, EDI connections, and integrations with ERP and SCM platforms. According to the guidelines outlined in NIST SP 800-161r1 (Boyens et al., 2022), effective supply chain security requires the implementation of mechanisms that safeguard connections and information exchange between organisational systems and those of their partners. This need is particularly critical in the context of collaboration among multiple entities operating within the so-called cyber supply chain. The technical complexity of such cooperation generates numerous challenges in ensuring consistent and threat-resistant security solutions (Henriksson, 2021). An additional source of technical vulnerabilities lies in inadequate authentication and authorisation mechanisms, including the absence of multi-factor authentication (MFA) and the use of shared accounts, both of which significantly increase the risk of unauthorised system access (*Threat Landscape for Supply Chain Attacks | ENISA*, 2021). Another significant challenge involves vulnerabilities present in APIs, which can be exploited to carry out injection attacks or enable users to escalate privileges. An additional area of risk is the limited capability for event monitoring and logging, which hinders effective detection, analysis, and response to security incidents (Boyens et al., 2022). The absence of robust mechanisms for detecting and analysing anomalies in network traffic or system logs results in delayed incident response, thereby increasing an organisation's vulnerability to the escalation of threats across the entire supply chain (Henriksson, 2021).

Organisational gaps in supply chain security primarily stem from the heterogeneous levels of security management maturity among partners involved in delivery processes. This disparity leads to inconsistencies in policies, procedures, and control mechanisms. One of the critical issues is the absence of standardised security policies and uniform operational practices, which hinders the implementation of coherent information protection measures across the entire collaboration ecosystem (ISO/IEC 27036-1, 2021, Cybersecurity–Supplier Relationships—Part 1: Overview and Concepts, 2021) (ENISA, 2022; ISO/IEC 27036-2, 2014). According to the Verizon DBIR 2025 (2025 Data Breach Investigations Report, 2025), the proportion of incidents involving third parties in security breaches has doubled within a year—from 15% to 30%—clearly indicating the growing significance of organisational risk in supply chains. In many cases, these incidents were caused by ineffective oversight of subcontractors and undefined or inconsistent supplier verification procedures, which resulted in the infiltration of vulnerable components or misconfigured services into the core infrastructure of primary organisations (Boyens et al., 2022).

An additional factor contributing to organisational gaps is insufficient communication among partners regarding incident response and risk management. The DBIR 2025 emphasises that in more than 60% of cases involving partner organisations, the incident response process was delayed due to the absence of clearly defined escalation channels and responsibilities. Such delays are critical in the context of complex supply chains, where response time directly affects the scale of losses and the ability to restore operations.

Ambiguous provisions in contracts and Service Level Agreements (SLAs), which often fail to clearly define responsibilities for incident handling, reporting procedures, or mitigation measures, further exacerbate this issue (Boyens et al., 2022). Moreover, data from the Verizon report indicate that ransomware remains one of the most prevalent consequences of such organisational gaps, accounting for 28% of all data breaches in 2025 and causing median financial losses of approximately USD 115,000 per incident. In organisations with a low level of security management maturity, these impacts are significantly higher, underscoring the strong correlation between the quality of organisational oversight and operational resilience.

The absence of clearly defined collaboration mechanisms, common standards, and systematic communication among partners in security management increases the risk of delays in threat response, thereby weakening the resilience of the entire supply chain. Consequently, the development of coherent security policies, the implementation of formal models for managing supplier relationships (Third-Party Risk Management), and the establishment of uniform requirements in contracts and SLAs should constitute a fundamental component of organisational security strategies within modern supply chain ecosystems.

Another category comprises *process-related gaps*, which refer to deficiencies in operational practices associated with IT system management and partner integration within the supply chain. These gaps typically arise from the lack of standardised processes supporting the security of an organisation's critical infrastructure. One of the most frequently observed phenomena is the presence of so-called shadow IT (Haag & Eckhardt, 2017), meaning unauthorised technological solutions or integrations developed outside the control of IT departments. Such practices lead to the absence of oversight over data flows and increase the risk of introducing vulnerable or non-compliant components into the production environment.

The Verizon DBIR 2025 (2025 Data Breach Investigations Report, 2025) indicates that as many as 20% of all data breaches resulted from the exploitation of known vulnerabilities, with remediation taking an average of 32 days. Notably, only 54% of these vulnerabilities were fully patched during the study period, demonstrating that delays in update and patch management processes pose a tangible threat to system continuity. At the same time, 22% of all vulnerability exploitation cases involved edge devices and VPN networks, whose configuration and management often remain outside the direct oversight of IT departments, thereby increasing the risk of compromising critical infrastructure.

Many organisations lack well-developed and regularly tested Business Continuity Plans (BCP) (Muflihah & Subriadi, 2019) and Disaster Recovery Plans (DRP), (Sardjono et al., 2024). Neglect in this area can lead to operational disruptions and destabilisation of the entire supply chain in the event of a security incident. Therefore, effective management of operational processes and their regular verification constitute a critical element in strengthening organisational resilience against threats within complex supply chain environments.

The human factor remains a critical element in the cybersecurity risk structure—both at the level of individual organisations and across entire supply chains. Data presented in DBIR 2025 (2025 Data Breach Investigations Report, 2025) indicate that as many as 60% of security incidents involved human participation, a figure that has remained relatively stable compared to previous years. The most common attack vectors exploiting human factors continue to be phishing, credential misuse, and employee errors, which frequently enable cybercriminals to gain access to organisational resources.

The report also shows that phishing and social engineering manipulation are among the dominant methods of acquiring credentials, which is particularly dangerous in a multi-party environment where access to partner and supplier systems is shared. A dynamic increase in the use of artificial intelligence in generating phishing content was also observed in 2025—the amount of synthetically created text in phishing emails doubled in two years, making it significantly more difficult for users to distinguish fake messages from genuine ones.

Another worrying trend is the growing risk associated with employee use of generative AI tools. According to the report, 15% of employees routinely accessed AI platforms on work devices, increasing the likelihood of sensitive data being leaked by unknowingly being passed to external models. Combined with the fact that 46% of the systems from which compromised credentials originated were unmanaged devices (e.g., employee personal computers), this creates a complex ecosystem of personal and organisational risks.

The issue of breaches of trust and a lack of a cohesive security culture between supply chain partners is also significant. Interpersonal dependencies and operational pragmatism often lead to the circumvention of security procedures—for example, by sharing login credentials to facilitate collaboration. Such behaviour, seemingly innocent, can be exploited to gain access to critical systems.

In the context of the supply chain, the human factor should therefore be viewed not only as a single risk element, but as a threat multiplier that, when combined with technical and organisational imperfections, can lead to systemic security breaches. Building a unified security culture, encompassing education, training in resilience to social engineering manipulation, and monitoring user behaviour in the inter-organisational environment, remains a key direction.

The existence of security vulnerabilities at the interface level can have serious consequences for the entire supply chain. These issues may lead to breaches in the confidentiality, integrity, and availability of data, delays in logistics processes, and a loss of trust among business partners. The cascading effect is especially concerning; when an incident impacts one entity, it can spread to other links in the chain, ultimately destabilising the entire collaboration system.

3.3 Consequences of Downtime and System Interruptions

Downtime and system disruptions caused by cybersecurity incidents pose a significant threat to supply chain continuity. Much like power grids, supply chains are highly interconnected systems that rely heavily on digital control layers (Rajkumar et al., 2023). The impact of these disruptions is felt almost immediately in operations, affecting both individual logistics nodes and the broader network of related entities. One notable characteristic of these disruptions is their cascading effect: a localised event—such as the loss of availability of IT (Information Technology) or OT (Operational Technology) control systems at one point in the network—can lead to successive disruptions in other parts of the supply chain. This can result in delays, schedule breakdowns, or even complete halts in processes across links that were not initially impacted by the incident.

The exposure of supply chains to various threats can lead to significant disruptions in execution and planning processes. This occurs due to the sudden loss of the control layer and input data, which are critical for modern storage operations and full process automation, as highlighted in warehouse security research (Meggiato et al., 2022). When access to systems like the Warehouse Management System (WMS), Transportation Management System (TMS), Radio Frequency Identification (EPC/RFID), Yard Management System (YMS), Manufacturing Execution System (MES), and Enterprise Resource Planning (ERP) is lost, the control cycle is abruptly interrupted. Additionally, the need to revert to emergency procedures—relying on paper documentation and manual management—leads to a significant decline in efficiency. This switch increases the likelihood of operational errors and creates a backlog that must be identified and resolved after the systems are restored before normal operations can resume.

A significant operational consequence is the loss of end-to-end visibility in the supply chain (Ivanov, 2024a). The lack of information about current inventory levels in ERP, about shipment locations in tracking systems (track & trace), about notification statuses transmitted via EDI or APIs, about real resource loads in Advanced Planning Systems or about the current container flow in port terminal operating systems (TOS) prevents inter-organisational coordination. The most common operational inefficiencies resulting from the loss of end-to-end visibility in the chain are:

- the bullwhip effect, as discussed by Sarac et al. (2010) occurs when limited or delayed visibility of demand and inventory leads to inflated or duplicate orders; this results in amplified demand fluctuations upstream, overproduction, excess inventory, and simultaneous shortages at other nodes;
- incorrect purchasing and planning decisions—arise when there is a lack of a complete and up-to-date "map" of the supply chain; this limitation affects the accuracy of planning and forecasting, leading to the need for corrections, emergency orders, or cancellations, which ultimately increases costs and lowers service levels (Joshi, 1998); the concept of end-to-end (E2E) visibility, which refers to a digital representation of the supply chain, is essential for effective planning and control, especially during disruptions such as the COVID-19 pandemic;
- incorrect slot reservations and congestion at ramps and terminals (Carlan et al., 2022)—stem from limited data exchange and poor synchronisation among systems like TMS, YMS, and TOS; this results in inadequate time window planning, frequent ad hoc changes, and a "first come, first served" approach, leading to waiting times, standstill costs, and schedule disruptions;
- the inadequate distribution of production and transport capacities (Dehoratius et al., 2008)—can result in a mismatch between the physical state and the data in systems; this mismatch may lead to poor resource allocation, causing excess capacity in some locations and shortages in others;

- cascading delays cause a "ripple effect" throughout the supply chain (Dolgui & Ivanov, 2021)—when visibility diminishes, the time required to detect disruptions and errors increases, which triggers secondary disturbances and delays in subsequent links.

System disruptions caused by cyber threats also create bottlenecks at the interface between physical and digital operations. In these situations, even well-functioning logistics processes in the physical infrastructure can slow down or come to a complete stop because they cannot be synchronised, registered, or authorised in IT systems. Simulation studies conducted on port infrastructure show that when key operating systems and external vendor servers lose functionality, there is a sudden shift to manual check-in modes. This transition leads to increased vehicle queues, delays in releasing cargo units, and a reduced throughput at gates and transshipment facilities (König et al., 2019). Digital disruption in partner synchronisation can lead to several challenges. For instance, the inability to send an Advance Shipping Notice (ASN), transmit an electronic waybill (the digital equivalent of a CMR), register receipts in the ramp subsystem, carry out customs clearance in broker systems, or input data into import-export platforms can result in the accumulation of loading units at terminals. This disruption can also cause vehicle downtime and incur additional fees for demurrage and exceeding operating windows.

Downtime significantly impacts quality and safety. When systems like quality management (QMS), operational technology (OT), industrial control (ICS), and enterprise resource planning (ERP) fail, organisations struggle to maintain control over key production and distribution stages. Cyber disruptions can cause uncontrolled changes in process parameters, incorrect device configurations, and loss of safety functionality, increasing risks to products, infrastructure, and personnel (Miller et al., 2021). As a result, there are more picking errors, disruptions to the cold chain, deviations in recipes, inconsistencies in shipping documents, and formal deficiencies that require additional checks, withdrawals, recalls, or even disposal of batches.

One serious and often underestimated consequence of system restoration is the lengthy recovery phase that follows. Simply restarting the application does not ensure an immediate return to the pre-disaster state (Steinberg et al., 2021). It involves several critical tasks, including rebuilding operational queues in the WMS, MES, and TMS. Additionally, it is essential to validate data integrity within the Enterprise Resource Planning (ERP) system, resynchronise Electronic Data Interchange (EDI) and Application Programming Interface (API) integrations, recalibrate slots in the Yard Management System (YMS), reconcile manual orders with system logs, and address any discrepancies that occurred during the emergency mode. Consequently, the recovery phase can significantly extend the actual downtime beyond the point when the system is technically restored.

From a supply chain perspective, interruptions in system availability have far-reaching operational consequences. They disrupt the flow of processes, destabilise coordination among partners, and lead to indirect costs resulting from corrections and delays. These interruptions can also give rise to additional consequences, including financial, relational, regulatory, and strategic impacts.

3.4 Risk Analysis and Vulnerability Assessment

Risk analysis in logistics builds on previous discussions about common cyber threats, security vulnerabilities among supply chain partners, and the impacts of system downtime. Modern logistics, relying on integrated IT systems and warehouse automation, depends heavily on proprietary and external technologies. Thus, risk analysis should be a fundamental aspect of strengthening the resilience of the entire supply chain. A systematic approach that includes threat identification, vulnerability assessment, and incident impact estimation is crucial for understanding the full extent of risks affecting both individual companies and the collaborative network.

Section 3.1 outlines various threats that are crucial for risk analysis. Key risk factors in the logistics sector include phishing attacks, malware (including ransomware), employee privilege abuse, and attacks on web applications and API/EDI interfaces. Risk analysis begins by connecting these threats to specific organisational vulnerabilities, both technical and human. In the logistics environment, these vulnerabilities are especially significant because systems like WMS, TMS, ERP, YMS, and EDI operate continuously and directly affect physical operations. Any instability in these systems can disrupt the order fulfilment process.

Attention has now been drawn to the issue of critical security gaps that arise not from a single organisation, but from the configuration of inter-organisational relationships. It is specifically these partner interfaces—whether technical (such as APIs, EDI, or B2B portals), process-based (such as shipping and delivery coordination), or human interactions—that introduce an additional layer of risk that cannot be overlooked. Often, the primary vulnerability does not originate from internal threats, but rather from disparities in cybersecurity maturity levels among partners. Therefore, risk analysis must take into account the risks transferred by:

- IT service providers;
- transport operators;
- system integrators;
- cloud service providers;
- companies utilising the same logistics platforms.

Research shows that supply chain attack incidents are becoming one of the main factors of operational disruptions, as they allow attackers to bypass the company's direct security measures and strike through the weakest link in the collaboration network (2025 Data Breach Investigations Report, 2025).

Risk analysis should consider the potential downtime of Information Technology (IT) and Operational Technology (OT) systems, as noted by Rajaram et al. (2022). This downtime can have significant negative effects in the logistics environment. The entire supply chain—ranging from goods receipt to warehousing, picking, shipping, and transport—depends on the continuous operation of digital tools. As a result, impact analysis must integrate elements typical of cybersecurity with operational assessments. It should address consequences such as loss of inventory visibility, blocked loading docks, incorrect orders, disruptions in transport planning, ripple effects throughout the distribution network, and the risk of violating quality standards. Often, the actual impact of an incident can exceed the immediate consequences of a system outage because manual data replenishment and process resynchronisation may be necessary once operations resume, which can delay the return to full performance (Ivanov, 2024b).

Risk analysis in logistics therefore encompasses three levels:

- the technological threat level (Section 3.1);
- the relational and integration weakness level (Section 3.2);
- the operational level (Section 3.3).

To create a realistic picture of risk, it is essential to combine three key dimensions. Methodologies such as ISO/IEC 27005 (*ISO/IEC 27005:2022 - Guidance on Managing Information Security Risks*, 2022), the NIST Cybersecurity Framework (The NIST Cybersecurity Framework (CSF) 2.0, 2024) and FAIR (*2025 State of Cyber Risk Management Report*, 2025) offer valuable tools for systematic threat identification, vulnerability assessment, and classification of risk severity. Logistics organisations are increasingly adopting a hybrid approach that integrates both quantitative and qualitative tools. This approach takes into account not only the financial value of potential losses but also the impact on operational continuity.

A key component of risk analysis is the assessment of risks associated with partners, known as Third-Party Risk Assessment (Keskin et al., 2021). It takes into account both technical aspects (API/EDI configurations, partner security procedures, authentication model), organisational aspects (compliance with standards, incident management), and process aspects (update deadlines, BCP/DRP tests) (Kadam, 2017). The ISO/IEC 27036 standard (ISO/IEC 27036-1:2021, Cybersecurity–Supplier Relationships—Part 1: Overview and Concepts, 2021) and ENISA guidelines (*Cybersecurity for SMES Challenges and Recommendations Cybersecurity for Smes About ENISA*, 2021) emphasise that partner risks cannot be treated as external—on the contrary, they constitute an integral part of the organisation's risk profile (Shonubi, 2025).

In the final phase, risk analysis leads to the development of a risk reduction strategy, according to which the highest probability and highest impact risks, especially those related to the integration of partner and critical operational systems, must be prioritised for protection. This includes implementing technical measures (network segmentation, Multi-Factor Authentication, Endpoint Detection and Response / eXtended Detection and Response, encryption), process measures (patching, penetration testing, BCP/DRP), and organisational measures (training, access management, security policies).

While these actions do not eliminate risk entirely, they do reduce it to an acceptable level consistent with the company's business requirements and the expectations of supply chain partners.

Risk analysis is a crucial component of logistics security management. It brings together insights from various areas, including cyber threats, weaknesses in collaboration between organisations, and the operational impacts of downtime. This comprehensive approach enables the planning of both preventive and reactive measures that safeguard not only individual companies but also the entire logistics ecosystem, where each participant plays an essential role.

3.5 Case Study: Supply Chain Attack on RFID Systems in an E-commerce Distribution Centre

This case study describes a complex, multi-stage cyber-physical attack on the radio frequency identification (RFID) infrastructure of a major European e-commerce distribution centre. The scenario combines patterns found in the cyber-physical security literature, existing vulnerabilities in industrial IoT systems, and emerging threat trends within the logistics sector (Boyes, 2015; Leligou et al., 2024; Humayed et al., 2017). It demonstrates how systemic vulnerabilities at the interfaces between partners can lead to cascading operational failures, directly referencing the concepts discussed in Sections 3.1–3.4.

3.5.1 Contex

The fictional company QuickGoods EU operated a fully automated, high-performance fulfilment centre that processed over 250,000 shipments daily. Its merchandise routing, picking, and shipping verification processes were built on a UHF RFID ecosystem, including (Figure 3.1):

- Passive GS1 EPC Gen2 (RAIN RFID) tags are designed according to the EPC UHF Gen2 Air Interface Protocol established by GS1 in 2025 (*EPC UHF Gen2 Air Interface Protocol | GS1*, 2025). GS1 EPC Gen2 is a global standard for passive RFID tags. The term EPC stands for Electronic Product Code, which is a unique code stored on the tag. An RFID reader can scan this unique EPC code and send it to

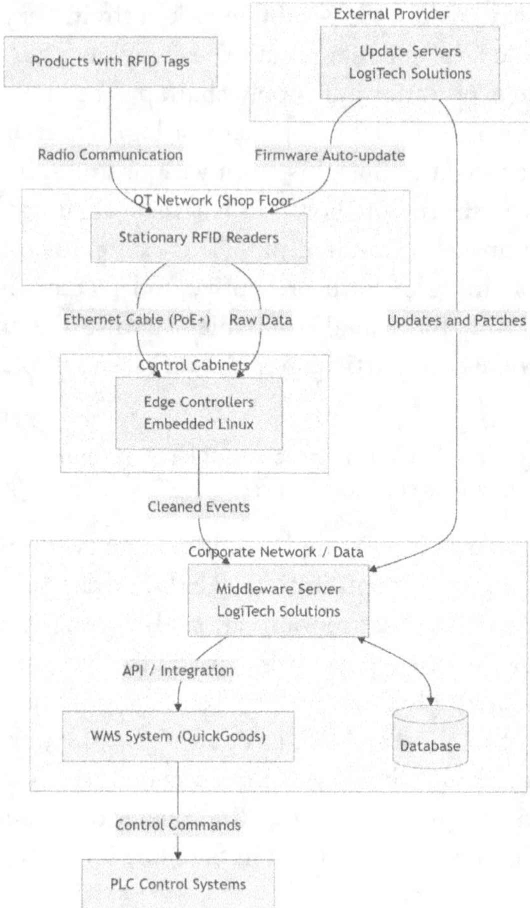

Figure 3.1 Simplified RFID system architecture at the QuickGoods EU distribution centre, illustrating the data flow from tags to the WMS and the key dependency on an external supplier (LogiTech Solutions) in the update process. Source: Own elaboration.

a system that identifies the product within a database. This process allows for accurate tracking of products' locations and conditions throughout the supply chain, ultimately enhancing operational efficiency (*Buy RFID Label - RFID Label*, 2025).

- Industrial stationary readers are connected to the operational technology (OT) network using Power over Ethernet (PoE).
- Edge controllers operating on an embedded Linux system are specialised industrial computers that conduct essential data processing directly on the shop floor through edge computing (Shi et al., 2016; Kumari & Lele, 2023).

- Middleware platform—central server software that acts as an integration and decision-making hub for the entire RFID system.

All components were provided and maintained by LogiTech Solutions, a third-party logistics technology provider. Reader firmware updates and middleware patches were delivered via LogiTech's cloud-based update server and deployed automatically—a common yet risky architecture in many supply chains Boyens et al., 2022).

Since the RFID system is directly connected to the warehouse management system (WMS), any malicious interference with tag readings or event streams could significantly affect real-time inventory accuracy, routing logic, and automated decision-making (Humayed et al., 2017; International Electrotechnical Commission, 2019; Aldossary & Elmedany, 2020).

3.5.2 Attack Vector and Course

Forensic evidence indicates that a highly skilled and financially motivated group is involved. The use of multi-stage malware (Figure 3.2), which is initially designed for covert data manipulation and later for coordinated operational paralysis, aligns with tactics seen in the preparation stages of ransomware attacks and data theft campaigns aimed at critical infrastructure (Mandiant, 2023; Dragos, 2025b).

3.5.2.1 Stage 1: Hacking into the Supplier's Systems

Attackers gained access to the LogiTech software update server by exploiting an unpatched, critical remote code execution (RCE) vulnerability in the administration panel of the customer portal. This access was likely obtained through the leak or capture of privileged vendor user credentials. Additionally, the absence of multi-factor authentication (MFA) and inadequate network segmentation contributed to the severity of the breach. As a result, the attackers were able to:

- escalate their privileges;
- move laterally within the LogiTech network;
- ultimately modify the firmware distribution directory.

The attackers infiltrated the official update channel for QuickGoods' flagship LTS-9000 reader by introducing infected firmware. While

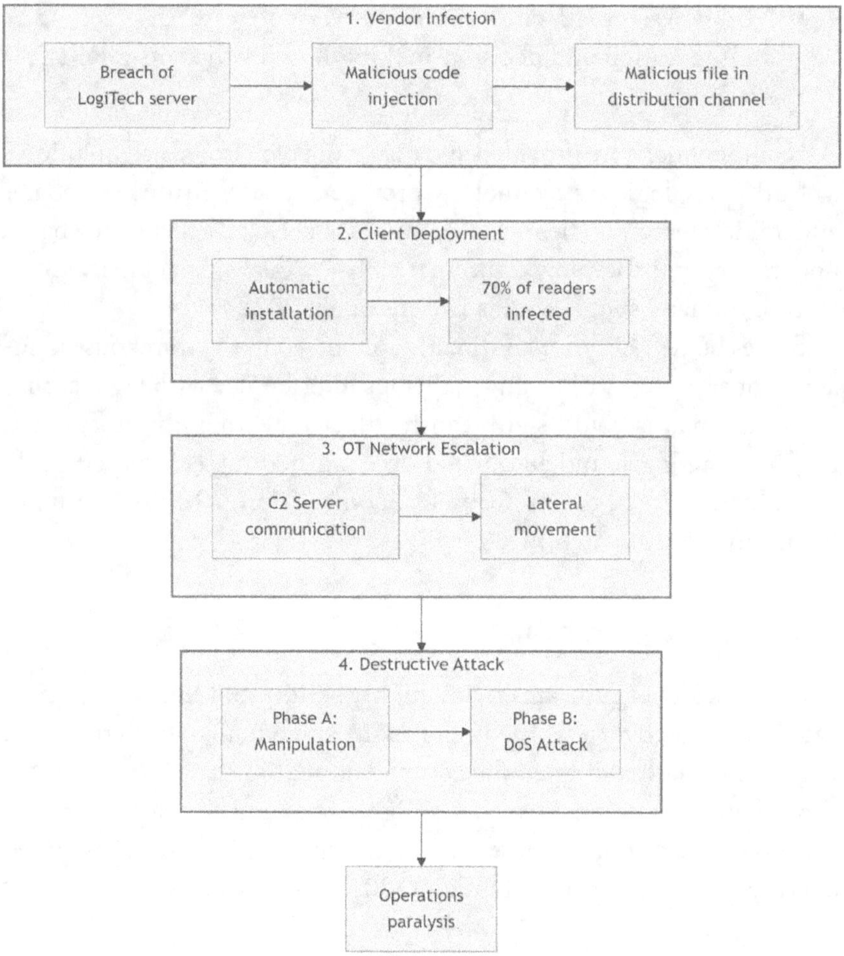

Figure 3.2 A sequential flow diagram of a supply chain, showing the key stages from supplier compromise to final operational paralysis. Source: Own elaboration.

the software appeared to function normally, it contained a concealed backdoor that allowed the attackers to maintain persistent access and control remotely. These kinds of attacks, which target the software supply chain to establish a lasting presence in operational technology (OT), signify a significant escalation in the threat landscape (2022 Top Routinely Exploited Vulnerabilities | CISA, 2022).

3.5.2.2 Stage 2: Deploying the Malicious Firmware

During a routine maintenance period, compromised firmware was automatically downloaded and installed on about 70% of QuickGoods desktop readers.

QuickGoods did not have essential firmware integrity checks in place, such as (Martínez & Durán, 2021).

- cryptographic signature verification—the company did not enforce validation of the supplier's (LogiTech's) digital signatures before installing updates (Souppaya et al., 2022);
- *hash* validation—even the most basic integrity check was skipped, i.e., comparing the cryptographic *hash* of the downloaded file with the value published by the supplier (Gilbert & Gilbert, 2025);
- pre-deployment testing in an isolated environment (staging/sandbox)—updates were pushed directly to production systems, bypassing the validation phase in a controlled, non-production environment (Cindric et al., 2025);
- real-time attestation mechanisms—the company did not monitor device state in real time for unauthorised changes in code (International Electrotechnical Commission, 2019).

As a result, the malicious image was deployed without being detected.

3.5.2.3 Stage 3: Lateral Movement through OT Weak Points

After activation, the firmware began covert communication (beaconing) with an external command-and-control (C2) server. This communication utilised encrypted outbound traffic that was disguised as telemetry data. The malware also took advantage of several vulnerabilities:

- default, hardcoded credentials on edge RFID controllers;
- unencrypted middleware communication through EPC event streams;
- a flat OT network without VLAN segmentation.

As a result, the malware was able to gain control of the RFID middleware server and move laterally between OT endpoints (Knowles et al., 2015; Hahn et al., 2013).

3.5.2.4 Stage 4: Operational Disruption through Data Integrity Attacks

The next phase of the attack carried out a two-stage disruption strategy:

1. Gradual data manipulation (Mancuso et al., 2013) ("low-and-slow," 72 hours). The malware selectively manipulated EPC read events using three mechanisms:
   - **tagspoofing**: altering tag IDs before forwarding them to the middleware (Spruit & Wester, 2013),
   - **silent drops**: discarding 10–20% of reads to trigger inventory discrepancies (de Medeiros & Burmester, 2007), cloning for "zone hopping" attacks: forging antenna zone IDs by using a cloned copy of an RFID tag to mislead the system about an item's actual physical location (Mustaffa et al., 2024).

   These manipulations undermined the routing algorithms, leading to mis-sorting of parcels, incorrect inventory states in the WMS, and failures in the automatic replenishment logic.
2. Synchronised reader shutdown: On the third day, the malware issued a synchronised "kill" command which (Kapoor et al., 2025):

- all infected readers into a boot loop;
- local configuration files;
- LLDP/CDP protocol frames, causing switches to fall back to lower power classes and effectively cutting power to the readers. This complete operational failure forced QuickGoods to halt automated operations—a characteristic escalation pattern in targeted OT attacks (Assante & Lee, 2015)

3.5.3 Detection, Consequences, and Impact

The attack went unnoticed by cybersecurity tools until operational anomalies were detected. On the third day at 3:14 a.m., automated inventory reconciliation alerts were triggered, revealing a 14.7% unexplained discrepancy in fast-moving stock (SKU: Stock Keeping Unit). Simultaneously, the night shift manager observed an unusual rise in the number of "exception bins" across multiple sorters.

The incident was not detected through cybersecurity tools; rather, it came to light due to the observation of irregularities in daily logistics operations. Warning signs emerged as sudden discrepancies in inventory and an increase in the number of exceptions on sorting machines. These anomalies were the first visible effects of the attack, prompting a crisis response within the organisation. Below, the main areas of impact—both operational and financial—are outlined, as illustrated in the attack impact diagram (Figure 3.3).

Operational impact:

- 48-hour suspension of automated sorting and picking systems;
- warehouse throughput reduced by over 90%;
- backlogs exceeded 520,000 orders, requiring extensive manual intervention;
- SLA violations with multiple trading partners.

Financial impact:

- Direct costs exceeding €2.5 million—an amount within the range of losses (>5M) reported by 25% of companies in the Kaspersky report (*Almost a Quarter of Industrial Companies Report Cyberattack Damages Exceeding $5 Million*, 2025).
- Indirect costs of €6–8 million—predicted in models where downtime and loss of trust are the main component (up to 52%) of financial losses from OT attacks (Dragos, 2025a).
- Cost per hour of downtime—consistent with sector benchmarks and a key parameter in global risk models, where downtime losses reach $172 billion annually (Fortinet, 2024).

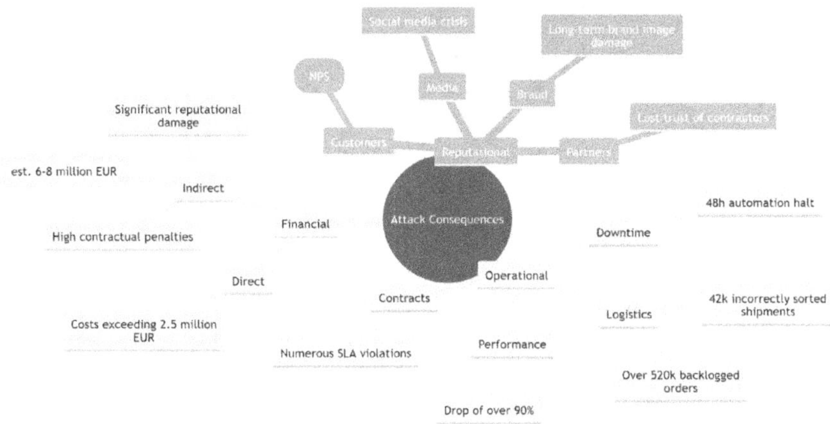

Figure 3.3 A comprehensive analysis of the incident's consequences, categorising its impact on three key areas: operational, financial, and image. Source: Own elaboration.

Impact on cybersecurity:

- Forensic analysis revealed exfiltration of raw RFID event data, including shipping metadata (Juels, 2006).
- Possible access to WMS API credentials stored on compromised edge nodes (Jin et al., 2022).
- Indicators of future attacks (Mazurczyk & Caviglione, 2021).

Impact on customer trust and brand:

Customer satisfaction rates declined, and social media monitoring indicated fluctuations in brand sentiment characteristic of significant logistics disruptions (Sharma, 2024).

3.5.4 Analysis of Root Causes

Post-reaction analysis traced the failure cascade to several systemic weaknesses, each highlighting a thematic vulnerability central to the framework of this chapter.

3.5.5 Common Vulnerabilities (Section 3.1)

The attackers exploited well-known vulnerabilities: unpatched vendor infrastructure, insecure firmware distribution, default credentials on OT devices, and a flat network architecture. These factors align with typical vulnerabilities noted in OT/IoT threat research (Boyens et al., 2022).

3.5.6 Security Gap at the Partner Interface (Section 3.2)

The main issue was inadequate cybersecurity oversight of subcontractors. This included a lack of formal requirements for secure update mechanisms, insufficient audit rights for LogiTech's development processes, and an absence of contractual clauses for security validation. At the time of the incident, QuickGoods did not have a contractual requirement for a Software Bill of Materials (SBOM), a gap that was later filled by making SBOM a standard provision in all new supplier contracts (The United States Department of Commerce, 2021).

3.5.7 Consequences of Downtime (Section 3.3)

The case demonstrates the non-linear, system-wide repercussions of downtime in a just-in-time logistics environment, where minor data integrity issues can spiral out of control and turn into major operational losses (Dolgui et al., 2018; Li & Zobel, 2020).

3.5.8 Risk Analysis Gap (Section 3.4)

QuickGoods' risk assessment, which focused on IT availability and physical risks, had a significant gap in its analysis by omitting key threats to cyber-physical systems. This oversight reflects the limitations of traditional, IT-centric risk management models (Srivastava et al., 2013).

3.5.9 Remedies and Conclusions

In response, the company implemented technical, process, and organisational controls consistent with industry standards (Figure 3.4):

Technical inspections:

- Tight segmentation and micro-segmentation of OT networks (Security for Industrial Automation and Control Systems—Part 3–2: Security Risk Assessment for System Design, 2020).
- Mandatory firmware cryptographic signing and validation (Boyens et al., 2022).
- Implementation of runtime attestation and secure boot mechanisms (International Electrotechnical Commission, 2019).
- Zero-trust access control for RFID middleware and controllers.

Process controls:

- Formal vendor risk management (VRM) programme with periodic security assessments.
- Mandatory disclosure of SBOM and security clearances by all third-party providers (The United States Department of Commerce, 2021).
- Establish a sandbox testing procedure for all firmware updates (*ANSI/ISA-62443-2-1-2024, Security for Industrial*

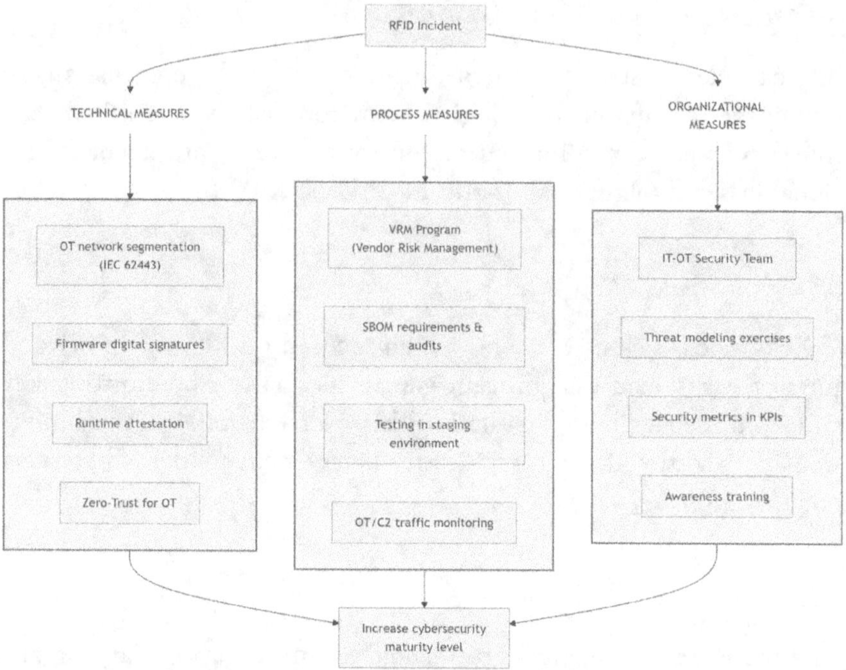

Figure 3.4 A framework of countermeasures implemented after an incident, including complementary technical, process, and organisational actions aimed at increasing the overall level of security maturity. Source: Own elaboration.

Automation and Control Systems – Part 2-1: Security Program Requirements for IACS Asset Owners, 2024).
- Continuously monitor OT network egress traffic for anomalous C2 communication patterns.

Organisational controls:

- Creation of a cross-functional IT-OT security team.
- Annual cybersecurity and physical threat modelling exercises.
- Incorporation of supply chain security metrics with operational KPIs.

3.5.10 Summary

This case study demonstrates that modern logistics cybersecurity must operate at the ecosystem level. As attackers increasingly target the weakest links in the supply chain—whether they are update servers, IoT providers, or integration partners—effective defence requires extending governance, monitoring, and risk assessment policies throughout the entire digital supply chain. This includes implementing secure development practices, validating vendor updates, and creating resilient operational technology (OT) architectures capable of detecting and containing covert manipulations. The incident underscores a significant shift: in cyber-physical environments.

Bibliography

2022 Top Routinely Exploited Vulnerabilities | CISA. (2022). Cybersecurity and infrastructure security agency. https://www.cisa.gov/news-events/cybersecurity-advisories/aa23-215a

2025 Data Breach Investigations Report. (2025). Verizon. https://www.verizon.com/business/resources/reports/dbir/

2025 State of Cyber Risk Management Report. (2025). FAIR Institute. https://www.fairinstitute.org/state-of-crm-2025

Acquah, I. S. K. (2023). Modelling the importance of collaborative culture and its dimensions for supply chain collaboration: A necessary condition analysis. *RAUSP Management Journal*, *58*(2), 125–142. https://doi.org/10.1108/RAUSP-05-2022-0153

Aldossary, L. A., & Elmedany, W. (2020). Security of RFID-based on Internet of Things (IoT) devices. *IET Conference Proceedings*, *2020*(6), 65–69. https://doi.org/10.1049/ICP.2021.0860

Alenezi, M. N., Alabdulrazzaq, H., Alshaher, A. A., & Alkharang, M. M. (2020). Evolution of malware threats and techniques: A review. *International Journal of Communication Networks and Information Security*, *12*(3), 326–337.

Alharbi, F., Zhou, Y., Qian, F., Qian, Z., & Abu-Ghazaleh, N. (2022). DNS poisoning of operating system caches: Attacks and mitigations. *IEEE Transactions on Dependable and Secure Computing*, *19*(4), 2851–2863. https://doi.org/10.1109/TDSC.2022.3142331

Almost a quarter of industrial companies report cyberattack damages exceeding $5 million. (2025). Kaspersky. https://www.kaspersky.com/about/press-releases/almost-a-quarter-of-industrial-companies-report-cyberattack-damages-exceeding-5-million

ANSI/ISA. (2024). *ANSI/ISA-62443-2-1-2024: Security for industrial automation and control systems – Part 2-1: Security program requirements for IACS asset owners*. International Society of Automation (ISA). https://www.isa.org/products/ansi-isa-62443-2-1-2024-security-industrial-automa

Arulkumar, S., Dhinakaran, S., Elamparithi, S., Balamanikandan, M., & Loganathan, R. (2024). Supply chain attacks in cybersecurity. *International Journal of Engineering Development and Research*, *12*(4), 86–91. https://rjwave.org/ijedr/viewpaperforall.php?paper=IJEDR2404007

Ashfaq, S., Chandre, P., Pathan, S., Mande, U., Nimbalkar, M., & Mahalle, P. (2024). Defending against vishing attacks: A comprehensive review for prevention and mitigation techniques. *Lecture Notes in Networks and Systems*, *896*, 411–422. https://doi.org/10.1007/978-981-99-9811-1_33

Assante, M. J., & Lee, R. M. (2015). The industrial control system cyber kill chain. https://www.lockheedmartin.com/content/dam/lockheed/data/corporate/documents/LM-White-Paper-Intel-Driven-Defense.pdf

Boyens, J., Smith, A., Bartol, N., Winkler, K., Holbrook, A., & Fallon, M. (2022). Cybersecurity supply chain risk management for systems and organizations. NIST SP 800-161r1. https://doi.org/10.6028/NIST.SP.800-161r1

Boyes, H. (2015). *Cybersecurity and cyber-resilient supply chains*. Technology Innovation Management Review. https://www.timreview.ca

Buy RFID Label – RFID Label. (2025). https://www.rfidlabel.com/

Carlan, V., Hintjens, J., Stuer, J., De Vylder, D., & Vanelslander, T. (2022). Why do slot booking systems still generate time-losses and is there a solution for it? *Research in Transportation Business & Management*, *44*, 100790. https://doi.org/10.1016/J.RTBM.2022.100790

Celtekligil, K. (2020). Resource dependence theory. *Contributions to Management Science*, 131–148. https://doi.org/10.1007/978-3-030-50131-0_7

Cindric, I., Jurcevic, M., & Hadjina, T. (2025). Operational technology sandbox environment for malware detection. MIPRO 2025, 800–805. https://doi.org/10.1109/MIPRO65660.2025.11132061

CISA. (2021). *Defending against software supply chain attacks*. Cybersecurity and Infrastructure Security Agency. http://www.cisa.gov/tlp/

Cybersecurity for SMEs: Challenges and recommendations. (2021). ENISA. https://doi.org/10.2824/770352

Dehoratius, N., Mersereau, A. J., & Schrage, L. (2008). Retail inventory management when records are inaccurate. *Manufacturing & Service Operations Management*, *10*(2), 257–277. https://doi.org/10.1287/MSOM.1070.0203

de Medeiros, B., & Burmester, M. (2007). *RFID security: Attacks, countermeasures and challenges*. 5th RFID Journal Conference – RFID Academic Convocation. https://www.researchgate.net/publication/228621244_RFID_Security_Attacks_Countermeasures_and_Challenges#fullTextFileContent

Dolgui, A., & Ivanov, D. (2021). Ripple effect and supply chain disruption management: New trends and research directions. *International Journal of Production Research*, *59*(1), 102–109. https://doi.org/10.1080/00207543.2021.1840148

Dolgui, A., Ivanov, D., & Sokolov, B. (2018). Ripple effect in the supply chain: An analysis and recent literature. *International Journal of Production Research*, *56*(1–2), 414–430. https://doi.org/10.1080/00207543.2017.1387680

Dragos, Inc. (2025a). OT security financial risk report: Assessing operational technology security efficacy with independent insurance industry analysis by Marsh McLennan. https://www.dragos.com/2025-ot-security-financial-risk-report

Dragos, Inc. (2025b). OT/ICS cybersecurity report: 8th annual. https://www.dragos.com/ot-cybersecurity-year-in-review

Eftimie, S., Moinescu, R., & Racuciu, C. (2022). Spear-phishing susceptibility stemming from personality traits. *IEEE Access*, *10*, 73548–73561. https://doi.org/10.1109/ACCESS.2022.3190009

EPCglobal / GS1. (2025). EPC UHF Gen2 air interface protocol. https://www.gs1.org/standards/rfid/uhf-air-interface-protocol

Falkevych, V., & Lisnyak, A. (2023). Internal and external threats in cyber security and methods for their prevention. *International Conference on Advanced Computer Information Technologies (ACIT)*, 414–419. https://doi.org/10.1109/ACIT58437.2023.10275516

Fonseca, O., Cunha, I., Fazzion, E., Meira, W., Silva, B. A. da, Ferreira, R. A., & Katz-Bassett, E. (2021). Identifying networks vulnerable to IP spoofing. *IEEE Transactions on Network and Service Management*, *18*(3), 3170–3183. https://doi.org/10.1109/TNSM.2021.3061486

Fortinet. (2024). State of operational technology and cybersecurity report. https://www.fortinet.com/content/dam/fortinet/assets/reports/report-state-ot-cybersecurity.pdf

Ghelani, D. (2022). Cyber security, cyber threats, implications and future perspectives: A review. *Authorea Preprints*, *3*(6), 12–19. https://doi.org/10.22541/AU.166385207.73483369/V1

Gilbert, C., & Gilbert, M. (2025). Exploring secure hashing algorithms for data integrity verification. *SSRN Electronic Journal*. https://doi.org/10.2139/SSRN.5251606

Haag, S., & Eckhardt, A. (2017). Shadow IT. *Business and Information Systems Engineering*, *59*(6), 469–473. https://doi.org/10.1007/S12599-017-0497-X

Hahn, A., Ashok, A., Sridhar, S., & Govindarasu, M. (2013). Cyber-physical security testbeds: Architecture, application, and evaluation for smart grid. *IEEE Transactions on Smart Grid*, *4*(2), 847–855. https://doi.org/10.1109/TSG.2012.2226919

Henriksson, J. (2021). Cyber supply-chain security challenges in the context of interorganizational collaboration. https://www.diva-portal.org/smash/get/diva2:1606249/FULLTEXT01.pdf

Hu, J., Hu, J., Wang, H., Chen, Z., Luo, J., Zheng, T., & Jiang, H. (2023). Password-stealing without hacking: Wi-Fi enabled practical keystroke eavesdropping. *Proceedings of the 2023 ACM SIGSAC Conference on Computer and Communications Security*, 239–252. https://doi.org/10.1145/3576915.3623088

Humayed, A., Lin, J., Li, F., & Luo, B. (2017). Cyber-physical systems security: A survey. *IEEE Internet of Things Journal*, *4*(6), 1802–1831. https://doi.org/10.1109/JIOT.2017.2703172

International Electrotechnical Commission (IEC). (2019). IEC 62443-4-2: Security for industrial automation and control systems – Part 4-2: Technical security requirements for IACS components.

ISO/IEC. (2021). ISO/IEC 27036-1:2021 — Cybersecurity — Supplier relationships — Part 1: Overview and concepts. https://www.iso.org/standard/82905.html

ISO/IEC. (2022). ISO/IEC 27005:2022 — Guidance on managing information security risks. https://www.iso.org/standard/80585.html

Ivanov, D. (2024a). Digital supply chain management and technology to enhance resilience by building and using end-to-end visibility during the COVID-19 pandemic. *IEEE Transactions on Engineering Management*, *71*, 10485–10495. https://doi.org/10.1109/TEM.2021.3095193

Ivanov, D. (2024b). Two views of supply chain resilience. *International Journal of Production Research*, *62*(11), 4031–4045. https://doi.org/10.1080/00207543.2023.2253328

Jamaluddin, F., & Saibani, N. (2021). Systematic literature review of supply chain relationship approaches amongst business-to-business partners. *Sustainability*, *13*(21), 11935. https://doi.org/10.3390/SU132111935

Jeske, D., & van Schaik, P. (2017). Familiarity with internet threats: Beyond awareness. *Computers & Security*, *66*, 129–141. https://doi.org/10.1016/J.COSE.2017.01.010

Jin, X., Katsis, C., Sang, F., Sun, J., Kundu, A., Kompella, R., & Research, C. (2022). Edge security: Challenges and issues. https://arxiv.org/pdf/2206.07164

Joshi, Y. V. (1998). Information visibility and its effect on supply chain dynamics. https://www.researchgate.net/publication/37989235_Information_visibility_and_its_effect_on_supply_chain_dynamics

Juels, A. (2006). RFID security and privacy: A research survey. *IEEE Journal on Selected Areas in Communications*, *24*(2), 381–394. https://doi.org/10.1109/JSAC.2005.861395

Kadam, M. S. (2017). Disaster Recovery Plan (DRP) and Business Continuity Plan (BCP) for financial cooperatives in new market economy. *SSRN Electronic Journal*. https://doi.org/10.2139/SSRN.2920431

Kapoor, S., Kumar, S., & Vardhan, H. (2025). Cyber security of OT networks: A tutorial and overview. https://arxiv.org/pdf/2502.14017

Keskin, O. F., Caramancion, K. M., Tatar, I., Raza, O., & Tatar, U. (2021). Cyber third-party risk management: A comparison of non-intrusive risk scoring reports. *Electronics*, *10*(10), 1168. https://doi.org/10.3390/ELECTRONICS10101168

Knowles, W., Prince, D., Hutchison, D., Disso, J. F. P., & Jones, K. (2015). A survey of cyber security management in industrial control systems. *International Journal of Critical Infrastructure Protection*, *9*, 52–80. https://doi.org/10.1016/J.IJCIP.2015.02.002

König, S., Rass, S., & Schauer, S. (2019). Cyber-attack impact estimation for a port. epubli. https://www.econstor.eu/bitstream/10419/209392/1/hicl-2019-28-164.pdf

Kumari, S., & Lele, V. (2023). Optimizing CRM and supply chain with edge computing: Real-time insights and scalable solutions. *International Journal of Computer Trends and Technology*, *71*(4), 19–26. https://doi.org/10.14445/22312803/ijctt-v71i4p104

Leligou, H. C., Lakka, A., Karkazis, P. A., Costa, J. P., Tordera, E. M., Santos, H. M. D., & Romero, A. A. (2024). Cybersecurity in supply chain systems: The farm-to-fork use case. *Electronics*, *13*(1), Article 215. https://doi.org/10.3390/ELECTRONICS13010215

Li, Y., & Zobel, C. W. (2020). Exploring supply chain network resilience in the presence of the ripple effect. *International Journal of Production Economics*, *228*, 107693. https://doi.org/10.1016/J.IJPE.2020.107693

Mancuso, V., Funke, G. J., Finomore, V., & Knott, B. A. (2013). Exploring the effects of "low and slow" cyber attacks on team decision making. *Proceedings of the Human Factors and Ergonomics Society*, 389–393. https://doi.org/10.1177/1541931213571084

Mandiant. (2023). M-Trends 2023: Mandiant special report. https://services.google.com/fh/files/misc/m_trends_2023_report.pdf

Martínez, J., & Durán, J. M. (2021). Software supply chain attacks, a threat to global cybersecurity: SolarWinds' case study. *International Journal of Safety and Security Engineering*, *11*(5), 537–545. https://doi.org/10.18280/IJSSE.110505

Mazurczyk, W., & Caviglione, L. (2021). Cyber reconnaissance techniques. *Communications of the ACM*, *64*(3), 86–95. https://doi.org/10.1145/3418293

Meggiato, G., Nterai, S., Skowronski, E., Gao, R., & Rahman, M. A. (2022). Warehouses against cyber-attack risks. https://ieomsociety.org/proceedings/2022istanbul/883.pdf

Mentzer, J. T., DeWitt, W., Keebler, J. S., Min, S., Nix, N. W., Smith, C. D., & Zacharia, Z. G. (2001). Defining supply chain management. *Journal of Business Logistics*, *22*(2), 1–25. https://doi.org/10.1002/J.2158-1592.2001.TB00001.X

Miller, T., Staves, A., Maesschalck, S., Sturdee, M., & Green, B. (2021). Looking back to look forward: Lessons learnt from cyber-attacks on industrial control systems. *International Journal of Critical Infrastructure Protection*, *35*, 100464. https://doi.org/10.1016/J.IJCIP.2021.100464

Muflihah, Y., & Subriadi, A. P. (2019). A basic element of IT business continuity plan: Systematic review. *Jurnal Informatika*, *12*(1), 17. https://doi.org/10.26555/jifo.v12i1.a8370

Mustaffa, M. Bin, Singh, M. M., & Selvaraj, K. (2024). RFID clone detection in supply chain using modified count-min and BASE protocol. *International Journal of Safety and Security Engineering*, *14*(2), 447–457. https://doi.org/10.18280/IJSSE.140212

Muzammil, M. Bin, Bilal, M., Ajmal, S., Shongwe, S. C., & Ghadi, Y. Y. (2024). Unveiling vulnerabilities of web attacks considering man in the middle attack and session hijacking. *IEEE Access*, *12*, 6365–6375. https://doi.org/10.1109/ACCESS.2024.3350444

Myataza, A., Mafunga, M., Mkhulisi, N. S., & Thango, B. A. (2024). A systematic review of ERP, CRM, and HRM systems for SMEs: Managerial and employee support. Preprints. https://doi.org/10.20944/PREPRINTS202410.0384.V1

Naser, M, Bazar, H. Al, & Abdel-Jaber, H. (2023). Mobile spyware identification and categorization: A systematic review. *Informatica*, *47*(8), 45–56. https://doi.org/10.31449/INF.V47I8.4881

Nawaz, M. S., Khan, S. U. R., Hussain, S., & Iqbal, J. (2023). A study on application programming interface recommendation: State-of-the-art techniques, challenges and future directions. *Library Hi Tech*, *41*(2), 355–385. https://doi.org/10.1108/LHT-02-2022-0103

Nelson, T., Nance, C., & Noteboom, C. (2023). Web injection and banking Trojan malware – A systematic literature review. *Proceedings of the 6th International Conference on Information and Computer Technologies (ICICT 2023)*, 45–53. https://doi.org/10.1109/ICICT58900.2023.00015

Newman, A., & Bruce, M. (2015). Electronic Data Interchange (EDI). *Wiley Encyclopedia of Management*, 1–1. https://doi.org/10.1002/9781118785317.WEOM090430

Odimarha, A. C., Ayodeji, S. A., & Abaku, E. A. (2024). Securing the digital supply chain: Cybersecurity best practices for logistics and shipping companies. *World Journal of Advanced Science and Technology*, *5*(1), 26–33. https://doi.org/10.53346/WJAST.2024.5.1.0030

Okoli, U. I., Obi, O. C., Adewusi, A. O., & Abrahams, T. O. (2024). Machine learning in cybersecurity: A review of threat detection and defense mechanisms. *World Journal of Advanced Research and Reviews*, *21*(1), 2286–2295. https://doi.org/10.30574/WJARR.2024.21.1.0315

Okoye, C. C., Ofodile, O. C., Tula, S. T., Nifise, A. O. A., Falaiye, T., Ejairu, E., & Addy, W. A. (2024). Risk management in international supply chains: A review with USA and African cases. *Magnascientia Research Review*, *10*(1), 256–264. https://doi.org/10.30574/MSARR.2024.10.1.0024

Priyanka, A. K., & Smruthi, S. S. (2020). Web application vulnerabilities: Exploitation and prevention. *Proceedings of the 2nd International Conference on Inventive Research in Computing Applications (ICIRCA 2020)*, 729–734. https://doi.org/10.1109/ICIRCA48905.2020.9182928

Rahman, M. L., Timko, D., Wali, H., & Neupane, A. (2023). Users really do respond to smishing. *Proceedings of the 13th ACM Conference on Data and Application Security and Privacy (CODASPY 2023)*, 49–60. https://doi.org/10.1145/3577923.3583640

Rajaram, P., Goh, M., & Zhou, J. (2022). Guidelines for cyber risk management in shipboard operational technology systems. *Journal of Physics: Conference Series*, *2311*(1), 012002. https://doi.org/10.1088/1742-6596/2311/1/012002

Rajkumar, V. S., Stefanov, A., Presekal, A., Palensky, P., & Torres, J. L. R. (2023). Cyber attacks on power grids: Causes and propagation of cascading failures. *IEEE Access*, *11*, 103154–103176. https://doi.org/10.1109/ACCESS.2023.3317695

Salim, M. M., Rathore, S., & Park, J. H. (2020). Distributed denial of service attacks and its defenses in IoT: A survey. *Journal of Supercomputing*, *76*(7), 5320–5363. https://doi.org/10.1007/S11227-019-02945-Z

Sarac, A., Absi, N., & Dauzere-Pérès, S. (2010). A literature review on the impact of RFID technologies on supply chain management. *International Journal of Production Economics*, *128*(1), 77–95. https://doi.org/10.1016/J.IJPE.2010.07.039

Sardjono, W., Perdana, W. G., & Putra, G. R. (2024). Disaster recovery plan implementation evaluation model at the corporation. *Procedia Computer Science*, *234*, 1658–1663. https://doi.org/10.1016/J.PROCS.2024.03.170

Sharma, A. (2024). The impact of cybersecurity breaches on big businesses. *International Journal of Advanced Research*, *12*(10), 10–25. https://doi.org/10.21474/IJAR01/19614

Shi, W., Cao, J., Zhang, Q., Li, Y., & Xu, L. (2016). Edge computing: Vision and challenges. *IEEE Internet of Things Journal*, *3*(5), 637–646. https://doi.org/10.1109/JIOT.2016.2579198

Shonubi, J. A. (2025). Multi-layered zero trust architectures for cross-domain data protection in federated enterprise networks and high-risk operational environments. *International Journal of Advance Research Publication and Reviews*, *2*, 146–169. https://doi.org/10.55248/gengpi.6.0725.2438

Singh, A., Choudhary, P, Singh, A. K., & Tyagi, D. K. (2021). Keylogger detection and prevention. *Journal of Physics: Conference Series*, *2007*(1), 012005. https://doi.org/10.1088/1742-6596/2007/1/012005

Souppaya, M., Scarfone, K., & Dodson, D. (2022). *Secure Software Development Framework (SSDF) version 1.1: Recommendations for mitigating the risk of software vulnerabilities*. National Institute of Standards and Technology. https://doi.org/10.6028/NIST.SP.800-218

Spruit, M., & Wester, W. (2013). RFID security and privacy: Threats and countermeasures. https://www.cs.uu.nl

Srivastava, A., Morris, T., Ernster, T., Vellaithurai, C., Pan, S., & Adhikari, U. (2013). Modeling cyber-physical vulnerability of the smart grid with incomplete information. *IEEE Transactions on Smart Grid*, *4*(1), 235–244. https://doi.org/10.1109/TSG.2012.2232318

Stefansson, G., & Russell, D. M. (2008). Supply chain interfaces: Defining attributes and attribute values for collaborative logistics management. *Journal of Business Logistics*, *29*(1), 347–359. https://doi.org/10.1002/J.2158-1592.2008.TB00083.X

Steinberg, S., Stepan, A., & Neary, K. (2021). *NotPetya: A Columbia University case study*. Columbia School of International and Public Affairs. https://www.sipa.columbia.edu/sites/default/files/2022-11/NotPetya%20Final.pdf

Szabo, A., & Hadad nextsecai, U. (2025). Crypto miner attack: GPU remote code execution attacks. https://arxiv.org/pdf/2502.10439

The NIST Cybersecurity Framework (CSF) 2.0. (2024). National Institute of Standards and Technology (NIST). https://doi.org/10.6028/NIST.CSWP.29

The United States Department of Commerce / NTIA. (2021). The minimum elements for a Software Bill of Materials (SBOM) pursuant to executive order 14028 on improving the nation's cybersecurity. https://www.ntia.gov/files/ntia/publications/sbom_minimum_elements_report.pdf

Threat Landscape for Supply Chain Attacks | ENISA. (2021, July 29). European Union Agency for Cybersecurity (ENISA). https://www.enisa.europa.eu/publications/threat-landscape-for-supply-chain-attacks

Töyli, H. L., Jonsson, P., & Mattsson, S.-A. (2013). The value of sharing planning information in supply chains. *International Journal of Physical Distribution & Logistics Management*, *43*(4), 282–299. https://doi.org/10.1108/IJPDLM-07-2012-0204

Ugbebor, F. O. (2024). Intelligent cloud solutions bridging technology gaps for small and medium-sized enterprises. *Journal of Artificial Intelligence General Science (JAIGS)*, *7*(1), 161–186. https://doi.org/10.60087/JAIGS.V7I01.307

Wang, Z., Zhu, H., & Sun, L. (2021). Social engineering in cybersecurity: Effect mechanisms, human vulnerabilities and attack methods. *IEEE Access*, *9*, 11895–11910. https://doi.org/10.1109/ACCESS.2021.3051633

Wu, I. L., Chuang, C. H., & Hsu, C. H. (2014). Information sharing and collaborative behaviors in enabling supply chain performance: A social exchange perspective. *International Journal of Production Economics*, *148*, 122–132. https://doi.org/10.1016/J.IJPE.2013.09.016

Zhang, M., Zheng, X., Shen, K., Kong, Z., Lu, C., Wang, Y., Duan, H., Hao, S., Liu, B., & Yang, M. (2020). Talking with familiar strangers: An empirical study on HTTPS context confusion attacks. *Proceedings of the ACM Conference on Computer and Communications Security*, 1939–1952. https://doi.org/10.1145/3372297.3417252

4

Managing Information Security in Logistics

This chapter introduces practical frameworks and methodologies for managing information security in logistics organisations. It begins by presenting key models such as the Information Security Management System (ISMS), which provides a structured approach to identifying, assessing, and mitigating cyber risks. The chapter explores internationally recognised standards, including ISO/IEC 27001, NIST Cybersecurity Framework, and TISAX, explaining their relevance and applicability to the logistics sector. It emphasises the importance of developing and maintaining organisational security policies that align with these standards and support continuous improvement. The chapter also addresses the need for effective collaboration among supply chain partners, highlighting how trust and information-sharing mechanisms can strengthen collective cybersecurity resilience. A detailed case study of an ISO 27001 certification process in a freight forwarding company illustrates the challenges and benefits of adopting formal security management practices. This example demonstrates how structured risk management can improve operational security, enhance customer trust, and ensure regulatory compliance. By providing both strategic and practical perspectives, the chapter guides logistics professionals in building robust security management systems tailored to their specific organisational needs.

In the era of digitalised logistics and hyperconnected supply chains, managing information security is no longer an auxiliary function—it has become a strategic necessity. As logistics systems evolve into complex ecosystems supported by cloud-based platforms, sensor networks, and artificial intelligence, the integrity, confidentiality, and availability of information assets determine not only operational efficiency but also the very resilience and credibility of logistics providers.

DOI: 10.1201/9781003685784-4

Historically, logistics security has been narrowly associated with physical risks—cargo theft, damage in transit, customs fraud, or the loss of paper-based documentation. However, the shift toward digital logistics has fundamentally altered the threat landscape. Today, a ransomware attack on a transportation management system (TMS), the leakage of sensitive shipment data from a warehouse management system (WMS), or unauthorised access to customs documentation via an API integration can have devastating effects. The impact is often immediate: halts in delivery flows, breach of SLAs, financial penalties, and long-term reputational damage.

These risks are compounded by the distributed and collaborative nature of modern logistics. A typical supply chain might include manufacturers, freight forwarders, 3PL operators, customs brokers, last-mile delivery services, and multiple IT service providers. Each entity introduces new systems, interfaces, and users—each of which expands the attack surface. In such environments, managing security is not only a question of protecting internal infrastructure, but also of ensuring that all partners adhere to common standards, enforce shared controls, and respond collectively to incidents. Trust, once built through handshake agreements and years of cooperation, must now be codified in security protocols, compliance reports, and digital certificates.

This chapter focuses on the mechanisms, models, and standards that logistics organisations can use to build and manage robust information security management systems (ISMS). It begins by outlining the theoretical foundations of ISMS, contextualising them for logistics operations where digital and physical assets are tightly intertwined. We explore how risk-based models such as the Plan–Do–Check–Act (PDCA) cycle can be applied not only to IT systems but also to operational technology (OT) in warehouses and transportation hubs. The discussion then turns to globally recognised frameworks—ISO/IEC 27001, the NIST Cybersecurity Framework, and the automotive-sector-specific TISAX—and their relevance for logistics actors that must comply with multiple regulatory regimes while maintaining agility and customer responsiveness.

Another essential element of this chapter is the exploration of internal security policies. As the first layer of defence, well-defined and consistently enforced policies determine how employees, systems, and contractors interact with sensitive data. We examine how logistics firms can develop, implement, and audit such policies in highly mobile, multicultural, and often decentralised operational settings.

However, managing information security in logistics goes beyond internal governance. Given the interdependent nature of global supply chains, collaboration between partners is critical. That includes vendor risk assessments, secure data-sharing agreements, joint incident response mechanisms, and efforts to build transparency across value chains. We analyse strategies to foster trust in integrated logistics networks, including the use of blockchain and attestation frameworks, and we reflect on the challenges posed by asymmetric capabilities and maturity levels among partners.

Finally, the chapter concludes with a detailed case study of ISO 27001 certification undertaken by a medium-sized freight forwarding company operating across the European Union. The case provides a realistic view of the practical steps involved, the challenges encountered—both technical and cultural—and the measurable outcomes achieved in terms of data protection and competitive advantage. It also highlights the importance of aligning security goals with broader organisational objectives and demonstrates how certification can become a catalyst for operational improvement and client trust-building.

This chapter, therefore, bridges theory and practice: it presents the models that inform security architecture, the standards that provide structure and legitimacy, the internal practices that ensure consistency, the partnerships that shape resilience, and the real-world experiences that validate the effort. Managing information security in logistics is not a static task, nor is it the sole responsibility of the IT department—it is an ongoing, organisation-wide commitment that determines how companies survive and thrive in the digital economy.

In the coming sections, we will dissect each layer of this framework—from formal ISMS models to the human and technological factors that shape their success. Through this, readers will gain a holistic understanding of how to navigate the intricate balance between operational efficiency, regulatory compliance, and digital risk resilience in modern logistics systems.

4.1 Information Security Management Models (ISMS)

The management of information security has evolved from a narrow technical function to a strategic pillar of organisational resilience, especially in industries that rely on complex, data-driven ecosystems such as logistics. As the logistics sector embraces digitisation—integrating enterprise resource planning (ERP) systems, transport management platforms, warehouse automation, and real-time sensor-based tracking—the sensitivity and volume of information processed across these systems have grown exponentially. This shift creates unprecedented exposure to cyber threats, data breaches, and operational disruptions. In this context, Information Security Management Systems (ISMS) provide a comprehensive, systematic approach to ensuring that information assets are protected in alignment with business objectives, regulatory expectations, and stakeholder trust requirements.

An ISMS is defined as a structured framework of policies, procedures, processes, technologies, and controls designed to manage information security in an organisation. Unlike isolated cybersecurity tools or ad hoc protective measures, ISMS provides an organisation-wide methodology that incorporates risk management, compliance, asset management, training, incident response, and continual improvement. Its core purpose is to establish, implement, operate, monitor, review, maintain, and improve the security of information using a risk-based approach tailored to the organisation's specific context.

For logistics organisations—especially third-party logistics (3PL) providers, freight forwarders, e-commerce warehouses, and cross-border operators—the value of ISMS lies in its capacity to bridge the gap between operational efficiency and cyber resilience. These companies routinely handle sensitive data such as shipping instructions, customs declarations, supplier contracts, delivery schedules, payment records, and personal information of drivers or customers. Moreover, they operate in highly interconnected environments where security vulnerabilities in one node of the chain can cascade rapidly across multiple partners. Traditional security models that focus solely on firewalls or antivirus tools are insufficient. ISMS, in contrast, offers a governance-driven framework that embeds security into organisational culture, decision-making, and strategic planning.

At the heart of every ISMS are the fundamental principles of information security, commonly referred to as the CIA triad:

Confidentiality—ensuring that information is accessible only to authorised individuals.
Integrity—safeguarding the accuracy and completeness of information and processing methods.
Availability—ensuring that authorised users have access to information and associated assets when required.

However, in logistics, two additional principles are increasingly critical:

Traceability (accountability)—the ability to trace data changes and identify who accessed or modified logistics records.
Resilience—the capacity of systems to recover from disruptions or breaches without significant impact on operations.

These principles are not abstract. For instance, a failure in confidentiality may lead to the leakage of customer shipping preferences to competitors. A breach of integrity could result in manipulated delivery quantities or destinations. Unavailability might halt transport scheduling entirely due to system downtime. Without traceability, unauthorised changes to customs declarations could remain undetected, risking legal penalties.

To illustrate the shift from traditional IT security to ISMS-based management in logistics, consider the following comparison:

The move toward ISMS in logistics is not driven solely by technological transformation—it is also a response to regulatory and contractual pressures. Data protection laws such as the General Data Protection Regulation (GDPR) in Europe, CCPA in California, and similar frameworks worldwide place legal obligations on companies handling personal and sensitive data. Meanwhile, clients—particularly large enterprises—now routinely require proof of security governance (such as ISO/IEC 27001 certification) from logistics vendors as a condition of business partnerships. A well-established ISMS not only protects against cyber risks but also supports regulatory compliance and enhances competitive positioning in tenders and audits.

Beyond compliance, ISMS also addresses internal risk factors stemming from human behaviour, decentralised operations, and fragmented

Table 4.1 Traditional IT Security vs ISMS Approach in Logistics

ASPECT	TRADITIONAL IT SECURITY	ISMS-BASED INFORMATION SECURITY MANAGEMENT
Focus	Technology (firewalls, antivirus)	Organisation-wide governance and continuous improvement
Scope	IT infrastructure only	Entire information ecosystem, including people & processes
Responsibility	IT department	Shared across all departments and levels
Security Objective	Prevent unauthorised access	Manage risks to acceptable levels
Methodology	Reactive and control-based	Proactive, risk-based, and adaptive
Documentation	Limited to technical policies	Comprehensive documentation and audit trail
Adaptability to Change	Static configurations	Dynamic, with regular review and updates
Integration with Logistics	Minimal	Fully integrated with logistics systems and operations

systems—common characteristics of logistics networks. Drivers using personal mobile devices to access WMS apps, warehouse staff sharing login credentials on shared workstations, or subcontractors connecting to internal ERP systems—all represent potential vulnerabilities that cannot be mitigated solely through technical controls. ISMS introduces structured policies, access control models, and security awareness programmes that align user behaviour with security objectives.

In conclusion, the adoption of ISMS in logistics is both a strategic and operational imperative. It enables organisations to take control of their security posture proactively, rather than reacting to incidents after they occur. By formalising security governance, aligning risks with business priorities, and institutionalising a culture of continuous improvement, logistics companies can ensure the trustworthiness of their digital operations and remain resilient in a landscape defined by complexity and uncertainty.

In the next section, we will explore the structure of a typical ISMS and how it can be mapped to logistics processes using the internationally recognised Plan–Do–Check–Act (PDCA) lifecycle.

Implementing an Information Security Management System within the logistics environment demands more than just the introduction of policies or technical safeguards. It requires the establishment of a robust operational framework that enables the organisation to dynamically adapt to evolving risks, regulatory expectations, technological shifts, and the needs of clients and partners. The most widely adopted structural model for ISMS, and the foundation of ISO/IEC 27001, is the Plan–Do–Check–Act (PDCA) cycle. Its iterative and scalable nature makes it especially suitable for the logistics industry, where responsiveness, operational agility, and resilience are key to maintaining competitive advantage.

The "Plan" phase marks the starting point of the ISMS lifecycle, in which the organisation develops its information security strategy. This includes identifying and classifying information assets such as ERP systems, transport management systems, warehouse management platforms, mobile terminals, vehicle sensors, IoT networks, and personal data sets related to customers and drivers. The organisation must then assess relevant threats and vulnerabilities, evaluate the probability and impact of adverse events, and define its risk appetite based on business continuity priorities. In logistics, this planning phase also requires alignment with the operational realities of decentralised sites, time-sensitive service delivery, seasonal demand fluctuations, and varying contractual obligations with clients and subcontractors.

During the "Do" phase, the organisation begins the operationalisation of the ISMS. This involves implementing selected security controls, deploying technical measures, and educating staff across all layers of the company. In a logistics setting, the implementation might include encryption of shipment data transmitted between hubs, segmentation of wireless networks for IoT devices in warehouses, application of secure access protocols for third-party contractors, or deployment of real-time intrusion detection systems in distribution centres. Human factor management becomes equally crucial—field staff, warehouse workers, drivers, and customer service teams must be trained in password hygiene, phishing recognition, data handling protocols, and device usage standards. These practices need to be adjusted depending on the type of logistics operation—air freight, last-mile delivery, 3PL warehousing, or customs brokerage.

The third stage, "Check," requires the organisation to audit and assess the effectiveness of the implemented controls and procedures. This includes ongoing internal audits, compliance assessments, vulnerability scans, penetration testing, and the analysis of logs from security systems and user activity. In the logistics sector, this might involve reviewing API activity logs between transport and inventory systems, testing the resilience of WMS access points, verifying that only authorised personnel have remote access to fleet management dashboards, and identifying anomalies in RFID-based stock records. The Check phase also enables feedback collection from clients, suppliers, and auditors, and highlights potential gaps between policy and practice.

In the final phase, "Act," the organisation must apply corrective actions based on the insights gathered during the evaluation process. This can include refining access control protocols, updating vendor management criteria, revising subcontractor security terms, improving encryption standards, or even restructuring internal reporting lines to ensure greater security accountability. Within the logistics context, the Act phase often includes redesigning processes following a security breach, re-training staff following non-compliance audits, or adopting new digital identity management systems for better control over multiple user roles and locations. This stage also serves to reinforce the continuous improvement cycle, making ISMS a living system that evolves with the operational and technological landscape.

The strength of the PDCA model lies in its adaptability. It is not designed as a one-time intervention but as a mechanism for ongoing security governance, perfectly aligned with the dynamic nature of logistics operations. Organisations that deploy the PDCA model as a core component of their ISMS can continually align their security posture with shifting business models, emerging threats, and technological innovations. In logistics, where real-time data, mobile workforces, and multi-tenant IT platforms are ubiquitous, this cyclical approach ensures that no component of the value chain becomes a systemic weak point.

Another significant element of ISMS implementation is the distribution of responsibility. In contrast to traditional IT security frameworks, where most responsibilities are confined to the IT department, ISMS promotes cross-organisational ownership. Operational managers, HR departments, warehouse supervisors, compliance officers, and even procurement specialists all contribute to the overall security posture. For instance, warehouse supervisors must ensure physical access controls, while procurement officers need to assess vendor compliance with cybersecurity standards. Only a collective approach can address the layered risks logistics organisations face, such as data leakage from subcontractors, phishing campaigns targeting drivers, or ransomware attacks on fleet management platforms.

Modern logistics organisations operate in a hybrid threat environment. They face not only cyber threats but also operational disruptions that may stem from security failures. From GPS spoofing affecting route optimisation to malware compromising barcode scanners or supply chain attacks inserted via insecure APIs with suppliers, the risk landscape is wide-ranging. ISMS is designed to cope with such diversity. Its strength lies in harmonising the management of these disparate risks under a single unified framework. The goal is not to eliminate all risk—which is neither possible nor cost-effective—but to reduce risk to a tolerable level while maintaining operational performance and customer trust.

The PDCA-based ISMS is also essential for regulatory compliance. With the expansion of data protection laws and industry-specific standards across jurisdictions, logistics providers increasingly face scrutiny regarding how they collect, process, store, and share data. ISO/IEC 27001 compliance, supported by a structured PDCA model, is not only a security strategy but also a market differentiator. Many clients, especially in the automotive, pharmaceutical, and aerospace industries, require evidence of an active ISMS as part of supplier qualification procedures. In this sense, ISMS becomes both a protective and promotional asset.

Ultimately, the structure and lifecycle of an ISMS enables logistics organisations to embed cybersecurity into their business model—not as a reactive function but as a strategic enabler. As information flows across platforms, warehouses, vehicles, and external partner systems, it is the ISMS that provides the oversight, discipline, and agility required to safeguard critical operations. In the next section, we will examine how such models can be scaled to fit the needs of logistics organisations of various sizes and complexities and how to measure ISMS maturity in environments with multiple risk layers and stakeholder dependencies.

As logistics operations expand across borders, integrate with partners, and digitise their core processes, a one-size-fits-all approach to information security quickly becomes insufficient. The adaptability of an Information Security Management System (ISMS) is essential to accommodate diverse operational models, organisational sizes, and risk profiles. While the ISO/IEC 27001 standard provides a universal framework, its real value lies in its ability to be tailored—scaled up for multinational 3PLs with thousands of endpoints and data flows, or scaled down for regional logistics providers with more limited but still critical infrastructure.

One of the most important aspects of tailoring an ISMS is aligning it with the complexity and digital maturity of the logistics provider. For small and medium-sized enterprises (SMEs), this might mean focusing on a limited set of core controls, such as secure authentication, regular backups, and awareness training. These organisations may not have full-time security staff or advanced technologies like SIEM systems, but they can still operate an effective ISMS through structured documentation, role-based access control, and periodic vulnerability assessments. On the other hand, large-scale logistics operators require enterprise-level integration, real-time monitoring, multi-jurisdictional compliance mechanisms, and dedicated governance structures. Their ISMS must address not only internal processes but also the extended risks introduced by subcontractors, joint ventures, and cloud service providers.

The customisation of ISMS also extends to governance models. Centralised ISMS governance can work effectively in organisations with strong corporate oversight and standardised operations across business units. However, many logistics providers operate in federated models with autonomous regional offices or business divisions. In these cases, a decentralised ISMS with local accountability and policy flexibility—backed by a global framework—can provide both responsiveness and alignment. For example, regional hubs may maintain their own asset registers, risk assessments, and incident handling procedures, while reporting to a central security function that ensures overall compliance and performance consistency.

Scalability is further influenced by the integration of ISMS with business continuity planning (BCP) and disaster recovery (DR). Given the operational sensitivity of logistics, any disruption—whether cyber-induced or environmental—can result in significant economic and reputational damage. A mature ISMS framework integrates risk management not just with day-to-day operations but also with long-term resilience planning. It ensures that critical information flows, such as shipment tracking, customs declarations, or inventory records, can be restored rapidly after an incident, with predefined recovery time objectives (RTOs) and recovery point objectives (RPOs). In larger organisations, ISMS controls may also include automated failover systems, data mirroring across geographic zones, and secure offline backups to protect against ransomware.

Another key dimension in ISMS customisation is defining and tracking performance through key performance indicators (KPIs) and security metrics. These metrics help ensure that security is not only compliant but also efficient, responsive, and continuously improving. Metrics relevant to logistics might include average time to detect incidents, frequency of policy violations by user role, success rate of phishing simulations among drivers or warehouse staff, number of vendor risk assessments completed per quarter, or the percentage of systems covered by regular patching.

To formalise growth and maturity, many logistics organisations adopt maturity models that assess their ISMS capabilities over time. These models typically progress through five stages: initial/ad hoc, repeatable, defined, managed, and optimised. In the initial stage, security practices are inconsistent and reactive, often driven by incidents rather than policy. As the ISMS matures, it becomes more structured, integrated into business processes, and data-driven. At the optimised stage, the ISMS is embedded into the organisational culture and strategically aligned with digital transformation and competitive positioning.

In logistics, reaching higher ISMS maturity levels offers not only improved security but also business benefits. Clients are increasingly prioritising secure partners in their procurement decisions. Regulatory bodies may impose fewer audits or offer certifications based on a company's ISMS standing. Internal efficiencies also increase as information governance improves and security responsibilities become better defined across departments.

This third part of the chapter has demonstrated that the ISMS framework is not rigid but highly adaptive to the needs of logistics providers regardless of scale. From the modest freight broker with minimal digital infrastructure to the global 4PL integrating hundreds of partners across cloud systems, ISMS offers a strategic structure to manage information risks. In the next section, we will delve into the most common barriers to implementation and identify critical success factors that help organisations overcome inertia and embed security into their logistics DNA.

While the benefits of implementing an Information Security Management System (ISMS) in logistics are increasingly recognised, the journey toward successful implementation is often complex, particularly due to the multifaceted operational environments of logistics service providers. From organisational resistance to technological gaps and partner misalignment, several barriers can hinder the effectiveness and timeliness of ISMS adoption. Understanding these challenges is essential not only to prepare mitigation strategies but also to define the conditions under which ISMS can thrive as a dynamic, value-generating framework.

One of the most common barriers is organisational inertia, particularly in traditional logistics companies with deeply embedded practices. In such environments, security may still be perceived as an IT-only responsibility or as a cost centre rather than a business enabler. This misperception can lead to resistance from middle and operational management, especially if the ISMS introduces new processes perceived as slowing down workflows. For example, warehouse supervisors may be reluctant to implement stricter access control protocols if these interfere with high-throughput operations. Similarly, transportation managers may deprioritise regular system audits in favour of meeting tight delivery deadlines. Overcoming this barrier requires leadership from the top—executive buy-in that communicates the strategic importance of information security and frames ISMS as integral to operational excellence and customer trust.

Another significant barrier is the lack of security awareness and training, especially among frontline employees and subcontracted partners. The logistics industry is heavily dependent on distributed workforces, including drivers, warehouse staff, temporary workers, and third-party vendors. Many of these actors interact daily with systems that store or process sensitive data—yet they are often the weakest link in the security chain. Social engineering attacks, lost credentials, and the improper use of mobile devices continue to be leading causes of breaches. Without consistent and practical training tailored to logistics roles, even the best-designed ISMS can fail at the point of execution. Overcoming this challenge demands a shift in culture and the creation of ongoing, role-specific training programmes that emphasise both technical controls and human vigilance.

A third barrier arises from technological fragmentation, particularly in organisations that have grown through mergers or operate across different IT platforms. The logistics sector is notorious for the diversity of systems used—legacy TMS platforms, proprietary ERP modules, third-party inventory apps, mobile field solutions, and cloud-based customer portals often coexist within a single organisation. Integrating ISMS controls across these systems—especially when they do not natively support modern security protocols—can be a daunting task. This challenge is magnified when external partners or government agencies are part of the data exchange chain. Overcoming fragmentation requires strategic IT planning, phased modernisation of systems, and the adoption of middleware or orchestration layers that allow centralised security management despite heterogeneous infrastructure.

Additionally, regulatory complexity can hinder ISMS implementation in multinational logistics organisations. Varying national and regional data protection laws, cybersecurity mandates, and industry-specific requirements (e.g., for pharmaceuticals or defence logistics) demand that ISMS frameworks remain agile and adaptive. Compliance with standards like GDPR, CCPA, or sectoral regulations such as TAPA or C-TPAT introduces additional administrative layers and documentation burdens. Smaller logistics providers, in particular, may struggle with aligning ISMS documentation and control sets to satisfy multiple audit requirements. Addressing this issue often necessitates the appointment of a compliance coordinator or the outsourcing of audit preparation and legal reviews to experienced consultants.

Partner alignment is another often-overlooked obstacle. The logistics industry is built on networks of interdependent players—freight forwarders, 3PLs, customs brokers, couriers, e-commerce platforms—each managing their own systems and standards. A robust ISMS must not only protect the organisation's internal environment but also extend outward through security clauses in contracts, third-party audits, secure API integrations, and shared incident response protocols. The failure to synchronise security expectations and procedures across partners can render an organisation vulnerable to supply chain attacks, such as the injection of malware through trusted vendors or the hijacking of communications channels used in scheduling or routing. Building mutual trust, harmonising standards, and fostering transparency are therefore critical for effective ISMS deployment across the extended logistics ecosystem.

Despite these barriers, several critical success factors can drive the effective implementation and long-term viability of ISMS in logistics environments. First and foremost is strong governance—establishing clear ownership for ISMS at the executive level, supported by a cross-functional security steering committee that includes operations, IT, legal, compliance, and business development units. This governance model ensures that information security is not isolated from broader strategic objectives and that accountability is distributed across all areas that handle sensitive information.

Secondly, risk-based prioritisation is essential. Not all risks are equal, and not all assets require the same level of protection. A well-designed ISMS in logistics will begin with a detailed asset inventory and business impact analysis that allows the organisation to focus its resources on the most critical areas—such as shipment visibility systems, customs data, and real-time vehicle telematics—rather than attempting to secure all systems uniformly. This selective approach ensures that the security budget is spent where it matters most, enhancing both effectiveness and efficiency.

Another success factor is progressive implementation through pilot projects, which allows organisations to test and refine ISMS components before scaling them organisation-wide. For example, a logistics firm may first apply ISMS principles to a single distribution centre or region, gather feedback, assess performance, and make adjustments before expanding the scope. This incremental method reduces disruption, enhances stakeholder buy-in, and accelerates the learning curve.

Furthermore, the integration of ISMS with broader digital transformation initiatives can significantly increase its acceptance and value. As logistics companies invest in automation, predictive analytics, smart warehousing, and IoT-driven fleet management, embedding security at the design stage of these projects aligns perfectly with the principles of a proactive ISMS. Security-by-design becomes not just a compliance measure but a catalyst for innovation, enabling the company to deploy new technologies confidently and responsibly.

Lastly, measurement and communication play a pivotal role in sustaining ISMS. Regular reporting of security KPIs—incident response times, audit findings, training completion rates, patching compliance—creates transparency and encourages accountability. More importantly, when security improvements are linked to operational outcomes, such as reduced system downtime, faster recovery from cyber events, or improved customer satisfaction scores, ISMS becomes a visible contributor to business success.

In conclusion, while the path to ISMS implementation in logistics is not without its challenges, these barriers are not insurmountable. By acknowledging organisational resistance, addressing training needs, bridging technological silos, managing regulatory obligations, and fostering partner alignment, logistics organisations can position themselves for long-term resilience. When combined with strong governance, prioritised investments, phased rollouts, integration with innovation, and performance-based monitoring, ISMS can transform from a compliance exercise into a strategic advantage in an increasingly digital and risk-prone supply chain environment.

4.2 Standards and Frameworks: ISO 27001, NIST, TISAX

The exponential increase in digitalisation across the global logistics sector has fundamentally redefined how companies manage not only the movement of goods but also the flows of data and information. As logistics processes become more interdependent, digitised, and vulnerable to cyber risks, organisations face mounting pressure to establish consistent and robust practices for managing information security. In this context, standardised frameworks and international norms offer a structured path forward—helping logistics organisations navigate the growing complexity of regulatory expectations, client demands, and risk landscapes.

The use of formal information security management standards provides a reliable basis for implementing organisational controls, auditing procedures, and governance mechanisms. These frameworks enable logistics companies to align with best practices in the protection of digital assets, personal data, system integrity, and the confidentiality of partner and client information. They are particularly vital in an environment where the logistics value chain includes multiple interconnected actors: manufacturers, distributors, third-party logistics providers (3PLs), freight forwarders, customs agents, and e-commerce platforms. Without a common language and reference model for managing cybersecurity, these actors risk falling into silos of fragmented or inconsistent protection—thereby weakening the entire chain.

Among the various standards available, three frameworks have emerged as particularly relevant for the logistics and supply chain sector: ISO/IEC 27001, the NIST Cybersecurity Framework, and TISAX (Trusted Information Security Assessment Exchange). Each of these standards presents a unique structure, scope, and philosophy, and they cater to different regional, industrial, and organisational needs.

ISO/IEC 27001 is widely recognised as the global benchmark for establishing an Information Security Management System (ISMS). It outlines a comprehensive, risk-based approach that can be scaled and adapted to organisations of varying sizes and complexities. Its strength lies in its universality and auditability, enabling logistics providers to demonstrate their commitment to information security in a formal and internationally accepted way. For logistics companies operating across multiple jurisdictions and dealing with high-value, sensitive shipments, ISO 27001 provides a standardised and certifiable structure for controlling cyber risks and ensuring business continuity.

In contrast, the NIST Cybersecurity Framework, developed by the US National Institute of Standards and Technology, offers a more flexible and descriptive model. Although originally designed for critical infrastructure sectors in the United States, its adoption has expanded globally, particularly among SMEs and in industries where prescriptive regulations are lacking. NIST emphasises functional alignment over certification, focusing on five core activities: Identify, Protect, Detect, Respond, and Recover. This makes it especially attractive for logistics organisations that seek to incrementally build their cybersecurity capabilities without the overhead of formal certification.

Meanwhile, TISAX responds to the specific needs of the automotive industry, where logistics plays a critical role in the just-in-time delivery of components, proprietary design data, and production tools. Initiated by the German automotive association VDA, TISAX provides a standard for assessing information security maturity within the supply chain and is often mandated by OEMs for logistics service providers. Unlike ISO 27001 and NIST, TISAX is not a general-purpose framework but is tailored to protect the confidentiality and integrity of data shared in automotive supply networks. It includes assessment levels based on sensitivity requirements and offers a centralised exchange platform where certification results can be accessed by authorised business partners.

While each of these standards serves distinct purposes, they share common goals: to improve the resilience of organisations against cyber threats, to foster trust among business partners, and to institutionalise security as a core business concern rather than an afterthought. For logistics organisations, which must often comply with multiple client-specific, industry-specific, and national security mandates, understanding the similarities and differences between these frameworks is not just beneficial—it is essential. Adopting one or more of these standards allows firms to signal their commitment to secure data management, meet regulatory obligations, and reduce liability exposure in case of a breach.

Moreover, these frameworks increasingly play a role in competitive positioning. Clients across sectors, from pharmaceuticals to high-tech manufacturing, now include cybersecurity and certification criteria in their logistics service contracts. An ISO 27001-certified logistics provider or a TISAX-validated warehousing partner is likely to be preferred over a competitor without such credentials. The ability to align with these frameworks thus becomes a strategic differentiator in an environment of growing customer scrutiny and cross-border compliance complexity.

The need for standardised approaches to cybersecurity is further underscored by the ongoing convergence between physical and digital logistics infrastructure. Smart warehouses, connected fleets, cloud-based shipment tracking, and AI-assisted route optimisation all generate unprecedented volumes of data. Securing these data flows and ensuring the integrity of digital interactions among systems and partners requires not just ad hoc protections but systemic and transparent security governance—exactly what these standards aim to provide.

This chapter segment begins with an in-depth analysis of ISO/IEC 27001 and its role as a foundational ISMS model. It then explores how the NIST Framework can complement or substitute formal certification efforts in logistics environments where flexibility or incremental implementation is preferred. The third part examines TISAX, its unique relevance for automotive logistics, and its growing recognition across European logistics providers. A comparative analysis will follow, highlighting the operational, strategic, and regulatory trade-offs among these standards. Finally, the chapter will outline practical roadmaps for logistics firms to implement and harmonise these frameworks based on their operational scope and client profiles.

In an era where cyber risk is no longer a remote possibility but a daily operational concern, the ability of logistics companies to navigate, adopt, and operationalise internationally recognised security standards will determine their resilience, reputation, and long-term viability. The following sections aim to equip practitioners, managers, and decision-makers in the logistics domain with the insights needed to make informed choices about these frameworks and to implement them in a way that strengthens—not complicates—their core logistics mission.

ISO/IEC 27001 is one of the most widely recognised and adopted international standards for information security management. It provides a systematic framework for managing sensitive information, ensuring confidentiality, integrity, and availability across organisational processes. Originally published by the International Organization for Standardization (ISO) and the International Electrotechnical Commission (IEC), ISO/IEC 27001 defines how an Information Security Management System (ISMS) should be structured, implemented, maintained, and continuously improved. For logistics companies, which operate in highly dynamic, partner-dependent, and data-intensive environments, ISO 27001 offers a structured path toward cyber resilience and regulatory alignment.

At the heart of ISO 27001 lies the concept of risk-based thinking. The standard does not prescribe specific controls but rather mandates that organisations assess their own risks and determine appropriate safeguards based on the criticality of their assets and the nature of their operations. This makes it particularly suitable for logistics providers, who may have vastly different risk exposures depending on their client base, technological maturity, scale of operations, and regulatory footprint. Whether a company manages international air freight or regional e-commerce deliveries, ISO 27001 can be adapted to secure its unique information flows and operational dependencies.

The ISMS defined by ISO 27001 follows the Plan–Do–Check–Act (PDCA) cycle, which promotes continuous improvement through iterative refinement. In the Plan phase, organisations establish their security objectives, define risk assessment methodologies, and identify applicable legal and contractual requirements. The Do phase involves the implementation of chosen controls and security measures. In the Check phase, the organisation evaluates the performance of its ISMS via internal audits and management reviews. Finally, in the Act phase, corrective and preventive actions are taken to address non-conformities and to refine the system based on performance data.

For logistics organisations, aligning their operational structure to ISO 27001 entails a comprehensive review of physical and digital assets—including warehouse management systems (WMS), transportation management systems (TMS), enterprise resource planning (ERP) platforms, RFID networks, and IoT-enabled tracking devices. It also requires addressing personnel risks, third-party exposures, data flow vulnerabilities, and disaster recovery strategies. ISO 27001 encourages the development of a formal Statement of Applicability (SoA), which lists all relevant controls from Annex A of the standard and indicates whether each control is implemented, not implemented, or excluded with justification.

The scope of ISO 27001 can vary significantly across logistics providers. Some firms choose to certify only their IT systems, while others extend the scope to include operational assets such as warehouses, distribution centres, and control towers. Increasingly, clients demand comprehensive certification that includes the entire supply chain interface, particularly in sectors such as automotive, electronics, and pharmaceuticals, where the confidentiality and integrity of shipment data are critical.

The standard includes 93 controls (as per ISO/IEC 27001:2022) grouped under four themes: organisational, people, physical, and technological. These controls include policies and procedures on access control, cryptography, asset management, physical security, secure system development, supplier relationships, and incident response. In the logistics domain, particular attention is paid to supplier risk management, secure data exchange between partners, and real-time system availability—factors critical to ensuring uninterrupted goods movement.

Below is Table 4.2 illustrating how selected ISO 27001 controls align with core logistics functions:

In practice, ISO 27001 certification involves a multi-step process. It begins with a gap assessment, where the organisation's current state is compared against the standard's requirements. Based on this, an implementation roadmap is developed, which typically spans 6 to 12 months, depending on the company's complexity and resource allocation. Internal audits are then conducted to ensure compliance before a formal certification audit by an accredited third party is scheduled. The certification is valid for three years and includes annual surveillance audits to verify ongoing conformity and continuous improvement.

Beyond technical measures, ISO 27001 emphasises the role of governance and leadership in maintaining information security. Top management is required to demonstrate commitment, assign clear responsibilities, allocate necessary resources, and integrate the ISMS into the organisation's strategic direction. This is crucial in logistics, where decisions affecting security often span multiple departments—operations, IT, HR, compliance, and procurement—and where external events (e.g., geopolitical disruptions, strikes, pandemics) can quickly shift risk landscapes.

From a business perspective, ISO 27001 certification provides a strong competitive advantage. Clients increasingly consider certified providers as more reliable, transparent, and resilient. Certification

Table 4.2 How Selected ISO 27001 Controls Align with Core Logistics Functions

ISO 27001 CONTROL DOMAIN	EXAMPLE LOGISTICS APPLICATION
Access Control	User roles in WMS/TMS restricted by function and location
Asset Management	Inventory of servers, mobile scanners, vehicle telematics devices
Communications Security	Secure APIs for data exchange with customs and clients
Supplier Relationships	Contractual clauses for security compliance in 3PL agreements
Physical Security and Environment	Surveillance, badge systems in warehouse perimeters
Incident Management	Incident response plan for system downtime or cyberattack
Operations Security	Patch management of transport scheduling software
Cryptography	Encrypted shipment documentation and cargo manifests

also simplifies compliance with data protection regulations such as GDPR, which apply to personal information processed in shipping, billing, or tracking systems. Moreover, ISO 27001 fosters trust in digital transformation projects by embedding security at the design stage, thereby reducing future rework and liability.

Finally, ISO 27001 plays a critical role in contractual negotiations and global partnerships. Multinational clients often require logistics providers to demonstrate compliance with ISO standards as a prerequisite for tender participation. Certification can also reduce the burden of repetitive security audits, as many customers accept ISO 27001 as evidence of due diligence. As supply chains become more interconnected, the ability to speak a common security language based on ISO standards greatly facilitates collaboration, risk sharing, and mutual accountability.

In conclusion, ISO/IEC 27001 serves as the cornerstone for building an effective and scalable ISMS in the logistics sector. Its flexibility, global recognition, and focus on continual improvement make it an indispensable framework for organisations seeking to secure their information assets, ensure regulatory compliance, and position themselves as trusted partners in the digital supply chain.

The NIST Cybersecurity Framework (CSF), developed by the US National Institute of Standards and Technology, is a widely accepted guideline that helps organisations of all sizes manage and reduce cybersecurity risks. Unlike ISO/IEC 27001, which is certifiable and prescriptive, the NIST Framework is a voluntary, flexible tool designed to support risk-based decision-making. Initially released in 2014 and updated in version 2.0 in 2024, it is particularly effective in industries such as logistics, where organisations vary greatly in size, maturity, technological sophistication, and regulatory exposure.

The primary value of the NIST CSF lies in its functional structure, which is organised into five high-level activities: Identify, Protect, Detect, Respond, and Recover. These categories, often visualised as a lifecycle, provide a clear and intuitive roadmap for building a comprehensive cybersecurity posture. Each function is subdivided into categories and subcategories that detail specific outcomes, supported by informative references to existing standards and guidelines. This structure makes the framework accessible even to organisations without prior cybersecurity experience.

The Identify function focuses on understanding and managing cybersecurity risks to systems, assets, data, and capabilities. In logistics, this involves mapping physical and digital assets across the supply chain—such as WMS platforms, driver tracking systems, freight management apps, and IoT-enabled sensors. The key objective is to develop a baseline understanding of business context, risk appetite, and resource dependencies. For example, a logistics provider may use this phase to determine which systems are mission-critical for daily operations and which third-party services represent significant data exposure.

The Protect function outlines safeguards to ensure the delivery of critical infrastructure services. This includes access control, data encryption, awareness training, and maintenance protocols. In logistics, protecting data can involve ensuring that only authorised personnel can update shipment manifests, that client delivery information is encrypted at rest and in transit, and that security patches for warehouse robotics software are installed on time. Employee training is especially vital in this phase, as frontline workers often handle mobile devices and interact with digital platforms under time pressure.

The Detect function emphasises real-time monitoring to identify cybersecurity events promptly. This may include anomaly detection in transportation management systems, unusual login behaviour from drivers in remote locations, or alerts from SIEM systems flagging malicious code in customs integration APIs. The ability to detect threats quickly can prevent minor vulnerabilities from escalating into major disruptions. In logistics, where time and continuity are crucial, early threat identification is essential for maintaining customer trust and operational integrity.

The Respond function focuses on developing and executing appropriate actions when a cybersecurity event is detected. It includes incident response planning, communication strategies, and mitigation procedures. A logistics operator, for instance, might need to isolate a compromised route optimisation server, switch to a backup, notify clients of possible delays, and initiate forensic analysis. The presence of a tested incident response plan ensures that reactions are timely, coordinated, and legally compliant.

The Recover function addresses the restoration of services impacted by a cybersecurity incident. This includes data recovery, system restoration, and communication with stakeholders. In logistics, rapid recovery might involve switching to an alternate distribution centre, restoring ERP data from backups, or enabling manual override processes in warehouse control systems. Effective recovery minimises business disruption and strengthens post-incident credibility.

Below is a summary table (Table 4.3) mapping NIST CSF functions to typical logistics operations:

Unlike ISO 27001, the NIST CSF is not a certifiable standard but rather a framework to guide continuous improvement. This has two major implications. First, it allows logistics firms to customise their approach based on available resources and specific business needs. Second, it lowers the barrier to entry for smaller logistics companies or startups that may not have the time or capacity to undergo formal certification but still wish to develop a structured cybersecurity programme. The modular nature of NIST allows companies to start with high-priority functions and expand progressively.

Another important advantage of the NIST CSF is its alignment with US critical infrastructure policy, including regulations from the Department of Homeland Security and the Transportation Security Administration. For logistics companies operating in or with the US, adopting NIST guidance supports compliance with sectoral expectations. Even beyond the US, many multinational corporations use NIST as a reference for supplier risk assessments, making it a valuable framework for logistics firms aiming to attract or retain global clients.

The flexibility of the NIST CSF also makes it ideal for hybrid integration. Organisations can align their NIST-based cybersecurity programmes with ISO 27001 or industry-specific frameworks like

Table 4.3 NIST CSF Functions to Typical Logistics Operations

NIST CSF FUNCTION	EXAMPLE LOGISTICS APPLICATION
Identify	Mapping of critical systems: WMS, TMS, RFID readers, telematics, data centres
Protect	Encryption of delivery data; user authentication for mobile apps; staff training
Detect	Real-time alerts for unauthorised access to ERP or WMS platforms
Respond	Incident response plan for ransomware attack on fleet tracking system
Recover	Restoring shipment data from backup; resuming operations from alternate DC

TISAX. For instance, a 3PL provider might use NIST CSF to manage internal IT controls while simultaneously preparing for ISO 27001 certification at its distribution centres. This dual-track approach can be cost-effective and strategically aligned with client demands and regional regulations.

The NIST framework emphasises the use of profiles, which are customised sets of cybersecurity outcomes tailored to a specific organisational context. A logistics company could define a "current profile" (existing capabilities) and a "target profile" (desired future state), then conduct a gap analysis to prioritise improvements. This strategic planning approach enables decision-makers to balance risk, cost, and operational impact when designing or upgrading security controls.

Despite its many advantages, the NIST CSF also presents challenges in adoption, particularly for logistics organisations with limited in-house cybersecurity expertise. Its voluntary nature can lead to underuse or superficial implementation if not supported by strong leadership and governance structures. Furthermore, the lack of certification may be viewed as a disadvantage by clients who prioritise auditability and formal credentials.

Nonetheless, the NIST CSF has been successfully adopted in various logistics scenarios. For example, a US-based freight terminal operator used the NIST model to assess cyber risks across its port systems. By mapping asset vulnerabilities and identifying gaps in response readiness, the operator was able to prioritise investments in endpoint detection systems and train staff in cyber incident handling. Although the company did not pursue ISO certification, the NIST-based improvements led to fewer system outages and greater confidence among customers and regulators.

In conclusion, the NIST Cybersecurity Framework offers logistics organisations a practical, accessible, and customisable approach to cybersecurity management. While it may not replace the formal rigor of ISO 27001 or the industry specificity of TISAX, it provides a strong foundation for building or enhancing cyber resilience—especially in dynamic, resource-constrained, or innovation-driven environments. Its lifecycle approach, emphasis on risk management, and integration with existing controls make it a powerful tool for aligning cybersecurity with operational goals in modern supply chains.

In recent years, the automotive industry has become one of the most security-sensitive sectors globally due to its increasing reliance on digital design processes, connected vehicles, just-in-time supply chains, and proprietary technological development. This complexity necessitates a heightened focus on data protection, particularly within supply chain logistics, where confidential information is exchanged continuously between manufacturers, suppliers, and logistics service providers. In response to this need, the Trusted Information Security Assessment Exchange (TISAX) was developed by the German Association of the Automotive Industry (VDA) in collaboration with the ENX Association, as a sector-specific standard to assess and exchange information security assessments among automotive stakeholders.

TISAX is not a standard in the traditional sense, like ISO/IEC 27001, but rather an assessment and exchange mechanism. Its goal is to ensure that all partners in the automotive value chain—especially third-party logistics providers (3PLs), IT service vendors, design contractors, and warehousing firms—meet a unified set of information security requirements tailored to the industry's specific risks. Unlike ISO 27001, which is internationally applicable and certifiable, TISAX assessments focus on benchmarking an organisation's maturity level against VDA ISA (Information Security Assessment) requirements, which are closely aligned with ISO 27001 but adapted to industry-specific use cases.

The TISAX framework evaluates three main domains: information security, prototype protection, and data protection. For logistics service providers, information security and prototype protection are especially critical. The first concerns the confidentiality, availability, and integrity of digital and physical data related to manufacturing, logistics coordination, or vehicle software. The second ensures that sensitive automotive parts—such as pre-release vehicle components—are stored, transported, and handled under strict confidentiality, often with elevated physical and procedural security measures.

TISAX assessments are conducted by accredited auditors and result in a label (rather than a certificate), which is published on a secure ENX portal. Business partners can access this portal to verify the security posture of a prospective or existing partner, avoiding redundant audits and saving time across the ecosystem. Importantly,

TISAX is recognised across Europe and increasingly by global OEMs (Original Equipment Manufacturers), which often mandate a valid TISAX assessment as a precondition for collaboration.

A distinguishing feature of TISAX is its *assessment level model*, which offers varying degrees of depth depending on the sensitivity of the data being handled:

Level 1: Self-assessment (not accepted for most professional applications);
Level 2: Assessment by an accredited auditor, focusing on standard information security;
Level 3: In-depth assessment including on-site visits, intended for highly sensitive environments such as prototype handling or production planning.

For a logistics provider offering *just-in-sequence delivery* of electronic components to an automotive plant, a Level 3 assessment may be required, especially if the goods involve pre-release parts or firmware. In such cases, physical security of the warehouse, access logs, employee vetting procedures, and vehicle security become part of the assessment criteria.

Table 4.4 summarises TISAX levels and their relevance for logistics companies:

One of the major advantages of TISAX is its *sector-specificity*. While ISO 27001 provides a strong foundation for general ISMS deployment, it may not address the nuanced risk scenarios encountered in automotive logistics, such as covert photography of pre-production vehicles, leaks of design documents, or industrial espionage at subcontracted storage sites. TISAX, on the other hand, embeds such threats into its design and assessment logic.

4.3 Security Policies in Logistics Organisations

In the rapidly evolving landscape of digital logistics, where supply chains are driven by real-time data, interconnected platforms, and automated decision-making systems, security policies emerge as one of the most essential pillars of cyber resilience. Security policies are formalised expressions of an organisation's intentions, expectations, and rules concerning the protection of its information assets

Table 4.4 TISAX Levels and Their Relevance for Logistics Companies

TISAX ASSESSMENT LEVEL	SCOPE	LOGISTICS RELEVANCE
Level 1	Self-assessment	Rarely sufficient; not recognised by OEMs
Level 2	External audit without on-site verification	Suitable for general logistics data handling (e.g., shipment info, invoices)
Level 3	External audit with on-site verification	Required for prototype handling, sensitive product components, design materials

and operational infrastructure. In logistics, these policies are not merely administrative documents—they are integral components of operational integrity and business continuity, particularly in light of increasing cyberattacks on transportation systems, data breaches involving customer information, and system outages caused by ransomware or third-party compromise.

At their core, security policies provide the foundation for standardised behaviour and consistent enforcement of cybersecurity measures. They serve as an internal legal framework that defines how information is to be handled, who is authorised to access what systems, under what conditions, and what actions must be taken in the event of anomalies or security incidents. While procedures and guidelines offer step-by-step instructions or best practices, security policies are more strategic and high-level in nature. They articulate principles and expectations, ensure regulatory compliance, and offer a benchmark against which employee conduct and system integrity can be evaluated.

In logistics organisations, the breadth and complexity of security requirements demand a diversified portfolio of policies that address both digital and physical domains. An effective security policy architecture encompasses various thematic areas, each designed to protect a specific category of assets or interactions. The most fundamental of these is the general information security policy. This policy typically outlines the company's commitment to safeguarding data, managing risk, and ensuring the confidentiality, integrity, and availability of operational systems across all departments. It also defines governance responsibilities, outlines the security objectives aligned with the organisation's mission, and clarifies accountability structures.

Another critical document is the access control policy, which is particularly relevant in the logistics sector due to the large number of users interacting with different platforms at various levels of the supply chain. Drivers accessing delivery schedules via mobile apps, warehouse staff scanning packages with RFID handhelds, planners manipulating transport management systems, and finance personnel accessing ERP modules—all require tailored access privileges. The access control policy formalises how these privileges are assigned, reviewed, revoked, and monitored, often in conjunction with identity and access management (IAM) tools and role-based access control (RBAC) mechanisms.

Similarly, acceptable use policies govern the behaviour of employees when using corporate devices, systems, and data. In logistics operations, where many employees work remotely, in transit, or across distributed sites, the risk of improper use of IT assets is significant. Acceptable use policies delineate what is considered permissible behaviour—such as avoiding unauthorised software installations, refraining from sharing passwords, or ensuring devices are locked when unattended. They also reinforce security awareness by communicating the consequences of policy violations.

The need to manage third-party risks necessitates a well-defined supplier and partner security policy. In modern logistics ecosystems, interactions with external vendors—customs agents, subcontracted 3PLs, IT system integrators, fleet maintenance firms—are continuous and operationally embedded. This policy establishes the security expectations placed on these partners, including requirements for secure data exchange, confidentiality agreements, onboarding assessments, and incident reporting. It may also reference industry standards such as TISAX or clauses mandating alignment with ISO 27001 controls, thereby integrating third-party management into the broader organisational ISMS.

Equally essential is the incident response policy, which defines the procedures to follow when a cybersecurity event occurs. Given the time-sensitive nature of logistics and the potentially devastating effects of service disruptions, a clearly defined response plan ensures that teams can react quickly and appropriately. This includes identifying incident categories, escalation paths, external communication guidelines (especially when clients or regulators must be notified), documentation requirements, and post-incident analysis routines. The presence of a mature incident response policy also supports regulatory compliance in jurisdictions requiring prompt breach notification.

Another area often overlooked is data retention and disposal. Logistics organisations handle massive volumes of data, including shipping manifests, invoices, driver logs, sensor readings, customer addresses, and customs documentation. Some of this data may have retention requirements under tax or trade regulations, while other information may need to be disposed of securely to minimise the risk of data leakage. A data retention and disposal policy establishes rules for classifying data, defining retention periods, designating archival methods, and outlining secure disposal processes—whether digital (e.g., wiping drives) or physical (e.g., shredding documents).

Finally, physical security policies address the protection of logistics infrastructure such as warehouses, distribution centres, yards, and offices. In an age where physical and cyber risks are intertwined—e.g., unauthorised access to server rooms enabling data theft—physical security is more than just a facility management concern. The policy may cover surveillance systems, badge access controls, visitor management, perimeter defences, environmental monitoring (temperature, humidity), and emergency procedures. In many organisations, these physical controls are now monitored and managed via digital building automation platforms, requiring careful coordination with IT and security departments.

To summarise the relationship between specific types of policies and their applications across logistics subsystems, Table 4.5 presents a representative mapping of how various documents protect operational areas:

Each of these policy types, when clearly articulated, regularly updated, and rigorously enforced, contributes to a security-aware culture across the logistics enterprise. In subsequent sections, the discussion will explore how these policies are developed, customised, communicated, and maintained, as well as the challenges faced by logistics organisations in their day-to-day implementation.

The effectiveness of any security policy hinges not only on its content but also on the process by which it is developed, communicated, and operationalised. In logistics organisations, where technological infrastructure intersects with dynamic human workflows and decentralised locations, crafting a security policy is an exercise in cross-functional collaboration and strategic alignment.

The development lifecycle of a security policy typically begins with the identification of the security need, often triggered by a risk assessment, a compliance requirement, a client demand, or a recent incident. For instance, a logistics operator experiencing unauthorised access to its warehouse management system might initiate the drafting of an access control policy as a remediation measure. Similarly, regulatory developments—such as updates to the EU's GDPR or new customs digitalisation protocols—might necessitate the creation or revision of data protection policies.

The next step is the policy scoping and design phase, during which the information security team—often under the guidance of a Chief Information Security Officer (CISO) or Security Manager—outlines the policy objectives, scope, and audience. This process must include input from multiple stakeholders. In a logistics company, this typically involves IT administrators, warehouse supervisors, fleet managers, legal advisers, compliance officers, and sometimes even client representatives. The objective is to ensure that the policy is not only technically sound but also operationally viable and understandable by all relevant personnel.

Alignment with international standards and frameworks is another critical part of this phase. Most logistics companies seek to anchor their security documentation within the structures provided by ISO/IEC 27001, which offers a detailed Annex A catalogue of control objectives, or use mappings from the NIST Cybersecurity Framework. If the organisation is part of the automotive supply chain, the VDA-ISA

Table 4.5 Representative Mapping of How Various Documents Protect Operational Areas

POLICY TYPE	LOGISTICS APPLICATION AREA
Information Security Policy	Enterprise-wide digital infrastructure and governance frameworks
Access Control Policy	WMS, ERP, TMS platforms; handheld scanners; driver portals
Acceptable Use Policy	Company-issued laptops, smartphones, telematics devices
Supplier Security Policy	Data exchange with customs, 3PL subcontractors, IT vendors, and digital freight marketplaces
Incident Response Policy	Handling cyberattacks on transport systems or client data breaches
Data Retention and Disposal	Shipment records, invoice archives, GPS data from completed deliveries
Physical Security Policy	Warehouse entry points, distribution centre fencing, CCTV coverage, biometric access

catalogue underlying TISAX assessments may also provide essential input. These frameworks offer consistent terminology, maturity benchmarks, and peer validation, which can reduce development time and increase policy legitimacy in audits or client reviews.

Once the draft is prepared, the policy undergoes internal review, often involving legal validation, risk committee discussion, and management sign-off. During this phase, practical considerations come to the forefront. For example, a clause mandating two-factor authentication for all system logins might need revision if a portion of drivers are using legacy tablets without support for OTP apps. Similarly, a data retention policy requiring monthly purging of outdated location data might conflict with customs record-keeping rules that demand data availability for up to six years.

Following approval, the policy enters the implementation phase, which includes distribution, training, technical integration, and enforcement planning. This is frequently where the greatest challenges emerge in logistics settings, due to several domain-specific characteristics. Firstly, logistics operations rely heavily on a diverse and distributed workforce—including drivers, warehouse staff, temporary labourers, and subcontractors—many of whom do not regularly access corporate email or intranet portals. This makes it difficult to ensure that everyone is not only informed about the policy but also understands it sufficiently to act in accordance with its provisions.

Secondly, the high turnover rates in certain logistics functions (particularly in warehousing and last-mile delivery) complicate long-term enforcement and require that policy orientation be embedded into onboarding procedures. Training programmes must therefore be brief, targeted, and repeatable. Video modules, laminated cheat-sheets, and supervisor-led daily briefings are among the approaches used to translate policy into practice for frontline workers.

Third, logistics environments are marked by decentralised decision-making and infrastructure. Security policies must therefore accommodate a variety of IT environments, from highly automated distribution centres with full SCADA integration to small rural depots operating on basic cloud-based dispatch tools. This fragmentation increases the complexity of both policy enforcement and performance monitoring.

Moreover, the logistics sector traditionally places a premium on operational efficiency and cost control, which can conflict with rigorous security enforcement. A policy requiring strict password rotation, for example, may be viewed as burdensome by shift workers who need to log in quickly during high-volume periods. Similarly, requirements for encrypted handheld devices might be met with resistance if legacy hardware is still in use and no capital investment is available to upgrade systems.

To navigate these challenges, organisations are increasingly turning to technology-enabled policy enforcement mechanisms. Identity and access management systems (IAM), mobile device management (MDM) solutions, and endpoint detection and response tools (EDR) can embed certain policy rules directly into system behaviour, reducing reliance on human discipline. For example, user roles in the ERP system can be configured to enforce least-privilege access automatically, while unauthorised USB ports on warehouse workstations can be disabled through policy profiles managed via the IT service desk.

However, technical enforcement cannot replace cultural adoption. Without a security-aware culture, even the best-written policies risk being ignored, bypassed, or misunderstood. Therefore, a dual strategy is essential: investing in enforcement technology while simultaneously nurturing a human-centred approach to security. This includes security champions programmes within logistics departments, gamified compliance training, and integrating security discussions into operational meetings.

As policies become embedded into daily operations, organisations must also develop mechanisms for compliance monitoring and feedback. This includes routine internal audits, spot checks, performance dashboards, and incident reports. Logistics companies often utilise security key performance indicators (KPIs) to measure policy adherence. These may include metrics such as the percentage of employees trained, the number of policy violations detected, average response time to incidents, and audit findings per business unit.

To sustain relevance, all policies require regular review and updating, particularly as threat landscapes evolve and technology infrastructures change. In logistics, this might occur annually or more frequently in response to client requirements, merger and acquisition activity, or regulatory shifts. Version control, stakeholder re-approval, and redistribution plans should be formalised within the organisation's ISMS documentation management process.

In sum, the successful deployment of security policies in logistics organisations requires a deep appreciation for sector-specific operational realities. It also demands a multi-level strategy that combines structured governance with agile communication and enforcement mechanisms. Policies must not only be written clearly and comprehensively but also made actionable across organisational layers—from the control room to the delivery truck—so that cybersecurity becomes an operational competency, not an abstract compliance objective.

4.4 Partner Collaboration and Trust Building

In today's global logistics environment, no single entity operates in isolation. Modern supply chains are built on complex, interdependent networks that rely on real-time information exchange, digital coordination, and shared technological platforms. This deep interconnectivity, while enabling unprecedented operational efficiency, also exposes logistics organisations to shared cyber risks and digital vulnerabilities. From manufacturers and third-party logistics providers (3PLs) to freight forwarders, customs agencies, and IT vendors, every participant represents a potential attack surface—and a point of entry for adversaries aiming to disrupt operations or exfiltrate sensitive data.

Given this ecosystemic nature of logistics, ensuring cybersecurity is no longer the responsibility of individual firms alone. Rather, it requires a cooperative approach in which partner collaboration and trust serve as the foundation for digital resilience. As data traverses organisational boundaries—via transport management systems (TMS), electronic data interchange (EDI), cloud-based inventory platforms, and telematics APIs—traditional methods of siloed security become insufficient. Cybersecurity becomes a shared concern, and with it emerges a critical paradox: partners must trust one another with sensitive data and system access while simultaneously protecting themselves from the possibility that those very partners may become sources of compromise.

This trust paradox is among the most pressing challenges in logistics cybersecurity. On one hand, business partnerships depend on seamless data integration and transparency. On the other hand, the more integrated two companies become, the more one's security posture depends on the other's hygiene. A small subcontractor with weak security practices can jeopardise an entire logistics chain, even when the primary contractors have robust controls in place. Real-world examples abound—from the infamous NotPetya attack (which entered global networks through a third-party software provider) to MOVEit Transfer breaches, where secure file transfers were exploited to steal logistics and government data worldwide.

This paradox illustrates why technical competence must be matched by trust frameworks, and why the design of supply chain collaborations should embed not only performance and cost metrics but also cyber resilience strategies. In this context, trust operates on multiple dimensions: technical trust in systems and protocols, legal trust codified in contracts and standards, and human trust built through communication, transparency, and reputation.

Technical trust is perhaps the most immediate requirement in logistics partnerships. It is established when partners utilise secure channels for data transfer (e.g., VPNs, encrypted APIs), enforce identity and access management (IAM), and implement complementary cybersecurity protocols. Trust is strengthened when partners can verify the security of the tools and systems used by others, for example, through code audits, API documentation, or access control summaries.

However, technical assurances are often insufficient without legal underpinnings. This is where legal trust becomes vital. Contracts between logistics organisations and their partners increasingly include cybersecurity-specific clauses. These may cover data ownership, incident response obligations, liability in the event of a breach, and requirements for compliance with frameworks like ISO 27001 or GDPR. Legal trust is particularly critical in cross-border supply chains, where partners may operate under different legal regimes and be exposed to differing levels of compliance enforcement.

Human trust, while intangible, plays a powerful role in maintaining secure logistics collaborations. This trust stems from prior business experience, clear communication practices, and a demonstrated willingness to disclose vulnerabilities or potential threats. Logistics managers are more likely to share early warnings about suspicious events or anomalies when they believe that partners will respond constructively rather than exploit weaknesses for commercial advantage.

In practice, a robust partner collaboration model integrates all three trust dimensions. For example, a logistics operator may require its IT service provider to sign a Data Processing Agreement (DPA) in line with GDPR, ensuring legal trust; conduct quarterly penetration testing reports to evaluate technical security, building technical trust; and participate in monthly operational reviews where any security concerns are openly discussed, reinforcing human trust.

As the complexity of logistics ecosystems grows, many organisations have begun adopting cybersecurity due diligence processes when selecting or renewing partnerships. These involve structured assessments of a partner's cybersecurity maturity. Evaluation tools include questionnaires based on ISO/NIST/TISAX controls, reviews of policy documentation, inspection of system logs or incident records, and—when warranted—third-party security audits. Due diligence is not a one-off event but a cyclical process, often aligned with contract renewals or triggered by risk events such as regional cyberattacks, regulatory changes, or the onboarding of new technologies.

To standardise this assessment, organisations use supplier risk matrices that assign weighted scores to various criteria. A simplified example of such a scoring model is presented Table 4.6.

This matrix allows decision-makers to evaluate and compare vendors objectively and to identify where security obligations need to be strengthened contractually or through joint initiatives. For instance, a freight carrier handling 60% of a company's outbound shipments but lacking any formal data encryption practices might trigger a compensating control, such as route anonymisation or enforced VPN tunnelling for their system logins.

Beyond assessment, *collaborative security governance* is emerging as a best practice in logistics. This involves designing *shared frameworks* for incident response, data sharing, and compliance monitoring. For example, partners may agree on a *joint incident response playbook*, detailing how breaches should be communicated, how forensic investigations will be conducted, and what responsibilities each side assumes in the containment and recovery process. Such arrangements help eliminate confusion during crises and ensure legal defencibility in post-incident audits.

Organisations also implement *shared monitoring protocols* using interoperable dashboards and log sharing platforms. This can be

Table 4.6 Example of Such a Scoring Model

CRITERIA	WEIGHT	EXAMPLE METRIC
ISO 27001 Certification	30%	Valid certificate or equivalent audit
Incident History	20%	Number of past breaches or delays
Data Handling Practices	20%	Encryption, backup, access controls
Business Criticality	20%	Volume of transactions handled
Legal & Compliance Fit	10%	GDPR, CCPA, customs security programs

particularly valuable in warehouse hubs or customs interfaces where multiple systems interact. A logistics company may grant its clients read-only access to relevant event logs or enable security alerts to be mirrored across partner SOCs (Security Operations Centres), enhancing real-time situational awareness.

Building trust is not only a matter of controls and contracts—it is a strategic cultural undertaking. In the next section, we will examine the *behavioural, organisational, and legal factors* that shape trust dynamics, including the role of transparency, ethical risk sharing, and managing asymmetries between partners.

4.5 Case Study: ISO 27001 Certification in a Freight Forwarding Company—Implementation Challenges and Outcomes

4.5.1 Case-Based Narrative: Concrete Problems in ISO 27001 Implementation in Logistics Companies

The story begins in a mid-sized freight forwarding company based in Central Europe, with branch offices in three countries and a digital infrastructure that had grown organically over the years. Despite expanding its operations rapidly and serving over 100 multinational clients, the company had long operated without a unified information security policy. When two clients began requiring ISO 27001 certification as a condition for renewing contracts, the management team decided it was time to act. What they didn't expect, however, was that the road to compliance would expose a fragile digital foundation—and a series of deeply embedded organisational issues.

The company's first major challenge emerged during the asset identification and risk analysis phase. The IT team, tasked with creating an asset register, discovered that no centralised inventory existed for digital assets across departments. Each branch managed its own devices, and many users had admin privileges on their workstations. In one warehouse, a supervisor had set up unauthorised Wi-Fi access points for "faster scanning," unknowingly exposing shipment data to interception. The external consultants assigned to lead the ISO 27001 process flagged this fragmentation as a critical gap, but resolving it required months of coordination and resistance from managers reluctant to give up local control.

As the project progressed, a second and perhaps more disruptive problem appeared: lack of staff awareness and engagement. During an internal survey, more than 60% of warehouse and transport employees claimed they didn't understand what information security meant in their daily work. Drivers regularly shared tablets, and some logged into TMS systems using shared credentials stuck on sticky notes inside glove compartments. Explaining ISO requirements to non-technical staff became a cultural project. The team attempted training workshops, but participation was low. Eventually, management had to link participation in cybersecurity sessions to quarterly performance bonuses—a move that created tension but ultimately increased engagement.

Another acute problem was policy overload and complexity. Consultants drafted over 30 new policies, from access control to media handling, most of which used regulatory language not suited to the company's operations. Middle managers complained they couldn't interpret the documentation, and workers simply ignored it. The ISMS lead had to halt the documentation process and initiate a full rewrite in collaboration with operational staff, translating legal and technical requirements into task-based instructions. For example, instead of stating "mobile media must be disposed of according to secure sanitisation procedures," the warehouse procedure now read: "Broken USB sticks and tablets must be returned to IT using a locked bin near the supervisor's office."

The company also struggled significantly with third-party risk management, an area neglected for years. A critical turning point occurred when an external software vendor managing customs documentation experienced a ransomware incident. While no data loss occurred on the company's end, it triggered client audits and public concern. When auditors reviewed the company's supplier risk assessments, they found only outdated spreadsheets and no contractual cybersecurity clauses. Correcting this required renegotiating over 40 contracts with software vendors, transport subcontractors, and temporary employment agencies—many of which were resistant or unfamiliar with ISO 27001 obligations. Some had to be replaced altogether.

A more subtle but damaging problem involved management commitment and scope creep. While senior leaders supported the certification initiative, they often failed to attend ISMS steering meetings or allocate staff time consistently. The ISMS coordinator described the process as "trying to build a cathedral with volunteers who can only show up one hour a week." As a result, project milestones slipped. What was initially supposed to be a 12-month implementation stretched into 19 months, with escalating costs and growing internal fatigue. To regain momentum, the company had to hire a full-time project manager mid-way through the implementation—an unplanned but necessary expense.

From a technical standpoint, the integration of legacy systems proved to be a major obstacle. The company's transport management system (TMS) dated back to 2009 and lacked native support for encryption or multi-factor authentication. Replacing it was not financially feasible, so the team developed workarounds, including VPN tunnels, role segregation, and manual log exports. This patchwork solution passed the audit but was recognised as a risk that would require long-term investment to address properly.

The audit preparation phase also revealed gaps in incident management practices. Although the company had experienced minor cyber events in the past—phishing attempts, delayed antivirus updates—these had never been formally recorded or analysed. When asked for incident logs, the IT team produced emails and chat logs from memory. Establishing a structured incident response process became a late-stage firefighting task. A basic logging and reporting system was eventually built using shared folders and email alerts, but it lacked automation and required constant manual oversight.

The internal audit process itself became a source of anxiety. Some departments saw it as a threat, fearing exposure of compliance failures. Others treated it as a formality and did not engage seriously. The internal audit report identified over 50 non-conformities, ranging from minor issues (e.g., unlocked cabinets with printed shipping documents) to major ones (e.g., unauthorised database access by subcontractors). Cleaning up these issues delayed the external audit by nearly four months.

Despite the difficulties, the company passed its external ISO 27001 certification audit with only a handful of minor non-conformities. But the road to that success had revealed the depth of the challenges inherent in translating international security standards into operational reality for a logistics company. Post-certification reviews highlighted additional problems: a drop-off in compliance monitoring once the certificate was issued, new staff joining without training, and periodic lapses in password management practices.

To address these risks, the company created a dedicated ISMS maintenance team and embedded information security KPIs into departmental scorecards. Annual refresher training was made mandatory, and internal phishing simulations were introduced as a way to keep awareness high. Over time, these changes helped shift the internal culture from reluctant compliance to cautious engagement.

4.5.2 Case Study: ISO 27001 Implementation in an E-commerce Logistics Hub—Chaos behind the Automation

In the heart of a major European capital, a rapidly growing e-commerce logistics provider operated a 24/7 distribution centre servicing next-day and same-day delivery for over 80 online stores. The company prided itself on automation, speed, and digital-first processes: barcode scanning, RFID tracking, warehouse robots, and real-time dashboards ruled the floor. To the outside world, it was a modern marvel. But inside the IT and compliance department, the infrastructure was fragile, documentation was outdated, and shadow IT was rampant.

When one of its largest international clients—a high-end electronics retailer—mandated ISO 27001 certification within 18 months as a condition to renew a €12 million contract, panic set in.

The core of the problem was not lack of technology—but lack of structure. The CTO described it as "having a spaceship with no instruction manual." Automated sorting systems ran on a patchwork of APIs and legacy middleware, some of which had not been updated in years. Access credentials were often hardcoded. Internal tools had no access control at all, and one developer joked that "the cleaner could probably reboot the WMS if she knew which button to click."

When the ISO consultant conducted the initial gap assessment, the verdict was clear: while technically impressive, the company lacked any formal risk management culture. There were no documented security policies, no data classification model, no backup policy, and no defined incident response workflow. The first action was to stop and stabilise.

But resistance came quickly—from operations.

"Security is slowing us down," said the Head of Fulfillment. "We deliver 20,000 packages a day. We can't stop to change passwords every two weeks or train pickers about cyber threats." The operational staff viewed the ISMS as a threat to performance KPIs, and cooperation between IT and logistics was minimal.

To break the deadlock, a cross-functional task force was created: IT, legal, warehouse ops, HR, and customer support. They met daily in the break room—often arguing. The breakthrough came when a minor data leak occurred: a junior employee uploaded a CSV file with customer phone numbers to an open cloud drive to "make printing labels easier." The file was indexed by search engines within 24 hours. Fortunately, the client noticed and warned them. That was the turning point. Suddenly, everyone understood what information security actually meant.

From there, real work began. A complete mapping of data flows showed over 25 systems exchanging personal and operational data—some via insecure protocols. A stopgap encryption solution was introduced using data masking for dashboards. Meanwhile, the HR team developed short cybersecurity modules in five languages for frontline staff, built around 3-minute videos and mobile quizzes.

One of the hardest technical problems was segmentation of the network. The main warehouse LAN was flat—every system talked to every other system. IoT devices, printers, scanners, and personal laptops all shared the same subnet. It took three months to design a segmented VLAN architecture with a zero-trust model, and another three months to implement it without stopping operations.

The audit trail issue was another nightmare. Most logs were either disabled or overwritten every 48 hours. To comply with ISO requirements, they had to implement a new centralised log server and configure all systems to retain logs for six months. This exposed dozens of unnoticed errors and misconfigurations. Suddenly, the IT team was flooded with alerts.

Despite all this, the most human problem persisted: turnover. The warehouse had 60% annual staff churn. Training new workers to follow security rules became an endless loop. The solution? Colour-coded wristbands. Green for trained, yellow for in progress, red for new. Supervisors could instantly see who needed mentoring, and the gamification boosted morale. Those with green bands got first pick of shift schedules.

When the day of the external audit came, tension was high. The auditors stayed for four days, combed through over 200 documents, and conducted interviews with night shift pickers and system admins. The result: certification granted, with five minor non-conformities.

Six months later, a follow-up review showed incident reporting had tripled (a good sign), failed logins were down 40%, and two new clients had signed on after seeing the ISO certificate.

The ISO 27001 journey didn't just secure the systems—it rebuilt trust across departments, exposed hidden fragilities, and ultimately strengthened the company's market position.

Bibliography

Atzori, L., Iera, A., & Morabito, G. (2010). The internet of things: A survey. *Computer Networks*, *54*(15), 2787–2805.

Bag, S., Pretorius, J. H. C., Gupta, S., & Dwivedi, Y. K. (2021). Role of institutional pressures and digital technologies in sustainable supply chain management. *International Journal of Production Economics*, *231*, 107830.

Ben-Daya, M., Hassini, E., & Bahroun, Z. (2019). Internet of things and supply chain management: A literature review. *International Journal of Production Research*, *57*(15–16), 4719–4742.

Büyüközkan, G., & Göçer, F. (2018). Digital supply chain: Literature review and a proposed framework for future research. *Computers in Industry*, *97*, 157–177.

Christopher, M. (2016). *Logistics & supply chain management* (5th ed.). Pearson.

Ghobakhloo, M. (2025). Industry 4.0 digital transformation and opportunities for supply chains. *International Journal of Production Research*. https://www.tandfonline.com/doi/full/10.1080/09537287.2023.2252376

Helo, P., & Szekely, B. (2024). Logistics 4.0 – digital transformation with smart connected technologies. *Journal of Manufacturing Systems*, *66*, 1–11.

Ivanov, D. (2020). Predicting the impacts of epidemic outbreaks on supply chains. *Transportation Research Part E: Logistics and Transportation Review*, *136*, 101922.

Ketchen, D. J., & Craighead, C. W. (2020). Research at the intersection of supply chain management and data science: Opportunities and challenges. *Journal of Operations Management*, *66*(7–8), 950–955.

Kamble, S. S., Gunasekaran, A., & Gawankar, S. A. (2019). Achieving sustainable performance in a data-driven agriculture supply chain: A review for research and applications. *International Journal of Information Management*, *48*, 39–50.

Klaus, P., & Müller, F. (2013). Supply chain finance and blockchain technology: The case of reverse logistics. *International Journal of Physical Distribution & Logistics Management*, *43*(10), 817–840.

Kshetri, N. (2018). Blockchain's roles in strengthening cybersecurity and protecting privacy in the digital supply chain. *International Journal of Information Management*, *39*, 80–89.

Kusi-Sarpong, S., Gupta, S., & Sarkis, J. (2019). A supply chain sustainability innovation framework and evaluation methodology. *International Journal of Production Research*, *57*(23), 7390–7408.

Lasi, H., Fettke, P., Kemper, H.-G., Feld, T., & Hoffmann, M. (2014). Industry 4.0. *Business & Information Systems Engineering*, *6*(4), 239–242.

Lee, H., & Whang, S. (2000). Information sharing in a supply chain. *Management Science*, *46*(5), 626–643.

Liu, C., et al. (2022). Blockchain-based digital twin for supply chain management: State-of-the-art review and future research directions. arXiv:2202.03966.

Melnyk, S. A., Davis, E. W., Spekman, R. E., & Sandor, J. (2010). Outcome-driven supply chains. *MIT Sloan Management Review*, *51*(2), 33–38.

Nguyen, T. N. N., & Buics, L. (2024). The evolution of digitalization transformation and Industry 4.0 in supply chain management: A systematic literature review. *Engineering Proceedings*, *79*(1), 65.

Nowicka, K., & Szymczak, M. (2020). *Logistics and supply chains in the light of industry 4.0.* Poznań University of Economics and Business Research Papers.

Osterwalder, A., & Pigneur, Y. (2010). *Business model generation: A handbook for visionaries, game changers, and challengers*. Wiley.

Preindl, R., Nikolopoulos, K., & Litsiou, K. (2020). Transformation strategies for the supply chain: The impact of Industry 4.0 and digital transformation. *Supply Chain Forum: An International Journal*, *21*(1), 26–34.

Radanliev, P., De Roure, D., Nurse, J. R. C., et al. (2019). Cyber risk at the edge: Current and future trends on cyber risk analytics and AI in IIoT and Industry 4.0 supply chains. *arXiv:1911.05726* .

Sanders, N. R. (2007). An empirical study of the impact of e-business technologies on organizational collaboration and performance. *Journal of Operations Management*, *25*(6), 1332–1347.

Schwab, K. (2017). *The fourth industrial revolution*. Crown Business.

Shafique, M. N., Arshad, Z., & Alavi Borazjani, S. A. (2025). Logistics 4.0 and digital supply chain: A systematic review. In J. L. Reis, M. K. Peter, L. P. Reis, & Z. Bogdanovic (Eds.), *Marketing and smart technologies* (pp. 143–156). Springer.

Siar, S. F., & Mohamad, M. (2019). Supply chain performance measurement: A structured literature review. *Benchmarking: An International Journal*, *26*(4), 1122–1153.

Stank, T. P., Autry, C. W., & Daugherty, P. J. (2015). Creating logistics value. *Journal of Business Logistics*, *36*(3), 195–209.

Tang, C. S. (2006). Perspectives in supply chain risk management. *International Journal of Production Economics*, *103*(2), 451–488.

Tortorella, G. L., Fogliatto, F. S., Gao, S., & Chan, H. K. (2021). Contributions of industry 4.0 to supply chain resilience. *The International Journal of Logistics Management*, *33*(2), 547–566.

Uckelmann, D., Harrison, M., & Michahelles, F. (2011). *Architecting the internet of things*. Springer.

Wamba, S. F., & Queiroz, M. M. (2020). Managing digital supply chain transformation: Challenges and strategies. *International Journal of Production Research*, *58*(7), 1–18.

Wang, Y., Gunasekaran, A., Ngai, E. W. T., & Papadopoulos, T. (2016). Big data analytics in logistics and supply chain management: Certain investigations for research and applications. *International Journal of Production Economics*, *176*, 98–110.

Wattanakul, S., Henry, S., Bentaha, M. L., Reeveerakul, N., & Ouzrout, Y. (2018). Improving risk management by using smart containers for real-time traceability. arXiv:1810.13332.

Wei, M. (2024). Digital transformation in supply chain 4.0: Challenges and opportunities for upstream and downstream enterprises. In *Proceedings of the 1st International Conference on Modern Logistics and Supply Chain Management (MLSCM 2024)*, 452–456.

Xu, L. D., He, W., & Li, S. (2018). Internet of things in industries: A survey. *IEEE Transactions on Industrial Informatics*, *10*(4), 2233–2243.

Zhu, K., & Kraemer, K. L. (2005). Post-adoption variations in usage and value of e-business technology in supply chains. *Management Science*, *51*(10), 1557–1576.

Żywiołek, J. (2018). Monitoring of information security system elements in the metallurgical enterprises. *MATEC Web of Conferences*, *183*, Article 01007. https://doi.org/10.1051/matecconf/201818301007

Żywiołek, J., & Nedeliaková, E. (2020). Personal data protection as an element of competitive advantage. *System Safety: Human–Technical Facility–Environment*, *2*(1), 55–61. https://doi.org/10.2478/czoto-2020-0008

5

Emerging Technologies and the Future of Cybersecurity

In the era of dynamic digitalisation and the Fourth Industrial Revolution, the logistics and supply chain sector is undergoing a profound transformation. The integration of advanced technologies such as the Internet of Things (IoT), artificial intelligence, machine learning, and complex platforms for real-time data exchange has become the foundation for modernising operations, aiming to increase their efficiency, transparency, and flexibility. However, alongside technological progress and growing connectivity, new, critical challenges in the realm of cybersecurity are emerging.

Modern supply chains, due to their complexity, global reach, and fundamental reliance on digital control systems and data exchange, are becoming increasingly vulnerable to cyber threats. These attacks can disrupt or completely paralyse critical processes—from fleet and warehouse management to shipment tracking and the coordination of production and distribution—directly threatening the functionality, reliability, and security of the entire system.

This chapter provides a comprehensive analysis of cybersecurity within the logistics and supply chain sector, structured around its core technological defences. The analysis will first establish the threat landscape and its consequences before detailing the key technologies that form the foundation of modern cyber resilience. The chapter will subsequently provide a detailed examination of the technological pillars of cybersecurity defence in logistics, focusing on: encryption, authentication, and identity management as the bedrock of data and access security; blockchain applications for ensuring tamper-proof transparency and traceability; the use of SIEM (Security Information

DOI: 10.1201/9781003685784-5

and Event Management), SOC (Security Operations Center), and AI (Artificial Intelligence) for advanced threat detection and incident response; and finally, the exploration of future trends and the vital link between robust cybersecurity practices and the achievement of ESG (Environmental, Social, Corporate Governance) and sustainable development goals.

5.1 Encryption, Authentication, and Identity Management

5.1.1 Encryption

Following the subject literature, we can define encryption as the process of converting a readable message (plaintext) into an unreadable cipher (ciphertext), which dates to antiquity. The main purpose of encryption is to allow two entities to communicate with each other in a safe manner without a third party being able to eavesdrop. One of the most famous early examples is the Caesar cipher, used by the Roman leader, which involved shifting the letters of the alphabet by a fixed number of positions. For centuries, cryptography developed in the "pre-computer era" through manual devices, such as the Enigma machine, used by the Germans during World War II. Its breaking by Allied cryptologists, including Alan Turing, was a turning point in the conflict and one of the milestones in the history of cryptography (Kahn, 1967).

The real revolution came in the 20th century with the advent of the digital age. Advanced mathematical encryption algorithms emerged, such as DES (Data Encryption Standard), and later its much more secure successor, AES (Advanced Encryption Standard), which to this day remains a cornerstone of digital security.

The most recent chapter is public-key (asymmetric) cryptography, initiated in the 1970s by, among others, Whitfield Diffie and Martin Hellman. This groundbreaking idea, which uses one-way mathematical functions, enabled secure communication over the dangerous medium that is the Internet and lies at the foundation of modern protocols such as SSL/TLS. Currently, intensive research is underway on the next generation of encryption—post-quantum cryptography, which is intended to be resistant to attacks using quantum computers.

5.1.2 Symmetric-key Algorithms

One of the most widely adopted and trusted encryption algorithms is the Advanced Encryption Standard (AES). Developed by cryptographers Joan Daemen and Vincent Rijmen, AES was selected by the National Institute of Standards and Technology (NIST) in 2001 as the successor to the ageing Data Encryption Standard (DES). AES is a symmetric-key algorithm, meaning that the same private key is used for both encryption and decryption processes, making it suitable for secure data transmission and storage (Swaminathan et al., 2024). In the setting of private-key encryption, two parties share a key and use this key when they want to communicate secretly.

One party can send a message, or plaintext, to the other by using the shared key to encrypt (or "scramble") the message and thus obtain a ciphertext that is transmitted to the receiver. The receiver uses the same key to decrypt (or "unscramble") the ciphertext and recover the original message. Note the same key is used to convert the plaintext into a ciphertext and back; that is why this is also known as the symmetric-key setting, where the symmetry lies in the fact that both parties hold the same key that is used for encryption and decryption (Figure 5.1). We can distinguish two types of symmetric-key cryptography:

- stream ciphers;
- block ciphers.

Stream cipher is a symmetric algorithm that encrypts each bit/byte of the message separately. It uses a secret key to seed a bitstream

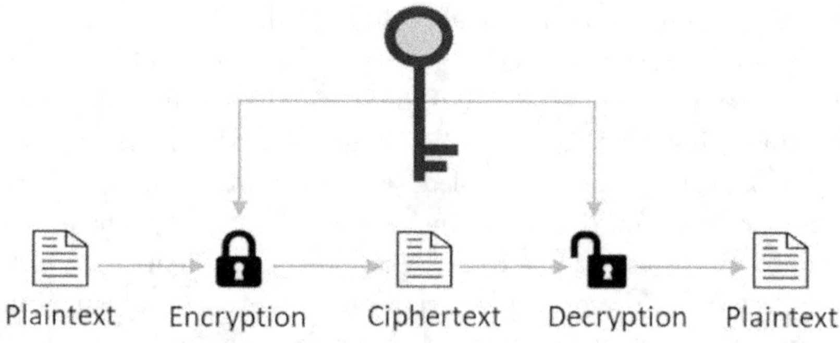

Figure 5.1 Symmetric-key algorithm. Source: https://medium.com/@.Qubit/symmetric-key-algorithm-in-cryptography-3d839bba8613.

pseudorandom generator, which produces a keystream. This keystream is then combined with the plaintext via an element like the XOR operation:

$C_i = S_i \oplus M_i$, (5.1)

where: S_i is a keystream, M_i is a plaintext and C_i is a ciphertext. Below you can find a simple example of an XOR stream cipher. For clarity, below you can find the definition of an XOR operation:

The XOR operation (exclusive OR) is one of the fundamental logical operations. It operates on two binary values (0 or 1) and returns:

- 1, if exactly one of the input values is equal to 1;
- 0, if both values are the same (that is, both 0 or both 1).

It is denoted symbolically as: A ⊕ B

Truth table for the XOR operation:Table 5.1 Truth Table for the XOR Operation

A	B	A ⊕ B
0	0	0
0	1	1
1	0	1
1	1	0

EXAMPLE 5.1: ENCRYPTION AND DECRYPTION USING XOR

STEP 1: PLAINTEXT CONVERSION

CHARACTER	ASCII	BINARY
H	72	01001000
E	69	01000101
L	76	01001100
L	76	01001100
O	79	01001111

STEP 2: KEYSTREAM (PSEUDORANDOM BITS)

11010010 10101100 01110011 10010110 00111001

STEP 3: XOR OPERATION (ENCRYPTION)

PLAINTEXT BINARY	KEYSTREAM	XOR RESULT (CIPHERTEXT)
01001000	11010010	10011010
01000101	10101100	11101001
01001100	01110011	00111111
01001100	10010110	11011010
01001111	00111001	01110110

Ciphertext:10011010 11101001 00111111 11011010 01110110

Step 4: XOR Operation (Decryption)

CIPHERTEXT	KEYSTREAM	XOR RESULT (PLAINTEXT)	CHARACTER
10011010	11010010	01001000	H
11101001	10101100	01000101	E
00111111	01110011	01001100	L
11011010	10010110	01001100	L
01110110	00111001	01001111	O

As shown in Example 5.1, the same keystream is used during the encryption and decryption phases, and the security depends on the keystream being unpredictable.

A real-life example of the most used stream ciphers is RC4. The cipher has gained immense popularity due to its design simplicity and has been widely adopted in various software and web applications. It is used in various network protocols such as WEP (Wireless Equivalent Privacy), WPA (Wi-Fi Protected Access), and SSL (Secure Socket Layer). Also, it is extensively used in Microsoft Windows, Apple OCE (Apple Open Collaboration Environment), secure SQL (a server for database management and data warehousing solution) etc (Jindal & Singh, 2015).

In supply chain context, symmetric-key algorithms are extensively used to protect data transmitted by IoT sensors monitoring shipment conditions, RFID tags tracking inventory, and automated warehouse systems communicating with central databases. The computational efficiency and low power consumption of AES encryption make it particularly suitable for resource-constrained IoT devices that operate on battery power while continuously collecting temperature, humidity, location, and other critical supply chain data (Chang et al., 2025).

5.1.3 Asymmetric Key Algorithms

A block cipher is an encryption function for fixed-size blocks of data. The current generation of block ciphers has a block size of 128 bits (16 bytes). These block ciphers encrypt a 128-bit plaintext and generate a 128-bit ciphertext as the result. The block cipher is reversible; there is a decryption function that takes the 128-bit ciphertext and decrypts it to the original 128-bit plaintext. The plaintext and ciphertext are always the same size, and we call this the block size of the block cipher (Figure 5.2).

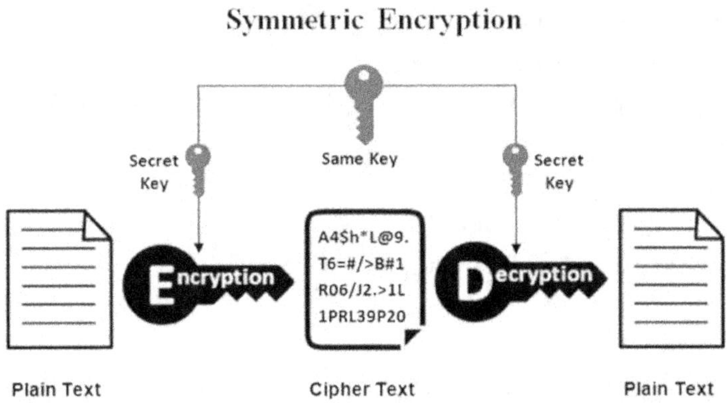

Figure 5.2 Asymmetric key algorithm. Source: https://nordvpn.com/blog/what-is-asymmetric-cryptography/.

To encrypt with a block cipher, we need a secret key. Without a secret key, there is no way to hide the message. Like the plaintext and ciphertext, the key is also a string of bits. Common key sizes are 128 and 256 bits (Ferguson et al., 2010).

Example 5.2: Asymmetric Key Algorithm—The "Lock Box" Analogy

In our example Alice wants to receive secret messages from Bob.

🔐 **Key Generation**

Alice creates a special lock box with two keys:

- Public Key (🔒): Anyone can use this to lock the box.
- Private Key (🔑): Only Alice has this to unlock the box.

✍️ **Encryption (Bob → Alice)**

Bob's Message: "HELLO"

Alice's Public Key: 🔒 (available to everyone)

Bob encrypts the message using Alice's public key:

"HELLO" + = 🔒"XJBSQ"

Bob sends the locked box to Alice.

Decryption (Alice reads the message)

Alice receives: 🔒"XJBSQ"

Alice uses her Private Key: 🔑

🔒"XJBSQ" + 🔑 = "HELLO"

Technical Example: Simplified RSA

🔧 **Key Generation**

Choose two primes: p = 3, q = 11

Compute n = p × q = 33

Compute $\varphi(n) = (p - 1)(q - 1) = 20$
Choose public key $e = 3$ (coprime with 20)
Compute private key $d = 7$ (since $3 \times 7 = 21 \equiv 1 \bmod 20$)
Keys:

- Public Key: $(e = 3, n = 33)$
- Private Key: $(d = 7, n = 33)$

Encryption (Bob encrypts message "2")
Ciphertext: $C = 2^3 \bmod 33 = 8$
Bob sends 8 to Alice.

Decryption (Alice decrypts)
Plaintext: $P = 8^7 \bmod 33 = 2$
Alice recovers the original message: "2"

While encryption ensures data confidentiality, it does not verify the legitimacy of the communicating parties. Protecting information from unauthorised access alone is insufficient; it is equally important to confirm the identity of the entities involved. This introduces the concept of authentication, which verifies message origin and establishes trust between participants.

5.1.4 Authentication

Following the literature, authentication is the process of verifying the identity of a user, device, or system in a computer environment, and it is a central component of any security infrastructure (Velásquez et al., 2018). While encryption protects the confidentiality of data against mostly passive attacks (e.g., eavesdropping), authentication is concerned with protecting against active attacks (e.g., falsification of data and transactions) and assuring that communication is authentic. For a single message, authentication ensures the recipient that the source is as claimed. For an ongoing connection, such as between a client and server, authentication involves two aspects (Stallings, 2020):

- verifying the identity of both entities when the connection starts;
- ensuring no third party can later masquerade as either party to send or receive data without authorisation.

Authentication mechanisms are typically based on one or more of the following factors (Stallings & Brown, 2018):

- something you know (e.g., passwords, PINs);
- something you have (e.g., smart cards, cryptographic tokens);
- something you are (e.g., biometric characteristics such as fingerprints).

In the context of supply chains, these principles apply to a diverse set of interacting entities, including suppliers, logistics providers, warehouse personnel, enterprise information systems, and IoT-enabled assets. As depicted in the authentication diagram (Figure 5.3), each supply chain entity must authenticate itself before gaining access to shared platforms or executing operational actions. The process begins with an access request, followed by the presentation of appropriate credentials that correspond to one or more authentication factors. These credentials are then verified against a trust registry or equivalent authority to determine their validity. Successful authentication establishes the entity as trusted and permits authorised actions within the supply chain, whereas failed verification results in access denial and the generation of security alerts. This illustrates how authentication mechanisms operationalise identity assurance in supply chain environments, mitigating the risk of impersonation, unauthorised access, and manipulation of transactions.

5.1.5 Identity Management

Identity Management (IdM) system is a set of services that support the creation, modification, and removal of identities and associated accounts, as well as the authentication and authorisation required to access resources. Identity management systems are used to protect online resources from unauthorised access and comprise an important part of a comprehensive security model (Wilson & Hingnikar, 2022). In supply chains, this extends beyond traditional employee access to include diverse entities: suppliers, logistics providers, warehouse personnel, enterprise systems, and IoT-enabled assets. The key challenges for identity management in supply chains are the fragmentation and risks of centralised systems, including poor user experience, vulnerability to breaches affecting both data and physical IoT infrastructure, and the difficulty of scaling securely for billions of IoT devices (Masip-Bruin et al., 2021).

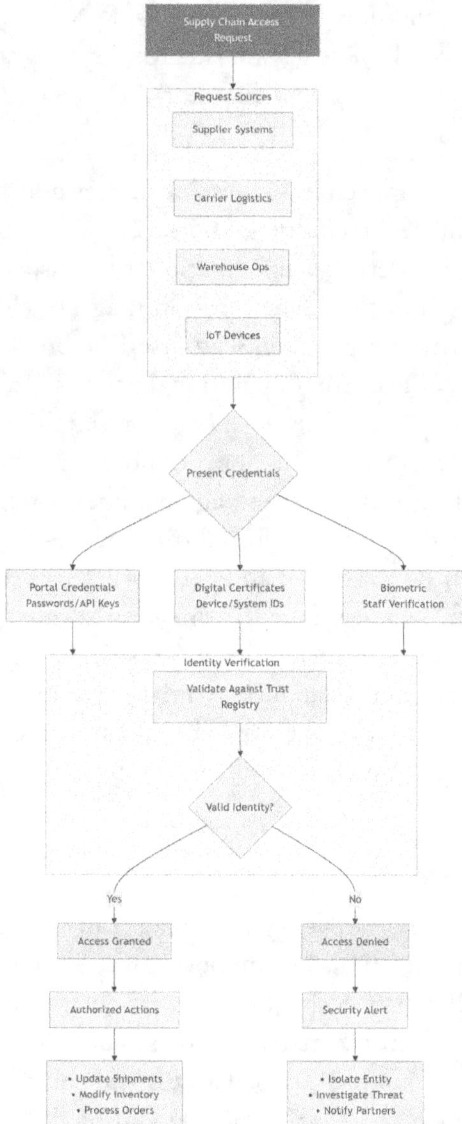

Figure 5.3 Supply chain authentication process. Source: Own elaboration.

In supply chain, managing thousands of human, system, and device identities requires diverse authentication methods, from biometric verification for warehouse access to cryptographic certificates for IoT sensors. Different entities within the supply chain use different authentication methods:

- human operators use multi-factor authentication with adaptive strategies based on risk levels (Dasgupta et al., 2016),
- system-to-system communication relies on API keys and mutual Transport Layer Security (mTLS) certificates (Thiyagarajan et al., 2025),
- IoT devices utilise hardware security modules embedded during manufacturing, creating a hardware-based root of trust that prevents counterfeiting (Guin et al., 2014).

These mechanisms implement the "never trust, always verify" principle essential to zero-trust architectures (Rose et al., 2020).

Emerging approaches in the area of identity management shift toward decentralised models. Blockchain-based verifiable credentials (Section 5.2) and self-sovereign identity frameworks allow partners to share verified information without relying on a central authority. Standards like GS1's digital linkage help connect physical assets with digital identities, improving traceability in supply chains.

However, implementing these new systems is challenging. Organisations face two main problems when putting these new security systems in place: meeting legal requirements and making sure new solutions work with old technology (integration issues). To deal with this, many companies use hybrid models, especially when working with partners.

Looking ahead, the focus is on two things:

- authentication methods that protect user privacy, so identities can be verified without exposing sensitive information (Camenisch & Lysyanskaya, 2001)
- cryptography that can withstand attacks from quantum computers, which is important for devices that need to stay secure for many years (L. Chen et al., 2016).

This shift means moving away from security models that only protect the network's outer edge ("perimeter-based") to models that verify every user and device individually ("entity-centric"). This approach helps fight problems like fake products, unauthorised access, and tampering with information in the supply chain.

5.2 Blockchain Applications in Supply Chain Tracking

At its core, a *blockchain* is a type of *distributed ledger technology (DLT)*. It can be best understood as a decentralised digital database or record-keeping system that is shared, replicated, and synchronised across a network of multiple participants (nodes). Unlike a traditional centralised database controlled by a single entity (e.g., a corporation or government), a blockchain ledger is maintained collectively by its network (Anascavage & Davis, 2018; Ghazi et al., 2022).

This technology derives its name from its structure: data is grouped into "blocks" that are *chronologically linked or "chained"* together using cryptographic hashes. Each block contains a timestamp, transaction data, and a unique cryptographic fingerprint (hash) of the previous block. This creates an immutable chain—altering any single record would require changing all subsequent blocks and gaining consensus from most of the network, which is computationally infeasible (Moosavi et al., 2024).

Figure 5.4 illustrates the blockchain technology within a supply chain context, demonstrating how the theoretical concepts translate into practical supply chain tracking applications. The diagram is organised into three connected layers that collectively explain the blockchain workflow.

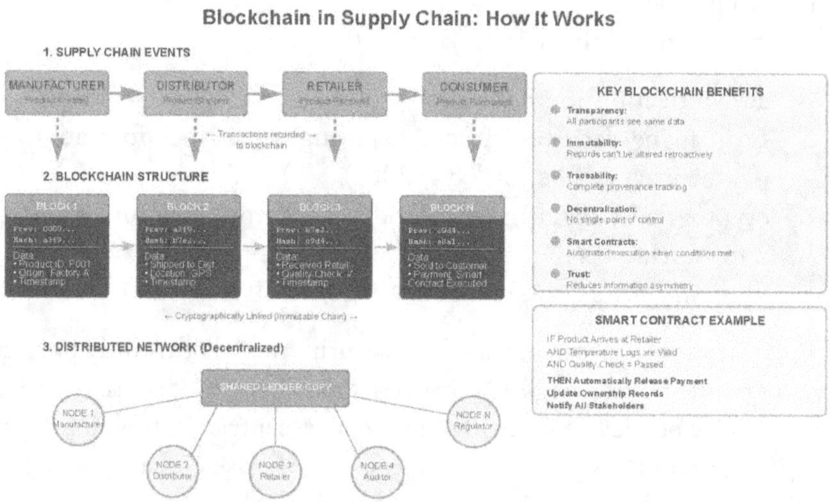

Figure 5.4 Blockchain in supply chain. Source: Own elaboration based on Hanqing (2022) and Ismail and Reza (2022).

The first layer of Figure 5.1 shows a typical supply chain flow from manufacturer to consumer. At each transition point, critical events occur—product creation, shipment, receipt verification, and purchase. Unlike traditional systems where each stakeholder maintains separate records, blockchain records each event as a transaction on a shared, immutable ledger visible to all authorised participants (Turjo et al., 2021).

The second layer illustrates the blockchain structure itself. Each transaction is recorded as a "block" containing three components:

- the previous block's cryptographic hash,
- the current block's hash,
- the transaction data (product ID, location, timestamp, quality metrics).

This cryptographic linking makes the blockchain tamper-evident—altering any earlier block changes its hash, breaking the chain and alerting the network. This ensures a complete, auditable history from origin to destination (Shamsuzzoha et al., 2025).

The third layer demonstrates the distributed network architecture. Rather than a single central server, identical ledger copies are maintained across multiple nodes representing different stakeholders (manufacturers, distributors, retailers, auditors, regulators). New transactions are validated through a consensus mechanism where the majority of nodes agree on validity. This distributed validation eliminates single points of failure and the need for a trusted central authority, creating transparency through cryptographic security rather than institutional trust (Karaduman et al., 2025).

This three-layer architecture enables blockchain's revolutionary characteristics for supply chain management:

- Decentralisation and Disintermediation: No single party has absolute control, reducing reliance on and the cost of central authorities or intermediaries for validation (Lumineau et al., 2021; Tan et al., 2021).
- Immutability & Auditability: Once recorded, data cannot be altered retroactively without detection, creating a permanent, tamper-evident history (Kshetri, 2018; Saberi et al., 2019).
- Transparency & Provenance: All permissioned participants can view the same ledger, provide a single version of truth and

enable end-to-end tracking of an asset's origin and journey (Montecchi et al., 2019; Sunmola & Burgess, 2022).

- Automation via Smart Contracts: Self-executing contracts with predefined rules (if-then logic) can automate processes (e.g., payments, compliance checks) when conditions are met, increasing efficiency and reducing fraud (De Giovanni, 2020).

Blockchain applications in supply chain tracking can be seen as mechanisms for reducing information asymmetry, improving inter-organisational trust, and lowering coordination and verification costs in complex, multi-actor networks. Rather than optimising physical logistics flows directly, blockchain primarily restructures how information about those flows is generated, shared, and governed across organisational boundaries (Babich & Hilary, 2018; Liu et al., 2025; Wang et al., 2019). The following subsections will focus on the blockchain application across different types of industries.

5.2.1 Food Supply Chain Traceability and Safety

The food industry represents one of the most mature applications of blockchain in supply chains, driven by food safety, regulations, and consumer demand for transparency (Sri Vigna Hema & Manickavasagan, 2024). These complex, multi-party (farmers, processors, distributors, retailers) systems create information gaps that hinder contamination response and enable fraud like origin mislabeling (Aung & Chang, 2014).

Blockchain addresses this by providing end-to-end visibility through an immutable record of each transaction. Systems like TE-FOOD track hundreds of thousands of transactions daily, enabling provenance tracing from retail to farm in seconds (Sri Vigna Hema & Manickavasagan, 2024). IBM Food Trust reduced traceability for mangoes from seven days to 2.2 seconds—a critical capability during contamination outbreaks (Kamath, 2018).

Some limitations in using blockchain in the food industry include:

1. Blockchain ensures data immutability, not initial accuracy—the "garbage in, garbage out" problem described in (Powell et al., 2022). To address this issue, complementary measures like IoT automation (which reduces human error and manual data

entry), third-party audits, and certification (which provides standardised baselines for quality and safety) are required.

2. The use of blockchain technology in the food supply chain is currently only practical, reasonable, and cost-effective for high-value livestock products and massive market players in the food industry. More research is required to study the potential of blockchain deployment in the food supply chain, with the emphasis on the challenges in blockchain integration in the food sector (Patel et al., 2023).

5.2.2 Pharmaceutical Supply Chain Traceability and Safety

Pharmaceutical supply chains face severe integrity issues, with an estimated 10–30% of medicines in developing countries being substandard or falsified. Blockchain solutions address this through unit-level digital serialisation and track-and-trace compliance. Each product unit receives a unique digital identity at manufacture, and every custody transfer requires dual authorisation, creating an immutable, auditable chain (Jamil et al., 2019).

Consortia like the MediLedger Project (involving Pfizer, McKesson, Walmart) demonstrate real-world application. It uses blockchain to verify returned medications in seconds instead of days, employing zero-knowledge proofs to confirm legitimacy without exposing commercial data. Smart contracts enable continuous real-time monitoring for diversion or expired sales, moving beyond periodic audits (Sample, 2023).

A key remaining challenge is scalability. Processing billions of annual global pharmaceutical transactions with the near-instantaneous speed required at the pharmacy counter pushes the limits of current technology (Jamil et al., 2019).

5.3 Use of SIEM, SOC, and AI in Incident Response

Robust identity management systems must be supported by continuous monitoring and rapid response capabilities to defend against evolving cyber threats. The Security Operations Center (SOC) serves as the organisational hub for coordinating defensive activities, while Security Information and Event Management (SIEM) platforms provide the technological foundation for aggregating and correlating security events from diverse systems spanning IT, IoT, and operational technology environments (Miller et al., 2010). In supply chain contexts, where thousands of distributed devices, third-party systems, and cross-organisational data flows create unprecedented complexity, manual monitoring becomes infeasible, necessitating automated and intelligent approaches to threat detection and response (González-Granadillo et al., 2021).

SIEM systems collect, normalise, and correlate log data from multiple sources to identify potential security incidents through pattern matching and behavioural analysis. Modern SIEM platforms have evolved significantly from simple log aggregation tools to sophisticated analytics engines capable of processing massive data volumes. However, they face persistent challenges including high rates of false positives, alert fatigue among analysts, and integration complexity when connecting heterogeneous systems common in supply chain environments (González-Granadillo et al., 2021). In supply chains specifically, SIEM platforms must ingest data from enterprise resource planning systems, warehouse management platforms, IoT sensors monitoring goods in transit, and operational technology controlling automated facilities, creating a unified security view across previously siloed domains. The SOC operates as the operational centre where human analysts and automated systems work together to monitor these alerts, investigate suspicious activities, and coordinate response actions. The effectiveness of a SOC depends not only on technological capabilities but also on well-defined processes, skilled personnel, and clear metrics for measuring performance (Forsberg & Frantti, 2023; Vielberth et al., 2020).

The incident response process within a SOC typically follows the structured lifecycle defined in the NIST Computer Security Incident Handling Guide, which encompasses preparation, detection and analysis, containment, eradication, recovery, and post-incident activities (Nelson et al., 2025). During the preparation phase, the SOC establishes tooling configurations, develops response playbooks for common scenarios, and trains team members on procedures. Detection and analysis activities involve monitoring SIEM alerts, enriching them with threat intelligence, and determining whether they represent genuine security incidents—a phase where the volume of data becomes particularly problematic and analyst expertise proves critical. Containment, eradication, and recovery require the SOC to orchestrate coordinated actions across IT and operational technology teams, often under time pressure to minimise business disruption. Post-incident activities enable the SOC to refine detection rules, update playbooks, and incorporate lessons learned into future defensive strategies.

Artificial intelligence and machine learning have become essential for overcoming the inherent limitations of traditional SIEM and SOC operations, particularly human fatigue and the inability to manually analyse vast data streams in real time. Figure 5.5 shows how all the parts cooperate. The SIEM platform forms the foundational data layer, aggregating and correlating events from IT, IoT, OT, and third-party systems across the supply chain. The AI/ML layer acts as an intelligent filter, applying anomaly detection to reduce false positives and prioritise threats. These enriched alerts flow to the SOC, which operates within the structured NIST incident response lifecycle (Nelson et al., 2025). Insights gained from SOC investigations are used to continuously improve both AI models and SIEM configurations, resulting in a dynamic defence system that can adapt to new and evolving threats within the supply chain.

Machine learning algorithms excel at detecting anomalies that may indicate security incidents, such as unusual data flows from an IoT device suggesting its identity credentials have been compromised, or unexpected access patterns indicating lateral movement by an attacker (Xin et al., 2018). Beyond detection, AI-driven automation through Security Orchestration, Automation, and Response (SOAR) platforms enables SOCs to automatically triage alerts, enrich them with contextual information from multiple threat intelligence sources, and

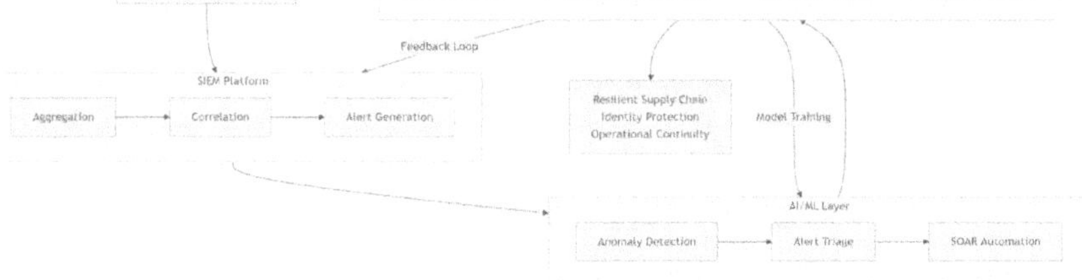

Figure 5.5 The integrated SIEM-SOC-AI cycle for supply chain security. Source: Own elaboration.

execute predefined containment playbooks without human intervention (Kinyua & Awuah, 2021). For instance, when a compromised logistics server is detected, automated workflows can immediately isolate the affected system, gather forensic evidence, and notify relevant stakeholders while human analysts focus on complex investigation tasks. However, the deployment of AI in security operations introduces its own challenges, including the need for high-quality training data, ongoing model refinement to adapt to evolving threats, and defences against adversarial machine learning attacks designed to evade detection (Apruzzese et al., 2018).

Supply chain incident response presents unique considerations that distinguish it from traditional enterprise security operations. Supply chain attacks often exploit trusted relationships and third-party access, targeting software dependencies or vendor systems to gain indirect access to primary targets, requiring SOCs to monitor for threats originating beyond their direct control (Lella et al., 2021). The convergence of information technology and operational technology in modern supply chains means that incidents may have immediate physical consequences—a cyberattack on a warehouse automation system could interrupt operations, while compromised IoT sensors could provide false data about shipment conditions (Knowles et al., 2015). This physical dimension necessitates frameworks like MITRE ATT&CK (Adversarial Tactics, Techniques, and Common Knowledge) for Industrial Control Systems, which guide analysts in understanding tactics and techniques specific to attacks on industrial environments (Jiang et al., 2025). An AI-augmented SOC, powered by a comprehensive SIEM platform capable of ingesting data from both digital and physical systems, represents an operational necessity for modern resilient supply chains. This integrated defensive capability protects the integrity of decentralised identity systems and the IoT infrastructure they secure, enabling organisations to detect identity compromise, unauthorised access attempts, and malicious activities across their extended supply chain ecosystems before they escalate into major breaches or operational disruptions.

5.4 Future Trends and Links to ESG and Sustainable Development

Looking ahead, the evolution of supply chain cybersecurity will be defined by its integration with strategic sustainability goals. Key technological trends are shaping this future. The convergence of IT, OT, and IoT security demands unified frameworks to protect smart physical infrastructure (ISA/IEC 62443 Series of Standards—ISA, 2021). The progression from AI-augmented to autonomous, AI-driven security promises real-time threat containment but introduces new adversarial risks (Brundage et al., 2018). Furthermore, quantum computing creates a necessity for a shift toward post-quantum cryptography (PQC) to safeguard long-lived supply chain data, as highlighted by the NIST standardisation project (Chhetri et al., 2025).

—These advancements are not merely technical but are increasingly critical for corporate Environmental, Social, and Governance (ESG) performance. Robust cyber governance directly protects shareholder value and is a key disclosure metric for ESG ratings, framing cybersecurity as a core board-level responsibility (Sustainability Accounting Standards Board, 2018; *The Global Risks Report 2022 17th Edition*, 2022). On the social front, securing data and ensuring the safety of cyber-physical systems are fundamental to maintaining consumer trust and protecting worker well-being (Martin et al., 2017). Environmentally, cybersecurity serves as a critical enabler of environmental protection and sustainable development by safeguarding the technological infrastructure essential for conservation efforts and preventing disruptive incidents that lead to waste and excessive energy consumption in recovery (Obasi et al., 2024), while the energy efficiency of security solutions themselves—"Green Security"—is gaining attention (Aslan et al., 2018).

Ultimately, cybersecurity is a foundational enabler of the United Nations Sustainable Development Goals (SDGs). SDGs are 17 goals launched in 2015 by the United Nations as a global initiative aimed at eradicating poverty, safeguarding the environment, and promoting peace and prosperity for all by 2030 (Sorooshian, 2024). While digital transformation accelerates progress toward these targets, it simultaneously creates vulnerabilities that can undermine development gains if cyber threats are not adequately addressed (Odumesi & Sanusi, 2023).

5.4.1 Cybersecurity and SDG 9: Industry, Innovation, and Infrastructure

SDG 9 aims to "build resilient infrastructure, promote inclusive and sustainable industrialisation and foster innovation." In the digital age, resilient infrastructure inherently includes cybersecurity protecting industrial systems, communication networks, and technological innovations from cyber threats. Innovations in cybersecurity, including the application of blockchain technology and the integration of artificial intelligence and machine learning, offer transformative potential to enhance digital security and support sustainable development across various sectors (Ige et al., 2024). Smart factories, automated manufacturing systems, and industrial control systems depend on secure digital foundations to operate without disruption. Major incidents like the 2021 Colonial Pipeline ransomware attack (Beerman et al., 2023) and the 2017 NotPetya malware (Fayi, 2018)—which caused billions in global manufacturing losses—demonstrate how cyberattacks directly impede industrial productivity and economic development (Dede et al., 2024).

5.4.2 Cybersecurity and SDG 8: Decent Work and Economic Growth

SDG 8 promotes "sustained, inclusive and sustainable economic growth, full and productive employment and decent work for all." The economic cost of information and technology asset security breaches in 2020 was estimated at USD 4–6 trillion, equivalent to approximately 4–6% of global GDP (Gillani et al., 2022). Cyberattacks on financial institutions, e-commerce platforms, and digital payment systems directly threaten economic growth by eroding trust in digital transactions and imposing massive recovery costs (Maurer & Nelson, 2021).

Small and medium enterprises (SMEs), which account for the majority of employment in most economies, are particularly vulnerable to cyber threats. By implementing cybersecurity measures to protect sensitive data and prevent attacks, SMEs can participate more securely in the digital economy, contributing to economic growth and job creation aligned with SDG 8 (Arroyabe et al., 2024). The shift toward remote work and digital labour markets has made cybersecurity critical for decent work conditions, protecting workers' personal data, intellectual contributions, and digital work environments from unauthorised access and exploitation (Ogugua, 2024).

5.5 Case Study: Artificial Intelligence for Threat Detection in a Global TMS Platform

A Transportation Management System (TMS) is a cloud-based logistics platform that manages inbound and outbound shipments across the supply chain. TMS solutions integrate with enterprise resource planning (ERP) and supply chain management (SCM) systems, facilitating transportation planning, freight management, real-time tracking, and payment processing (Griffis & Goldsby, 2007). Modern TMS platforms are critical infrastructure that handle sensitive commercial data, coordinate multi-party operations across organisational boundaries, and process financial transactions—making them high-value targets for cyber-attacks. The distributed, real-time, and collaborative nature of TMS operations presents unique cybersecurity challenges that traditional IT security approaches struggle to address.

5.5.1 Executive Summary

—LogiChain Global, a leading cloud-based TMS provider, faced escalating cyber threats targeting its global logistics platform. Traditional security measures proved inadequate against AI-powered attacks, credential stuffing, and supply chain compromises. This case study presents the implementation of "Sentinel AI"—a comprehensive AI-driven cybersecurity framework integrating machine learning, cryptographic innovations, blockchain transparency, SIEM capabilities, and zero-trust principles. The initiative achieved a 99.5% reduction in threat detection time, prevented over $2 million in annual fraud, and transformed security from reactive to proactive intelligence.

5.5.2 Introduction: The Evolving Cyber Threat Landscape

The digital transformation of global supply chains has created unprecedented cyber vulnerabilities. According to data cited by Statista from the Identity Theft Resource Center, the number of supply chain attacks increased by 115% year-over-year between 2022 and 2023. These 2,116 attacks in 2023 affected a total of 2,769 organisations (*Annual Number of Supply Chain Cyber Attacks U.S. 2023| Statista*, 2023). Between 2021 and 2023, supply chain attacks surged by a staggering 431%, demonstrating the explosive growth of this threat vector (*Supply Chain Breaches Increased from 2022 to 2023 | SupplyChainBrain*, 2023). The financial impact has proven to be severe. According to IBM's Cost of a Data Breach 2025 report, the global average cost of a data breach reached $4.44 million, with supply chain-related breaches often exceeding this average due to their cascading effects across multiple organisations (Khalil, 2025). Recent high-profile incidents demonstrate the devastating real-world impact: the August 2025 cyberattack on Jaguar Land Rover resulted in estimated losses of £1.9 billion ($2.5 billion) to the UK economy, while Asahi Group's October 2025 breach suspended operations for months with full logistics recovery not expected until February 2026 (Fitzgerald & Bonnie, 2025; Mondal, 2025).

The transportation and logistics industry has become particularly vulnerable, with cyberattacks spiking by over 400% in three years (Snape, 2025). Transportation Management Systems (TMS) are high-value targets due to their central role—compromising a TMS can enable cargo theft, shipment diversion, or complete operational paralysis (Gil, n.d.; Under Attack: Why Transportation & Logistics Are Top Cyber Targets, n.d.). LogiChain's legacy security infrastructure proved inadequate against modern supply chain attacks, including:

- IoT device exploitation—IoT devices commonly ship with inadequate security configurations, creating exploitable entry points (Neshenko et al., 2019),
- credential stuffing attacks with infrastructure-level analysis showing compromised credentials are used in nearly 50% of all login attempts (Radwan & Zejnilovic, 2025), attacks that increasingly target APIs to bypass traditional controls.

The company faced annual financial losses exceeding $2.5 million and falling customer trust. Supply chain-specific vulnerabilities compounded these challenges: data sharing across organisational boundaries, integration with carriers of varying security maturity, public-facing APIs, and proliferating IoT devices (Hammi et al., 2023; Islam et al., 2022). Traditional perimeter-based security models proved fundamentally incompatible with distributed supply chain operations, as modern paradigms must "assume that the security perimeters have been breached" (Sobb et al., 2020).

5.5.3 The Pre-implementation Security Posture

LogiChain's security infrastructure suffered from fundamental deficiencies:

1. Reactive Threat Detection
   - Signature-based intrusion detection systems are fundamentally limited as they can only identify known attack patterns and fail against novel or modified threats (Buczak & Guven, 2016).
   - Mean Time to Detect (MTTD) exceeding 14 days with 72-hour response times.
   - 42% false positive rate—high false positive rates lead to staff fatigue and lower numbers of detected incidents (Tariq et al., 2025).
2. Fragmented Identity Management
   - Separate authentication systems for customers, carriers, and staff create identity silos. When identity data is trapped in isolated systems, security teams cannot effectively correlate activities across different environments, leaving the organisation vulnerable to sophisticated attacks (Wang et al., 2025).
   - Password-only authentication for non-critical users without risk-based controls. Multi-factor authentication (MFA) is strongly recommended by the National Institute of Standards and Technology (Temoshok et al., 2025).
   - No automated user provisioning/deprovisioning, leading to orphaned accounts and privilege creep (Subramanyam, 2025).
   - Static role-based access control (RBAC) without contextual factors causes cyber threats (Alexander & Chikwarti, 2021; Atakari, 2025).
3. Inadequate Cryptography
   - Basic TLS 1.2 without a unified data protection strategy, exemplifying a dangerous decoupling of network and

data security that modern frameworks warn against (Tait, 2025).
- Weak key management with keys stored in configuration files, which violates recommendations from the National Institute of Standards and Technology (Barker, 2020).
- No end-to-end encryption for sensitive data, which makes the platform vulnerable to cyberattacks (Karaduman et al., 2025).

4. Missing Security Operations
    - No SIEM: Security logs scattered across 12+ systems with no correlation capability (Section 5.3).
    - No SOC: No 24/7 monitoring or dedicated security operations team (Section 5.3).
    - Limited visibility across the supply chain ecosystem—this causes blind spots that can be exploited by potential attackers, as was shown in (Meegammana & Kumara, 2025).
    - Manual, ad-hoc incident response without documented playbooks. Playbooks are highly recommended by the Cybersecurity & Infrastructure Security Agency (CISA, 2021).
5. Network Vulnerabilities
    - Insufficient network segmentation enabling lateral movement. Network segmentation is strongly suggested by Zero Trust Architecture (Rose et al., 2020).
    - Unencrypted internal service-to-service communications (Section 5.1.1).
    - Inadequate cloud security posture management, which opens several different ways for potential attackers as shown in (Matrix—Enterprise—Cloud | MITRE ATT&CK®, 2025).

5.5.4 The Sentinel AI Solution: Multi-Layered Architecture

Sentinel AI implemented a comprehensive defence-in-depth system across seven integrated layers, grounded in zero-trust principles (Rose et al., 2020).

5.5.4.1 Layer 0: Blockchain-Enabled Trust Foundation

Immutable Audit Logs:

- Hyperledger Fabric Implementation: critical events (shipment releases, payment authorisations, contract modifications) recorded on a permissioned blockchain creating tamper-proof audit trails. Hyperledger Fabric is an enterprise-grade permissioned distributed ledger platform designed for use in enterprise contexts (Androulaki et al., 2018).
- Smart Contract Enforcement: automated multi-party authorisation verification before high-risk actions, e.g., international shipments >$50K required three cryptographic signatures.
- RAFT Consensus: Achieved sub-2-second transaction finality using crash-fault-tolerant RAFT consensus (Ongaro & Ousterhout, 2014).

Distributed Identity Verification:

- A consortium blockchain was implemented, where regulatory agencies serve as credential issuers for carrier licences, insurance, and safety ratings (Chen et al., 2024).
- Eliminated centralised identity provider dependencies and credential forgery risks.

5.5.4.2 Layer 1: Behavioural Analysis and Advanced Identity Context (Figure 5.6)

Graph Relationship Analysis:

- Mapped relationships between users, carriers, devices, and bank accounts to uncover hidden fraud rings. Recent research demonstrates that Graph Neural Networks (GNNs) are exceptionally adept at capturing complex relational patterns and dynamics within financial networks, significantly outperforming traditional fraud detection methods (Cheng et al., 2024; Wu et al., 2024).

Communication Security:

- Fine-tuned BERT (Bidirectional Encoder Representations from Transformers) models scanned communications for phishing, social engineering, and account takeover indicators.

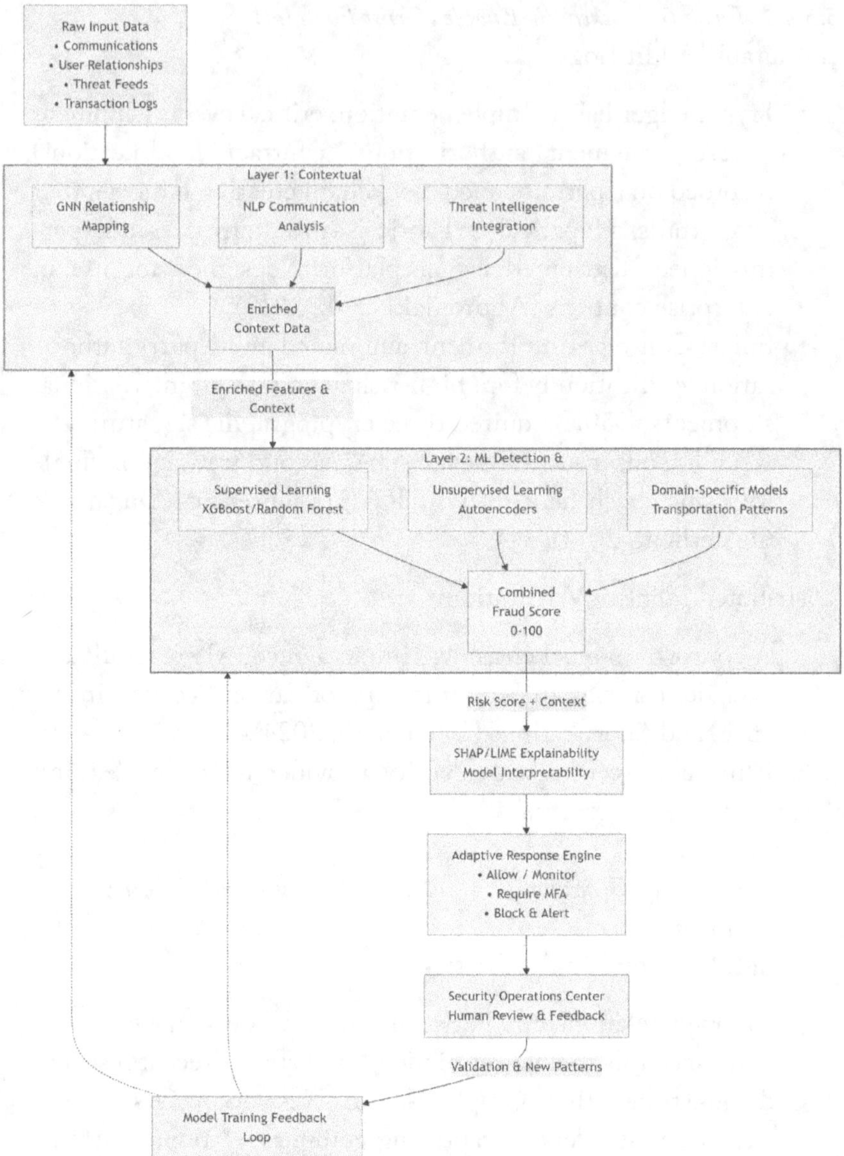

Figure 5.6 Flow between Layer 1 and 2 of the "Sentinel—AI". Source: Own elaboration based on Samaneh Sorournejad et al. (2016).

BERT-based models have demonstrated remarkable effectiveness in phishing detection, with studies reporting F1 scores above 0.93 for email classification tasks (Devlin et al., 2019; Diyasi et al., 2023). Systematic literature reviews confirm the efficacy of transformer-based approaches for phishing detection, with fine-tuned models outperforming baseline BERT implementations (Jamal et al., 2023).

Threat Intelligence (Alzahrani et al., 2024).

- Real-time feeds from commercial providers, OSINT (Open-Source Threat Intelligence feed), and logistics ISACs (Information Sharing and Analysis Center).
- Automated IoC matching against global threat databases.

5.5.4.3 Layer 2: Machine Learning Detection and Decision Engine (Figure 5.6)

Known Threat Detection:

- XGBoost models classified known fraud patterns from historical transportation data (Tayebi & El Kafhali, 2025).

Novel Anomaly Detection:

- Autoencoder neural networks identified behavioural anomalies through reconstruction error analysis (Chalapathy & Chawla, 2019).

Domain-Specific Intelligence:

- Transportation-aware models focused on logistics-specific fraud vectors and patterns (Middae et al., 2024).

Explainable Governance:

- SHAP framework provided model explanations for compliance and analyst trust (Barredo Arrieta et al., 2020).

5.5.4.4 Layer 3: Cryptographic Controls and Identity Protection

Comprehensive Encryption (Section 5.1):

- AES-256-GCM for all data at rest; TLS 1.3 mandatory for data in transit,
- End-to-end encryption for sensitive multi-party shipment data with party-controlled private keys.

Centralised Key Management:

- HSM providing FIPS 140-3 Level 3 validated key storage (FIPS 140-3, Security Requirements for Cryptographic Modules | CSRC, 2019).
- Hierarchical key structure with automated 90-day rotation (Barker, 2020).
- All key access operations logged immutably on blockchain.

Zero-Trust Identity Framework:

- Universal MFA with phishing-resistant FIDO2/WebAuthn prioritisation (Temoshok et al., 2025).
- Just-in-time privileged access with automatic expiration.
- Attribute-based access control (ABAC) considering user, resource, environment, and action attributes dynamically (Hu et al., 2019).
- Automated provisioning/deprovisioning integrated with HR systems.

5.5.4.5 Layer 4: SIEM and SOC (Section 5.3)

Security Information and Event Management (Figure 5.7).

- Elastic Security SIEM aggregating logs from 87+ sources (cloud, applications, databases, network, endpoints, APIs, blockchain).
- 150+ correlation rules mapped to the MITRE ATT&CK framework (Strom et al., 2020), with specialised detection for software supply chain compromise techniques (T1195) as defined in the Mitre Attack (Matrix—Enterprise—Cloud, 2025).
- Machine learning anomaly detection establishing behavioural baselines.
- Automated threat intelligence enrichment.

Virtual Security Operations Center (Figure 5.7):

- 24/7 follow-the-sun monitoring with tiered response model.
- 40+ SOAR (Security Orchestration, Automation and Response) playbooks automating common incident scenarios (credential compromise, malware, API abuse, phishing).

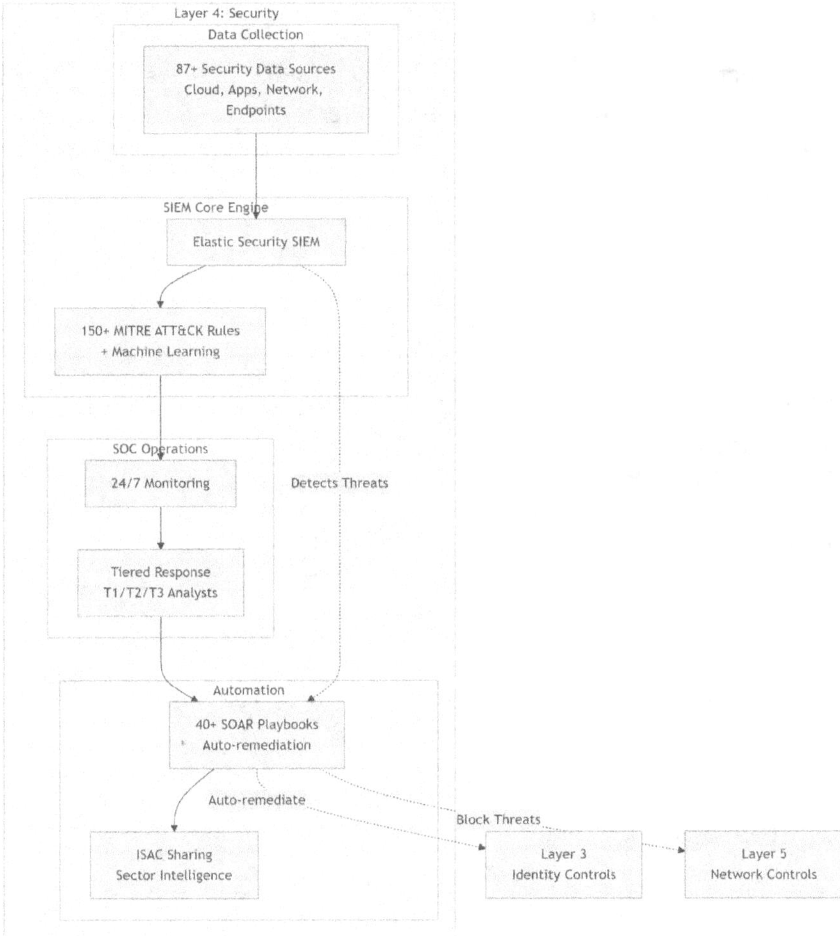

Figure 5.7 SIEM and SOC. Source: Own elaboration.

- Active ISAC (Information Sharing and Analysis Center) participation for sector-wide threat intelligence sharing.

5.5.4.6 Layer 5: Network and Infrastructure Security

Service Mesh with mTLS:

- Istio service mesh providing transparent mutual TLS for all service-to-service communications (Istio/Security, 2025).
- Automatic certificate management with 24-hour validity periods.
- Identity-based policies replacing IP-based rules in zero trust architectures (Rose et al., 2020).

Software-Defined Perimeter:

- Micro-segmentation with explicit allow-list policies.
- Default-deny posture preventing lateral movement.
- Strict egress filtering blocking C2 (Command and Control) communications (Myers, 2025).

5.5.5 Measurable Results and Impact

TABLE 5.2 QUANTITATIVE SECURITY IMPROVEMENTS

METRIC	PRE-IMPLEMENTATION	POST-IMPLEMENTATION	IMPROVEMENT
Mean Time to Detect (MTTD)	14.2 days	1.8 hours	99.5% ↓
Mean Time to Respond (MTTR)	72 hours	25 minutes	94.8% ↓
Mean Time to Contain (MTTC)	96 hours	45 minutes	99.2% ↓
False Positive Rate	42%	3.7%	91.2% ↓
Annual Fraud Losses	$2.5M	$400K	$2.1M saved
SIEM Log Sources	12	87	625% ↑
SOC Alert Automation	45%	98%	118% ↑
Blockchain Transactions	0	2.3M/month	New capability

Source: Own elaboration.

Bibliography

2022 Top Routinely Exploited Vulnerabilities | CISA. (2022). Cybersecurity and Infrastructure Security Agency. Retrieved from: https://www.cisa.gov/news-events/cybersecurity-advisories/aa23-215a

Ahmed, I., Zhang, Y., Jeon, G., Lin, W., Khosravi, M. R., & Qi, L. (2022). A blockchain- and artificial intelligence-enabled smart IoT framework for sustainable city. *International Journal of Intelligent Systems*, *37*(9), 6493–6507. https://doi.org/10.1002/INT.22852

Alexander, D., & Chikwarti, D. K. (2021). Self-learning AI models for behavior-driven access management in zero trust architectures. https://www.researchgate.net/publication/393696404_Self-Learning_AI_Models_for_Behavior-Driven_Access_Management_in_Zero_Trust_Architectures

Alzahrani, I., Lee, S., & Kim, K. (2024). Practical cyber threat and OSINT analysis based on implementation of CTI sharing platform. https://doi.org/10.20944/PREPRINTS202405.0277.V

Anascavage, R., & Davis, N. (2018). Blockchain technology: A literature review. *Electronic Journal*. https://ssrn.com/abstract=3173406

Androulaki, E., Barger, A., Bortnikov, V., Muralidharan, S., Cachin, C., Christidis, K., De Caro, A., Enyeart, D., Murthy, C., Ferris, C., Laventman, G., Manevich, Y., Nguyen, B., Sethi, M., Singh, G., Smith,

K., Sorniotti, A., Stathakopoulou, C., Vukolić, M., & Yellick, J. (2018). *Hyperledger fabric: A distributed operating system for permissioned blockchains*. Proceedings of the 13th EuroSys Conference, EuroSys. https://doi.org/10.1145/3190508.3190538

Annual number of supply chain cyber attacks U.S. 2023| Statista. (2023). https://www.statista.com/statistics/1367208/us-annual-number-of-entities-impacted-supply-chain-attacks/

Apruzzese, G., Colajanni, M., Ferretti, L., Guido, A., & Marchetti, M. (2018). *On the effectiveness of machine and deep learning for cyber security*. International Conference on Cyber Conflict, CYCON, 2018–May, 371–389. https://doi.org/10.23919/CYCON.2018.8405026

Arroyabe, M. F., Arranz, C. F. A., Fernandez De Arroyabe, I., & Fernandez de Arroyabe, J. C. (2024). Exploring the economic role of cybersecurity in SMEs: A case study of the UK. *Technology in Society*, *78*, 102670. https://doi.org/10.1016/J.TECHSOC.2024.102670

Aslan, J., Mayers, K., Koomey, J. G., & France, C. (2018). Electricity intensity of internet data transmission untangling the estimates. *Journal of Industrial Ecology*, *22*(4), 785–798. https://doi.org/10.1111/JIEC.12630

Atakari, C. (2025). Adaptive role-based access control and policy enforcement in ERP systems for governmental and military applications. *International Journal of Emerging Research in Engineering and Technology*, *6*. https://doi.org/10.63282/3050-922X.IJERET-V6I3P109

Aung, M. M., & Chang, Y. S. (2014). Traceability in a food supply chain: Safety and quality perspectives. *Food Control*, *39*(1), 172–184. https://doi.org/10.1016/J.FOODCONT.2013.11.007

Babich, V., & Hilary, G. (2018). *Forthcoming in manufacturing & service operations management distributed ledgers and operations: What operations management researchers should know about blockchain technology*. Forthcoming in Manufacturing & Service Operations Management. https://ssrn.com/abstract=3131250

Barker, E. (2020). Recommendation for key management: Part 1 – General. https://doi.org/10.6028/NIST.SP.800-57PT1R5

Barredo Arrieta, A., Díaz-Rodríguez, N., Del Ser, J., Bennetot, A., Tabik, S., Barbado, A., Garcia, S., Gil-Lopez, S., Molina, D., Benjamins, R., Chatila, R., & Herrera, F. (2020). Explainable Artificial Intelligence (XAI): Concepts, taxonomies, opportunities and challenges toward responsible AI. *Information Fusion*, *58*, 82–115. https://doi.org/10.1016/J.INFFUS.2019.12.012

Beerman, J., Berent, D., Falter, Z., & Bhunia, S. (2023). *A review of colonial pipeline ransomware attack*. Proceedings - 23rd IEEE/ACM International Symposium on Cluster, Cloud and Internet Computing Workshops, CCGridW 2023, 8–15. https://doi.org/10.1109/CCGRIDW59191.2023.00017

Brundage, M., Avin, S., Clark, J., Toner, H., Eckersley, P., Garfinkel, B., Dafoe, A., Scharre, P., Zeitzoff, T., Filar, B., Anderson, H., Roff, H., Allen, G. C., Steinhardt, J., Flynn, C., Héigeartaigh, S. Ó., Beard, S.,

Belfield, H., Farquhar, S., … Amodei, D. (2018). The malicious use of artificial intelligence: Forecasting, prevention, and mitigation. https://arxiv.org/pdf/1802.07228

Buczak, A. L., & Guven, E. (2016). A survey of data mining and machine learning methods for cyber security intrusion detection. *IEEE Communications Surveys and Tutorials*, *18*(2), 1153–1176. https://doi.org/10.1109/COMST.2015.2494502

Camenisch, J., & Lysyanskaya, A. (2001). An efficient system for non-transferable anonymous credentials with optional anonymity revocation. *Lecture Notes in Computer Science (Including Subseries Lecture Notes in Artificial Intelligence and Lecture Notes in Bioinformatics)*, *2045*, 93–118. https://doi.org/10.1007/3-540-44987-6_7

Chalapathy, R., & Chawla, S. (2019). Deep learning for anomaly detection: A survey. https://arxiv.org/pdf/1901.03407

Chang, Q., Ma, T., & Yang, W. (2025). Low power IoT device communication through hybrid AES-RSA encryption in MRA mode. *Scientific Reports*, 15(1), 14485. https://doi.org/10.1038/s41598-025-98905-0

Chen, L., Jordan, S., Liu, Y.-K., Moody, D., Peralta, R., Perlner, R., & Smith-Tone, D. (2016). Report on post-quantum cryptography. https://doi.org/10.6028/NIST.IR.8105

Chen, X., He, S., Sun, L., Zheng, Y., Wu, C. Q., Chen, X., He, S., Sun, L., Zheng, Y., & Wu, C. Q. (2024). A survey of consortium blockchain and its applications. *Cryptography*, 8(2), 12. https://doi.org/10.3390/CRYPTOGRAPHY8020012

Cheng, D., Zou, Y., Xiang, S., & Jiang, C. (2024). Graph neural networks for financial fraud detection: A review. *Frontiers of Computer Science*, *19*(9), 1–17. https://doi.org/10.1007/s11704-024-40474-y

Chhetri, G., Brotee, S., Das, S., Somvanshi, S., & Hebli, P. (2025). Post-quantum cryptography and quantum-safe security: A comprehensive survey. In *ACM computing surveys* (Vol. 1). https://doi.org/10.48550/arXiv.2510.10436

CISA. (2021). Federal government cybersecurity incident and vulnerability response playbooks. https://www.cisa.gov/resources-tools/resources/federal-government-cybersecurity-incident-and-vulnerability-response-playbooks

Dasgupta, D., Roy, A., & Nag, A. (2016). Toward the design of adaptive selection strategies for multi-factor authentication. *Computers and Security*, *63*, 85–116. https://doi.org/10.1016/j.cose.2016.09.004

De Giovanni, P. (2020). Blockchain and smart contracts in supply chain management: A game theoretic model. *International Journal of Production Economics*, *228*, 107855. https://doi.org/10.1016/j.ijpe.2020.107855

Dede, G., Petsa, A. M., Kavalaris, S., Serrelis, E., Evangelatos, S., Oikonomidis, I., Kamalakis, T., Dede, G., Petsa, A. M., Kavalaris, S., Serrelis, E., Evangelatos, S., Oikonomidis, I., & Kamalakis, T. (2024). Cybersecurity as a contributor toward resilient Internet of Things (IoT) infrastructure and sustainable economic growth. *Information*, *15*(12). https://doi.org/10.3390/INFO15120798

Devlin, J., Chang, M. W., Lee, K., & Toutanova, K. (2019). BERT: Pre-training of deep bidirectional transformers for language understanding. *NAACL HLT 2019 - 2019 Conference of the North American Chapter of the Association for Computational Linguistics: Human Language Technologies - Proceedings of the Conference*, *1*, 4171–4186.

Diyasi, S., Ghosh, A., & Dey Dipankar. (2023). Cyber-resilient phishing detection: BERT-driven NLP for advanced email security. *International Journal of HIT Transaction on ECCN*. https://www.researchgate.net/publication/389190315_Cyber-Resilient_Phishing_Detection_BERT-Driven_NLP_for_Advanced_Email_Security

Fayi, S. Y. A. (2018). What Petya/NotPetya ransomware is and what its remidiations are. *Advances in Intelligent Systems and Computing*, *738*, 93–100. https://doi.org/10.1007/978-3-319-77028-4_15/FIGURES/10

Ferguson, N., Schneier, B., & Kohno, T. (2010). *Cryptography engineering: Design principles and practical applications* (pp. 41–62). John Wiley & Sons.

FIPS 140-3, Security Requirements for Cryptographic Modules | CSRC. (2019). https://csrc.nist.gov/pubs/fips/140-3/final

Fitzgerald, A., & Bonnie, E. (2025). Supply chain attacks: Recent examples, trends & how to prevent them in 2026. https://secureframe.com/blog/supply-chain-attacks

Forsberg, J., & Frantti, T. (2023). Technical performance metrics of a security operations center. *Computers & Security*, *135*, 103529. https://doi.org/10.1016/J.COSE.2023.103529

Ghazi, A., Alisawi, M., Wahab, Y. M., Al-Dawoodi, A., Abdullah, S. S., Hammood, L., & Nawaf, A. Y. (2022). A systematic literature review of blockchain technology. *International Journal of Interactive Mobile Technologies*, *16*(10), 97–108. https://doi.org/10.3991/ijim.v16i10.30083

Gil, L. (n.d.). Security in the TSL industry: Threats to Transportation and Logistics | nFlo Blog. Retrieved December 27, 2025, from https://nflo.tech/knowledge-base/cyber-security-in-logistics-and-transportation-tsl-how-to-protect-the-digital-supply-chain/

Gillani, S., Dermish, A., & Grossman, J. (2022). The role of cybersecurity and data security in the digital economy. https://policyaccelerator.uncdf.org/all/brief-cybersecurity-digital-economy?

González-Granadillo, G., González-Zarzosa, S., Diaz, R., González-Granadillo, G., González-Zarzosa, S., & Diaz, R. (2021). Security Information and Event Management (SIEM): Analysis, trends, and usage in critical infrastructures. *Sensors*, *21*(14). https://doi.org/10.3390/S21144759

Griffis, S. E., & Goldsby, T. J. (2007). Transportation management systems: An exploration of progress and future prospects. *Journal of Transportation Management*, *18*(1), 18–32. https://doi.org/10.22237/jotm/1175385780

Guin, U., Huang, K., Dimase, D., Carulli, J. M., Tehranipoor, M., & Makris, Y. (2014). Counterfeit integrated circuits: A rising threat in the global semiconductor supply chain. *Proceedings of the IEEE*, *102*(8), 1207–1228. https://doi.org/10.1109/JPROC.2014.2332291

Hammi, B., Zeadally, S., & Nebhen, J. (2023). Security threats, countermeasures, and challenges of digital supply chains. *ACM Computing Surveys*, *55*(14 S). https://doi.org/10.1145/3588999

Hanqing, W. U. (2022). Big data sharing and high-efficiency traceability for blockchain-based supply chain management. https://theses.lib.polyu.edu.hk/bitstream/200/11970/3/6455.pdf

Hu, V., Ferraiolo, D., Kuhn, R., Schnitzer, A., Sandlin, K., Miller, R., & Scarfone, K. (2019). Guide to Attribute Based Access Control (ABAC) definition and considerations. https://doi.org/10.6028/NIST.SP.800-162

Ige, A. B., Kupa, E., & Ilori, O. (2024). Aligning sustainable development goals with cybersecurity strategies: Ensuring a secure and sustainable future. *GSC Advanced Research and Reviews*, *19*(3), 344–360. https://doi.org/10.30574/GSCARR.2024.19.3.0236

ISA/IEC 62443 Series of Standards - ISA. (2021). https://www.isa.org/standards-and-publications/isa-standards/isa-iec-62443-series-of-standards

Islam, T., Niger, M., Kynatun, M., & Mission, M. R. (2022). Systematic review of cybersecurity threats in IoT devices focusing on risk vectors vulnerabilities and mitigation strategies. *American Journal of Scholarly Research and Innovation*, *1*(1), 108–136. https://doi.org/10.63125/WH17MF19

Ismail, S., & Reza, H. (2022). *Security challenges of blockchain-based supply chain systems*. 2022 IEEE 13th Annual Ubiquitous Computing, Electronics and Mobile Communication Conference, UEMCON. https://doi.org/10.1109/uemcon54665.2022.9965682

Istio / Security. (2025). https://istio.io/latest/docs/concepts/security/

Jamal, S., Wimmer, H., & Sarker, I. H. (2023). An improved transformer-based model for detecting phishing, spam, and ham: A large language model approach. *Security and Privacy*, *7*(5). https://doi.org/10.1002/spy2.402

Jamil, F., Hang, L., Kim, K., Kim, D., Jamil, F., Hang, L., Kim, K., & Kim, D. (2019). A novel medical blockchain model for drug supply chain integrity management in a smart hospital. *Electronics*, *8*(5). https://doi.org/10.3390/ELECTRONICS8050505

Jiang, Y., Cyber Special Ops, N. R., Thi Hong Minh, S. LE, Wei Lim, H., Meng, Q., Shang, F., Oo, N., Thi Hong Minh, L., & Sikdar, B. (2025). MITRE ATT&CK applications in cybersecurity and the way forward. 1(1). https://arxiv.org/pdf/2502.10825

Jindal, P., & Singh, B. (2015). RC4 encryption - A literature survey. *Procedia Computer Science*, *46*, 697–705. https://doi.org/10.1016/j.procs.2015.02.129

Kahn, D. (1967). *The codebreakers. The story of secret writing*. The New American Library.

Kamath, R. (2018). Food traceability on blockchain: Walmart's pork and mango pilots with IBM. *The Journal of the British Blockchain Association*, *1*(1), 1–12. https://doi.org/10.31585/jbba-1-1-(10)2018

Karaduman, Ö., Gülhas, G., Karaduman, Ö., & Gülhas, G. (2025). Blockchain-enabled supply chain management: A review of security, traceability, and data integrity amid the evolving systemic demand. *Applied Sciences*, *15*(9), 5168. https://doi.org/10.3390/APP15095168

Khalil, M. (2025). Supply chain attack statistics 2025: Costs & defenses. https://deepstrike.io/blog/supply-chain-attack-statistics-2025

Kinyua, J., & Awuah, L. (2021). AI/ML in security orchestration, automation and response: Future research directions. *Intelligent Automation & Soft Computing*, *28*(2), 527–545. https://doi.org/10.32604/iasc.2021.016240

Knowles, W., Prince, D., Hutchison, D., Disso, J. F. P., & Jones, K. (2015). A survey of cyber security management in industrial control systems. *International Journal of Critical Infrastructure Protection*, *9*, 52–80. https://doi.org/10.1016/j.ijcip.2015.02.002

Kshetri, N. (2018). 1 Blockchain's roles in meeting key supply chain management objectives. *International Journal of Information Management*, *39*, 80–89. https://doi.org/10.1016/j.ijinfomgt.2017.12.005

Lella, Ifigeneia., Theocharidou, Marianthi., Tsekmezoglou, Eleni., Malatras, Apostolos., García, S., & Valeros, Veronica. (2021). *ENISA threat landscape for supply chain attacks*. European Union Agency for Cybersecurity. https://www.enisa.europa.eu/sites/default/files/publications/ENISA%20Threat%20Landscape%20for%20Supply%20Chain%20Attacks.pdf

Liu, S. S., Ma, B. J., Zhang, W., Cheng, E. T. C., Li, X., & Ng, C.-T. (2025). Eliminating information asymmetry in supply chains: Blockchain-driven or not. *Transportation Research Part E: Logistics and Transportation Review*, *201*. https://doi.org/10.1016/j.tre.2025.104208

Lumineau, F., Wang, W., & Schilke, O. (2021). Blockchain governance: A new way of organizing collaborations? *Organization Science*, *32*(2), 500–521. https://doi.org/10.1287/orsc.2020.1379

Martin, K. D., Borah, A., & Palmatier, R. W. (2017). Data privacy: Effects on customer and firm performance. *Journal of Marketing*, *81*(1), 36–58. https://doi.org/10.1509/JM.15.0497

Masip-Bruin, X., Marín-Tordera, E., Ruiz, J., Jukan, A., Trakadas, P., Cernivec, A., Lioy, A., López, D., Santos, H., Gonos, A., Silva, A., Soriano, J., & Kalogiannis, G. (2021). Cybersecurity in ict supply chains: Key challenges and a relevant architecture. In *Sensors* (Vol. 21, Issue 18). MDPI. https://doi.org/10.3390/s21186057

Matrix - Enterprise – Cloud, Mitre Attack. (2025). https://attack.mitre.org/matrices/enterprise/cloud/.

Maurer, T., & Nelson, A. (2021). Cyber threats to the financial system are growing, and the global community must cooperate to protect it global cyber threat. https://www.esrb.europa.eu/pub/pdf/reports/esrb.report200219_systemiccyberrisk

Meegammana, N. W., & Kumara, V. (2025). SolarWinds attack 2020: A cyber security and legal perspective. https://www.researchgate.net/publication/397324855_SolarWinds_Attack_2020_A_Cyber_Security_and_Legal_Perspective

Middae, V. L., Kumar Appachikumar, A., Lakhamraju, M. V., & Yerra, S. (2024). *AI-powered fraud detection in enterprise logistics and financial transactions: A hybrid ERP-integrated approach*. Computer Fraud and Security. https://computerfraudsecurity.com/index.php/journal/article/view/673/455

Miller, D., Harris, S., Harper, A., VanDyke, S., & Blask, C. (2010). *Security Information and Event Management (SIEM) Implementation (Network Pro Library)*. McGraw-Hill.

Mondal, P. (2025). The true cost of the top cyberattacks of 2025: Inside the losses and fallout - ET Edge Insights. https://etedge-insights.com/technology/cyber-security/the-true-cost-of-the-top-cyberattacks-of-2025-inside-the-losses-and-fallout/

Montecchi, M., Plangger, K., & Etter, M. (2019). *It's real, trust me! Establishing supply chain provenance using blockchain*. Business Horizons. https://www.sciencedirect.com/science/article/abs/pii/S0007681319300084?via%3Dihub

Moosavi, N., Taherdoost, H., Mohamed, N., Madanchian, M., Farhaoui, Y., & Khan, I. U. (2024). Blockchain technology, structure, and applications: A survey. *Procedia Computer Science*, *237*, 645–658. https://doi.org/10.1016/j.procs.2024.05.150

Myers, M. (2025). The critical role of egress filtering in preventing unauthorized outbound traffic. https://sbscyber.com/technical-recommendations/egress-filtering-unauthorized-outbound-traffic-prevention

Nelson, A., Rekhi, S., Souppaya, M., & Scarfone, K. (2025). Incident response recommendations and considerations for cybersecurity risk management: A CSF 2.0 community profile. https://doi.org/10.6028/NIST.SP.800-61R3

Neshenko, N., Bou-Harb, E., Crichigno, J., Kaddoum, G., & Ghani, N. (2019). Demystifying IoT security: An exhaustive survey on IoT vulnerabilities and a first empirical look on internet-scale IoT exploitations. *IEEE Communications Surveys and Tutorials*, *21*(3), 2702–2733. https://doi.org/10.1109/COMST.2019.2910750

Obasi, S. C., Solomon, N. O., Adenekan, O. A., & Simpa, P. (2024). Cybersecurity's role in environmental protection and sustainable development: Bridging technology and sustainability goals. *Computer Science & IT Research Journal*, *5*(5), 1145–1177. https://doi.org/10.51594/CSITRJ.V5I5.1140

Odumesi, J. O., & Sanusi, B. S. (2023). Achieving sustainable development goals from a cybersecurity perspective. *Advances in Multidisciplinary and Scientific Research Journal Publication*, *2*(1), 1–10. https://doi.org/10.22624/aims/csean-smart2023p3

Ogugua, O. C. (2024). ESG, cybersecurity, and the remote workforce: Navigating the new realities of corporate governance. *SSRN Electronic Journal*. https://doi.org/10.2139/SSRN.5055739

Ongaro, D., & Ousterhout, J. (2014). *In search of an understandable consensus algorithm*. Proceedings of the 2014 USENIX conference on USENIX Annual Technical Conference. USENIX ATC'14: Proceedings of the 2014 USENIX Conference on USENIX Annual Technical Conference. https://dl.acm.org/doi/10.5555/2643634.2643666

Patel, A. S., Brahmbhatt, M. N., Bariya, A. R., Nayak, J. B., & Singh, V. K. (2023). Blockchain technology in food safety and traceability concern to livestock products. *Heliyon*, *9*(6), e16526. https://doi.org/10.1016/j.heliyon.2023.e16526

Radwan, R., & Zejnilovic, S. (2025). Password reuse is rampant: Nearly half of observed user logins are compromised. https://blog.cloudflare.com/password-reuse-rampant-half-user-logins-compromised/

Rose, S., Borchert, O., Mitchell, S., & Connelly, S. (2020). Zero trust architecture. https://doi.org/10.6028/NIST.SP.800-207

Saberi, S., Kouhizadeh, M., Sarkis, J., & Shen, L. (2019). Blockchain technology and its relationships to sustainable supply chain management. *International Journal of Production Research*, *57*(7), 2117–2135. https://doi.org/10.1080/00207543.2018.1533261

SamanehSorournejad, Zojaji, Z., Atani, R. E., & Monadjemi, A. H. (2016). A survey of credit card fraud detection techniques: Data and technique oriented perspective. https://arxiv.org/pdf/1611.06439

Sample, M. (2023). MediLedger DSCSA pilot project. https://www.fda.gov/media/168283/download

Shamsuzzoha, A., Shahzad, K., Nousiainen, E., Ranta, M., Helo, P., & Govindan, K. (2025). Ensuring supply chain transparency by deploying blockchain-enabled technology: An overview with demonstration. *International Journal of Intelligent Systems*, *2025*(1), 7304193. https://doi.org/10.1155/int/7304193

Snape, G. (2025). Supply chain cyber attacks surge over 400%, expected to continue rising – Cowbell report | Insurance Business. https://www.insurancebusinessmag.com/us/news/cyber/supply-chain-cyber-attacks-surge-over-400-expected-to-continue-rising--cowbell-report-525369.aspx

Sobb, T., Turnbull, B., Moustafa, N., Sobb, T., Turnbull, B., & Moustafa, N. (2020). Supply chain 4.0: A Survey of cyber security challenges, solutions and future directions. *Electronics*, *9*(11), 1–31. https://doi.org/10.3390/electronics9111864

Sorooshian, S. (2024). The sustainable development goals of the United Nations: A comparative midterm research review. *Journal of Cleaner Production*, *453*, 142272. https://doi.org/10.1016/j.jclepro.2024.142272

Sri Vigna Hema, V., & Manickavasagan, A. (2024). Blockchain implementation for food safety in supply chain: A review. *Comprehensive Reviews in Food Science and Food Safety*, *23*(5), e70002. https://doi.org/10.1111/1541-4337.70002;pagegroup:string:publication

Stallings, W., & Brown, L. (2018). *Computer security principles and practice*. Pearson Education Limited. https://support.pearson.com/getsupport/

Stallings, W. (2020). *Cryptography and network security: Principles and practice* (8th ed.). Pearson.

Strom, B. E., Applebaum, A., Miller, D. P., Nickels, K. C., Pennington, A. G., & Thomas, C. B. (2020). Mitre attack: Design and philosophy. https://attack.mitre.org/docs/attack_Design_and_Philosophy_March_2020.pdf

Subramanyam, S. P. (2025). Zero trust in practice: Enhancing privileged access security with Just-in-Time (JIT) and self-service models. *International Research Journal of Innovations in Engineering and Technology*, *9*(12), 13–18. https://doi.org/10.47001/irjiet/2025.912003

Sunmola, F., & Burgess, P. (2022). Transparency by design for blockchain-based supply chains. *Procedia Computer Science*, *217*, 1256–1265. https://doi.org/10.1016/j.procs.2022.12.324

Supply Chain Breaches Increased from 2022 to 2023 | SupplyChainBrain. (2023). https://www.supplychainbrain.com/articles/38672-supply-chain-breaches-increased-from-2022-to-2023

Sustainability Accounting Standards Board. (2018). Software & IT services industry standard. https://sasb.ifrs.org

Swaminathan, B., Reddy, A. P., Reddy, S. T., & Scholar, U. G. (2024). Text and image encryption decryption using AES algorithm. *Strad Research*, *11*(5). https://doi.org/10.5281/Zenodo.11108844

Tait, S. (2025). It's data, stupid: Unifying a modern data security approach. https://www.forbes.com/councils/forbestechcouncil/2025/12/23/its-data-stupid-unifying-a-modern-data-security-approach/

Tan, T. M., Salo, J., Ahokangas, P., Seppänen, V., & Sandner, P. (2021). Revealing the disintermediation concept of blockchain technology (pp. 88–102). https://doi.org/10.4018/978-1-7998-7603-8.ch006

Tariq, S., Chhetri, M. B., Nepal, S., & Paris, C. (2025). Alert fatigue in security operations centres: Research challenges and opportunities. *ACM Computing Surveys*, *57*(9), 38. https://doi.org/10.1145/3723158;website:website:dl-site;requestedjournal:journal:csur;taxonomy:taxonomy:acm-pubtype;pagegroup:string:publication

Tayebi, M., & El Kafhali, S. (2025). A novel approach based on XGBoost classifier and Bayesian optimization for credit card fraud detection. *Cyber Security and Applications*, *3*, 100093. https://doi.org/10.1016/J.CSA.2025.100093

Temoshok, D., Fenton, J. L., Choong, Y.-Y., Lefkovitz, N., Regenscheid, A., Galluzzo, R., & Richer, J. P. (2025). Digital identity guidelines: Authentication and authenticator management. https://doi.org/10.6028/NIST.SP.800-63B-4

The Global Risks Report 2022 17th Edition. (2022). https://www3.weforum.org/docs/WEF_The_Global_Risks_Report_2022.pd

Thiyagarajan, G., Bist, V., & Nayak, P. (2025). Strengthening gRPC security in microservices: A proxy-based approach for mTLS, JWT, and RBAC enforcement. *International Journal of Computer Applications*, *187*(28), 975–8887.

Turjo, M. Das, Khan, M. M., Kaur, M., & Zaguia, A. (2021). Smart supply chain management using the blockchain and smart contract. *Scientific Programming*, *2021*(1), 6092792. https://doi.org/10.1155/2021/6092792

Under Attack: Why Transportation & Logistics Are Top Cyber Target's. (2025). https://vilogics.com/blog/under-attack-why-transportation-logistics-are-a-top-cyber-targets

Velásquez, I., Caro, A., & Rodríguez, A. (2018). Authentication schemes and methods: A systematic literature review. *Information and Software Technology*, *94*, 30–37. https://doi.org/10.1016/J.INFSOF.2017.09.012

Vielberth, M., Bohm, F., Fichtinger, I., & Pernul, G. (2020). Security operations center: A systematic study and open challenges. *IEEE Access*, *8*, 227756–227779. https://doi.org/10.1109/ACCESS.2020.3045514

Wang, Y., Castillejo, P., Martínez-Ortega, J. F., & Hernández Díaz, V. (2025). A survey on Identity and Access Management for future IoT services. *Computer Networks*, *272*, 111718. https://doi.org/10.1016/J.COMNET.2025.111718

Wang, Y., Han, J. H., & Beynon-Davies, P. (2019). Understanding blockchain technology for future supply chains: a systematic literature review and research agenda. In *Supply chain management* (Vol. 24, Issue 1, pp. 62–84). Emerald Group Holdings Ltd. https://doi.org/10.1108/SCM-03-2018-0148

Wilson, Y., & Hingnikar, A. (2022). Solving identity management in modern applications. In *Solving identity management in modern applications: Demystifying OAuth 2, OpenID connect, and SAML 2* (2nd ed.). Apress Media LLC. https://doi.org/10.1007/978-1-4842-8261-8

Wu, B., Chao, K. M., & Li, Y. (2024). Heterogeneous graph neural networks for fraud detection and explanation in supply chain finance. *Information Systems*, *121*, 102335. https://doi.org/10.1016/j.is.2023.102335

Xin, Y., Kong, L., Liu, Z., Chen, Y., Li, Y., Zhu, H., Gao, M., Hou, H., & Wang, C. (2018). Machine learning and deep learning methods for cybersecurity. *IEEE Access*, *6*, 35365–35381. https://doi.org/10.1109/ACCESS.2018.2836950

For Product Safety Concerns and Information please contact our EU representative GPSR@taylorandfrancis.com
Taylor & Francis Verlag GmbH, Kaufingerstraße 24, 80331 München, Germany

www.ingramcontent.com/pod-product-compliance
Lightning Source LLC
Chambersburg PA
CBHW070249230726
48635CB00030B/360

* 9 7 8 1 0 4 1 1 6 6 7 1 9 *